Financial Determinants in Local Re-Election Rates:

Emerging Research and Opportunities

Ana Maria Cunha
Polytechnic Institute of Cávado and Ave, Portugal

Augusta Ferreira
University of Aveiro, Portugal

Maria José Fernandes
Polytechnic Institute of Cávado and Ave, Portugal

Patrícia Gomes
Polytechnic Institute of Cávado and Ave, Portugal

A volume in the Advances in Public Policy and Administration (APPA) Book Series

IGI Global
DISSEMINATOR OF KNOWLEDGE

Published in the United States of America by
IGI Global
Business Science Reference (an imprint of IGI Global)
701 E. Chocolate Avenue
Hershey PA, USA 17033
Tel: 717-533-8845
Fax: 717-533-8661
E-mail: cust@igi-global.com
Web site: http://www.igi-global.com

Library of Congress Cataloging-in-Publication Data

Names: Cunha, Ana Maria, 1974- editor. | Ferreira, Augusta da Conceicao Santos, 1966- editor. | Fernandes, Maria Jose, 1967- editor.
Title: Financial determinants in local re-election rates: emerging research and opportunities / Ana Maria Cunha, Augusta Ferreira, Maria Jose Fernandes, and Patricia Gomes, editors.
Description: Hershey, PA : Business Science Reference, [2019] | Includes index.
Identifiers: LCCN 2018037203| ISBN 9781522578208 (hardcover) | ISBN 9781522578215 (ebook)
Subjects: LCSH: Local elections. | Finance, Public--Accounting. | Political participation.
Classification: LCC JS221 .F56 2019 | DDC 324.9--dc23 LC record available at https://lccn.loc.gov/2018037203

This book is published in the IGI Global book series Advances in Public Policy and Administration (APPA) (ISSN: 2475-6644; eISSN: 2475-6652)

British Cataloguing in Publication Data
A Cataloguing in Publication record for this book is available from the British Library.

All work contributed to this book is new, previously-unpublished material.
The views expressed in this book are those of the authors, but not necessarily of the publisher.

For electronic access to this publication, please contact: eresources@igi-global.com.

Advances in Public Policy and Administration (APPA) Book Series

ISSN:2475-6644
EISSN:2475-6652

MISSION

Proper management of the public sphere is necessary in order to maintain order in modern society. Research developments in the field of public policy and administration can assist in uncovering the latest tools, practices, and methodologies for governing societies around the world.

The **Advances in Public Policy and Administration (APPA) Book Series** aims to publish scholarly publications focused on topics pertaining to the governance of the public domain. APPA's focus on timely topics relating to government, public funding, politics, public safety, policy, and law enforcement is particularly relevant to academicians, government officials, and upper-level students seeking the most up-to-date research in their field.

COVERAGE

- Government
- Law Enforcement
- Political Economy
- Politics
- Public Administration
- Public Funding
- Public Policy
- Resource Allocation
- Urban Planning

IGI Global is currently accepting manuscripts for publication within this series. To submit a proposal for a volume in this series, please contact our Acquisition Editors at Acquisitions@igi-global.com or visit: http://www.igi-global.com/publish/.

The Advances in Public Policy and Administration (APPA) Book Series (ISSN 2475-6644) is published by IGI Global, 701 E. Chocolate Avenue, Hershey, PA 17033-1240, USA, www.igi-global.com. This series is composed of titles available for purchase individually; each title is edited to be contextually exclusive from any other title within the series. For pricing and ordering information please visit http://www.igi-global.com/book-series/advances-public-policy-administration/97862. Postmaster: Send all address changes to above address.

Titles in this Series

For a list of additional titles in this series, please visit:
https://www.igi-global.com/book-series/advances-public-policy-administration/97862

Community Risk and Protective Factors for Probation and Parole Risk Assessment Tools Emerging Research and Opportunities
Edwina Louise Dorch (Texas A&M Universty, USA)
Information Science Reference • © 2020 • 165pp • H/C (ISBN: 9781799811473) • US $165.00

Political Propaganda, Advertising, and Public Relations Emerging Research and Opportunities
Samet Kavoğlu (Marmara University, Turkey) and Meryem Salar (Kastamonu University, Turkey)
Information Science Reference • © 2020 • 212pp • H/C (ISBN: 9781799817345) • US $195.00

Political, Economic, and Social Factors Affecting the Development of Russian Statehood Emerging Research and Opportunities
Bogdan Ershov (Voronezh State Technical University, Russia) Natalia Muhina (Voronezh State Technical University, Russia) and Igor Ashmarov (Voronezh State Institute of Arts, Russia)
Information Science Reference • © 2020 • 155pp • H/C (ISBN: 9781522599852) • US $155.00

Participation of Young People in Governance Processes in Africa
Jeffrey Kurebwa (Bindura University of Science Education, Zimbabwe) and Obadiah Dodo (Bindura University of Science Education, Zimbabwe)
Information Science Reference • © 2019 • 350pp • H/C (ISBN: 9781522593881) • US $195.00

Information Systems Strategic Planning for Public Service Delivery in the Digital Era
Emanuel Camilleri (University of Malta, Malta)
Information Science Reference • © 2019 • 372pp • H/C (ISBN: 9781522596479) • US $225.00

For an entire list of titles in this series, please visit:
https://www.igi-global.com/book-series/advances-public-policy-administration/97862

IGI Global
DISSEMINATOR OF KNOWLEDGE

701 East Chocolate Avenue, Hershey, PA 17033, USA
Tel: 717-533-8845 x100 • Fax: 717-533-8661
E-Mail: cust@igi-global.com • www.igi-global.com

Editorial Advisory Board

Table of Contents

Preface

ABOUT THE SUBJECT

The New Public Management paradigm has enabled public entities to make major changes at the organizational level, encouraging organizations to adopt new approaches and management practices followed by private sector entities, introducing new concepts associated with management, in particular, performance, economy, efficiency and effectiveness, both at the accounting level, namely through organizational best practices and accountability.

Accounting information allows, on the one hand, public managers to obtain better information to support decision-making, greater transparency and accountability. On the other hand, accounting information also allows citizens greater knowledge of how public resources are being managed and used by public managers. Accounting is an instrument that enables citizens to assess the performance of public managers and can be used to communicate the economic effects associated with policymaking (Ingram & Copeland, 1981).

In this context, we consider that the study has implications at two levels: (i) from the point of view of public managers, to the extent that the mayors have become aware that accounting information and others factors, such as social and economic influence their re-election on the one hand, introduce measures that contribute to a better fulfillment of the needs of the electorate citizens, on the other hand, to develop a model for predicting electoral results; (ii) from the point of view of citizens, as knowledge of public management practices can help citizens to better understand their environment and to involve them more closely in local civil society, with a view to obtaining greater satisfaction and quality of life.

EXPECTATIONS

The editors expect this book to be useful for academics, researchers, policy makers, public managers and citizens who are involved in or are responsible for the transparency and public accountability.

In light of the assumptions of agency theory and public choice theory, the main goal of this book is to assess whether accounting information and others factors have an impact on electoral results, with impact on re-election, on local government.

This book shall contribute to the existing gap in the literature on the influence of accounting information in elections results and to serve as a basis for new empirical studies whose objective is to evaluate the relationship between accounting information and electoral results.

ORGANIZATION OF THE BOOK

This book is organized into seven chapters.

The first two chapters are focused on the financial information and its impact on local elections:

Chapter 1: The Impact of Financial Information on Voting Behavior
Chapter 2: Financial Indicators as Determinants of the Mayoral Election – Evidence From Italian Local Governments

In the context of Portugal, the third chapter addresses the determinants of re-election, with emphasis on public finance, and assess if the Law Term Limits has brought any change:

Chapter 3: Does It Pay Off to Mayors to Accurately Manage Finance on Municipalities? The Case of Portugal

The fourth chapter aims to assesses the financial sustainability of local governments in the context of Portugal and if accounting information enables public governance with greater transparency and accountability, in particularly, Portuguese local governments financial sustainability:

Chapter 4: Sustainability Assessment of Portuguese Local Governments (2009 to 2017): Accounting Information and Public Governance

The fifth chapter evaluates the dimensions of political factors and the constituent elements of financial condition sustainability in the context of the recent Great Recession, in particularly, in Spain:

Chapter 5: Analysis of the Association Between Political Change in Local Government and Municipal Financial Condition in Spain During the Great Recession

The sixth chapter is an analysis of what types of information the citizen wants and how, and what communication tools and forms the citizen wants to receive information:

Chapter 6: Popular Financial Reporting – A New Information Tool for Local Public Groups

The seventh chapter reviews and discusses the case of investments in infrastructural assets and local government, in particularly, in New Zealand:

Chapter 7: The Case of Accounting Information for Infrastructural Assets Reporting – Local Government Borrowings and Investment Choices in the Context of Moral Hazard and Local Government Politics

Ana Maria Cunha
Polytechnic Institute of Cávado and Ave, Portugal

Augusta Ferreira
University of Aveiro, Portugal

Maria José Fernandes
Polytechnic Institute of Cávado and Ave, Portugal

Patrícia Gomes
Polytechnic Institute of Cávado and Ave, Portugal

REFERENCES

Ingram, R., & Copeland, R. (1981). Municipal Accounting Information and Voting Behavior. *The Accounting Review*, *56*(4), 830–843.

Acknowledgment

The editors would like to thank the support of all the people involved in this project and, more specifically, the authors and reviewers who took part in the review process. Their effort was an outstanding contribution to this publication process. Without their support, this book would not have become a reality.

First, the editors would like to thank each of the chapters' authors who contributed with their time and expertise to this book.

Second, the editors wish to acknowledge the excellent and valuable work of the Editorial Advisory Board members regarding the improvement of quality, coherence, and content presentation of chapters which ensured the highest accuracy in the double-blinded review process. Most of the authors also served as referees; we highly appreciate their double task.

Ana Maria Cunha
Polytechnic Institute of Cávado and Ave, Portugal

Augusta Ferreira
University of Aveiro, Portugal

Maria José da Silva Fernandes
Polytechnic Institute of Cávado and Ave, Portugal

Patrícia Gomes
Polytechnic Institute of Cávado and Ave, Portugal

Chapter 1
The impact of Financial Information on Voting Behaviour

Isabel Brusca
University of Zaragoza, Spain

Margarita Labrador
University of Zaragoza, Spain

Jorge Olmo
University of Zaragoza, Spain

ABSTRACT

In the public sector, citizens have been recognized as potential users of financial reporting elaborated by governments. A specific use of financial reporting by citizens is voting decisions, where they can approve or disapprove of the politicians' management. Political budget cycles literature contains many studies that evidence that politicians manage the budget in order to increase their possibilities of being reelected, but there is no consensus about the outcome. This chapter aims to study to what extent financial management influences electoral outcomes and if there is any evidence that the financial management of governments has an impact on election results. The study is focused on Spanish local governments and uses data from the elections of 2011 and 2015. The results indicate that governments with higher capital investments or fewer deficits have no advantages in the elections. However, citizens reward government policies with higher levels of social expenditures and punish higher fiscal pressure.

DOI: 10.4018/978-1-5225-7820-8.ch001

INTRODUCTION

The introduction of an electoral system in which citizens can elect their political representatives is typical of democracy and tries to guarantee the functioning of political systems. It allows the political party in power to obtain the necessary legitimacy to carry out its fiscal, social and economic policies. The citizens can use elections to decide about the type of governments they prefer, as they are at the same time resource providers to governments and user of the services provided by them. Because of this, statements of concepts of accounting standard boards state that taxpayers and citizens are potential users of public administration financial reporting. Accounting literature about the usefulness of governmental financial reporting has also included this group of users and found a strong interest. A specific use of financial reporting by citizens is voting decisions, where they can approve or disapprove of the politicians' management.

Political budget cycles literature maintains that the need to have voters' support may lead political managers to adopt policies that enhance their possibilities of being re-elected. Politicians may have incentives to try to influence voting intentions. It is argued that this can lead to increase public spending before elections to improve the chances that they (or their party) will be re-elected (Drazen & Eslava, 2010).

Some authors have tried to study the effect of political budget cycles on the management of expenses and revenues (Boetti et al., 2012; Klein, 2010; Sakurai & Menezes-Filho, 2011; Cioffi et al., 2012; Wagner, 2012; Wang & Hou, 2012; Guillamón et al., 2013; Lopez, 2013; Sjahrir et al., 2013; Vicente et al., 2013). They study whether governments adopt policies of expense and revenue manipulation in the year prior to elections, either from the perspective of total expenditure or from its composition. The results are not conclusive.

From this perspective, there is also a stream of the literature that has tried to analyze the effect of political cycles, that is if governments that use expenditures to increase their possibilities of being reelected really obtain advantages in the voting box. This implicates to assess if citizens and users perceive the financial management of governments and the signals that politicians send them. As financial management is shown in financial statements, this could indicate that financial information have an impact on voting decisions and therefore the usefulness that they can have for citizens and other users to evaluate the public policies.

This chapter addresses two empirical research questions: (1) Does financial management influence electoral outcomes, that is, to what extent can it be said that voters perceive accounting data? (2) What impact does the socioeconomic context have on electoral outcomes? While numerous factors might affect election outcomes, the paper considers only accounting ratios that can be calculated on the basis of the information included in the financial report and socioeconomic variables. The chapter does not try to construct a model of voting behaviour but only to test if there is a relationship between elections outcomes and accounting information or not. There are possible restrictions, because a decision to vote and how to vote will probably not be based on accounting numbers alone.

The analysis is focused on local government because it is the administration that is closest to citizens, which could make it more likely that management perceives them as a costumer, obliged to pay taxes but with the power to evaluate municipal management in the ballot box, with enough power to substitute politicians if they consider that management is not proper or correct.

The study is carried out for 103 Spanish local governments and uses data for the elections of May 2011 and May 2015. To this end it is used OLS regression and logit regression to test whether or not there is a relationship between the financial reporting of local authorities and the electoral results of the political party governing the council.

Two dependent variables are used: the change in the percentage of votes that the political party has had in the elections and the re-election of the political party (that is, a dicotomous variable showing if the political party has been or not re-elected).

The independent variables selected consisted firstly of financial data representative of budgetary management and the financial and economic situation. A number of these ratios are similar to those specified in municipal financial stress literature as being indicative of budgetary and financial analysis. Secondly, the study includes some socio-demographic characteristics to analyze whether the local governments included in the study are homogeneous or not. The variables used are: population, unemployment rate and immigration. Unfortunately, information about performance indicators or service efforts and accomplishments are not available because of which is not included in the study although this is the most important information for citizens.

The results can enrich literature about the effect of financial management of governments in electoral outcomes, and also about the effectiveness of political budget cycles of governments.

THEORETHICAL FRAMEWORK AND LITERATURE REVIEW

Public Choice Theory

Public Choice has been defined as the application of the methodology of economics to the study of politics, including the voting behaviour (Mueller, 1976). Since its origin, the literature in public choice has been divided into two groups: normative and positive (Mueller, 1976). The normative analysis is related to the problems and identification of improvements of constitutional rules, while the positive public choice literature studies decision making processes of individuals, such as voters or politicians, and their interactions (Nordhaus, 1975). It supports that voters prefer administrations and policies that benefit them, while politicians pursue policies that allow them to win elections.

In this framework, research about participation in elections within democracy has been based on the positive Public Choice theory, specifically in the assumption of voter rationality, based on the works of Black (1948) and Arrow (1951), which has given the methodological foundation to understand the rational behaviour of voters in elections within a democratic system. The literature has evidenced the rationality of the vote of the citizens in relation to the application of the fiscal policies of the party in power, which can condition the continuity of the party, as stated by Rogoff and Sibert (1988) and Rogoff (1990). For example, Rogoff (1990)'s model suggests that observed pre-election expenditures may serve as a sign of the incumbent's competence, meaning its ability to provide more public services for a given tax revenue.

Shi and Svensson (2006) argue that informed voters are rational because they can deduce government ability, but their uninformed voters are also rational because they can form rational expectations about government behaviour. Financial reporting can be used to reduce the information difference between voters and government.

In accordance with Chan and Rubin (1987), this allows researchers to study the role of information in a democracy and government operations. The authors state that public choice provides a framework for addressing the role of accounting information in the demand for and supply of government output. Taking into account this assumption, our first research question is to analyze the impact that financial information has on the electoral outcomes and in consequence in voting behaviour in order to test if voters perceive financial management and accounting data. As the institutional context may be also important, our second research question analyzes the impact of socioeconomic factors on the electoral outcomes, such as the size, the level of unemployment and the rate of immigration.

Financial Management and Voting Behaviour

The application of the Public Choice Theory has been the base of the Political Budget Cycles Theory, which argues that politicians adopt policies that enhance their possibilities of being re-elected, that is incumbent politicians can use public spending policies to improve the chances of being re-elected. From this perspective, Shichk (1969) points out that revenues, expenses and debt in the budget can be used to create fiscal illusion. In accordance with the theory of opportunistic rational political budget cycles politicians would spend on the most visible items attractive to voters. This idea is based on a rational behaviour of the voter, who bases his/her expectations of future policies on current policies.

Several empirical studies have tried to test this theory both at the central and local government. For example, Blais and Nadeu (1992) show that total expenditure and deficit increase slightly in the electoral year. Galli and Rossi (2002) find that total expenditure and each spending category were lower in non-election years, while the deficit was higher. Lago and Lago (2008) analyze upward deviations in the deficit and show a tendency to increase it in election years. Alesina and Paradisi (2017) also found Political Budget Cycles (PBC) in the case of Italian cities, with municipalities choosing lower tax rates when close to elections, but the size of the cycle was smaller for cities with elections in which deficits were higher.

In Spain, Guillamón et al. (2013) confirm that incumbents increase spending the year before the elections, and Vicente et al. (2013) show that PBC can be modified by the legislation and that in the case of Spanish local government, the law of budgetary stability has introduced some changes, with the result that deficit and spending increases are confined to the election year.

Another stream of the literature argues that whatever the total volume, politicians want to manipulate the proportions of current expenses and capital expense. Authors in this line consider that voters are averse to high levels of total expenditure and deficit. As a consequence, governments will have to concentrate their manipulation on the composition of expenditure and avoid increases in the total expenditure. Within this line of reasoning, two possible directions can explain how expenditure can be managed. The first argues that as current expenditure is more visible, politicians will use this item to influence voters (Rogoff, 1990). A second line argues that capital expenditure rather than current expenditure could be used to impress voters.

Empirical research has tried to study the outcomes of PBC, that is how public expenditure policies affect electoral results. The results are not conclusive. A part of the literature suggests that governments do not obtain benefits from the manipulation of expenditure before elections (Peltzman, 1992; Alesina, Peroti & Tavares, 1998; Brender, 2003). For example, Alvarez and Delgado (2006) detect signs of PBC in total expenditure and in specific expenditure, but they do not find clear evidence that this manipulation leads to positive results for the governing party.

However, Pelzman (1992) shows that the electorate penalizes those governments that increase public spending and condition the deficit. Klomp and De Haan (2013) study whether political budget cycles increased the share of votes received by the parties in government in the elections. The results suggest that voters punish politicians who create budget deficits during their term in office.

However, there are authors that maintain that the increase in public spending before the elections increases the possibility of re-election of the governors (Akhmedov & Zhuravskaya, 2004; Veiga & Veiga, 2007; Sakurai & Menezes-Filho, 2008; Aidt et al., 2011). Drazen and Eslava (2005) results support that capital expenditures are rewarded by voters while the current expenditure does not influence the decisions of the voters. In a later study, Drazen and Eslava (2010) find evidence of a pre-electoral increase in targeted expenditures and a contraction of other types of expenditure, and a positive voter response to targeting. More recently, Chortareas et al. (2016) studied the influence of opportunistic policies on incumbents' reelection prospects and found that increased expenditures and election year opportunistic excesses are electorally rewarding.

In Spain, the influence of financial management on voting decision has been supported by Brusca and Montesinos (2006) and Balaguer-Coll and Brun-Martos (2013). The latter found that the electorate values capital expenditures in a positive way, while current expending does not influence the decisions of the voters, concluding that a higher municipal public spending has a positive effect on the possibility that the government be reelected.

There are also studies that highlight that information to citizens can reduce or eliminate PBC. In accordance to James and John (2007), this situation can be changed with performance information: if incumbents give information to the voters they can make judgments and reward and punish them accordingly. They found that performance information communicated to citizens can have an effect on election results. Incumbents in local authorities in the poor performance category experience a substantial reduction in aggregate vote share at the election following publication, but there is no similarly sized reward for those in the highest performance category (James & John, 2007). Repetto (2018) studied whether having more informed voters affects the political budget cycle, and their results suggest that mayors react to more informed voters by reducing spending manipulation. Because of this, transparency of financial reporting is fundamental. In this respect, popular reports are gaining interest in this framework which according to the GASB (1992) should focus on analysis rather than disclosure, be objective, and user-friendly

More recently, Cunha (2018) carried out a study for two budget cycles in Portuguese local governments, evidencing that the level of financial independency, the percentage of expenditure executed and the total expenditures per capita influence electoral outcomes. The author includes also in the analysis some socio-economic variables, evidencing that the density of population, the level of unemployment and the rate of primary and superior education of population have a statistically significant effect in the re-election of government.

In summary, although many authors have evidenced the existence of PBC, there is no clear confirmation on the effect that these may have on the electoral results, so that contributions in this area may be relevant. This chapter makes a contribution on the impact of financial management on electoral behaviour and tries to analyze the extent to which citizens may be interested in financial management and the financial information produced by local governments. The results can enrich literature about the effect of financial management of governments in electoral outcomes, and also about the effectiveness of political budget cycles.

Agency Theory and Citizens as Users of Financial Reporting

The research question defined about the impact of financial management on electoral outcome can be also related with the Theory of Agency, whose application indicates that politicians are the agents that try to maximize their welfare and re-election, while voters are the politician's principals, whose welfare is tied to the actions of their agents. Each voter has an incentive to monitor the behaviour of the politician and use it for decision making. Nevertheless, Zimmerman (1977) points out some problems that can arise in the control of the agent by the principal in this case. Because of the small probability of a voter influencing an election, each voter will incur a small expected cost. Voters do not require much monitoring-type information, but they have an incentive to establish rigid, explicit operating procedures to constrain the politician's actions. Politicians try to maximize votes for elections and want to formulate policies that will please their constituents.

Citizens provide resources through taxes and receive the services provided by public administrations. This implies that governments are accountable for management and use of the resources. The Conceptual Framework for General Purpose Financial Reporting by Public Sector Entities elaborated by the International Public Sector Accounting Standards Board (IPSASB, 2018) states that citizens are the primary users of financial reporting. They should use the information for decision making purposes, and among others, about voting preferences. Obviously economic awareness and rationality on the part of voters and politicians are assumed as preconditions for the utility of municipal accounting numbers (Ingram & Copeland, 1981).

RESEARCH DESIGN

Aims and Variables

The aim of this chapter is twofold: a) To test the impact of financial management on the voting decisions of the citizens. b) To consider the influence of socioeconomic factors on electoral decisions. Two dependent variables are used to measure the electoral outcomes of governments: the change in the percentage of votes that the incumbent party has had in the elections and whether the political party is re-elected (that is, a dichotomous variable showing whether the political party has or not been re-elected). The following Research Questions (RQ) related to the two dependent variables used in the analysis are defined:

RQ1: What is the impact of financial reporting and socioeconomic factors on the change or re-election of the local government?

In accordance with the Public Choice Theory, citizens are rational and will perceive the financial management of politicians and use it in voting decisions (Nordhaus, 1975). This will lead to a positive effect of Political Budget Cycles, so that governments that increase targeted expenditures or reduced fiscal pressure can benefit (Rogoff & Sibert, 1988; Rogoff, 1990). Our analysis will check whether the financial managements reflected in financial figures and information available affects the change of the political party of the local government. In this section, if we finally verify that the financial information available can influence the change of the local government, we can argue the strong importance of this kind of information in the electoral decisions.

RQ2: What is the impact of financial information and socioeconomic factors on the variation in the percentage of votes for the political party in power? This complements the first objective. Accounting and budgetary information available may not involve a change of government but may have repercussions in the voting decisions the citizens and in the percentage of votes obtained. In this case, depending of the financial and budgetary management reflected in the public accounting information, the mayors can have greater or lesser expectations of an increase in the percentage of votes for the political party.

Table 1 shows all the dependent and independent variables used in the empirical analysis.

Table 1. Definition of variables

Variable	Calculation	Description
Change of Political Party of the Local Government (***Changegov***)	By the municipal elections of the year 2015, checking if the political party that had governed during the previous political cycle has changed. Dummy variable: 0- There is no change of government political party in 2015. 1- There is a change of political party in 2015 respect to the previous political cycle.	Ministry of Interior (2015a)
Variation in the Percentage of Votes of the Political Party (***Varvoto***)	First, the percentage of votes obtained by the political party that governed after the elections of the year 2011 is calculated. Second, the percentage of votes obtained by that political party in the elections of the year 2015 is calculated. With these figures the variation percentage is determined: Percentage of votes in 2015 - percentage of votes in 2011. If the variation is negative the political party loses percentage of participation.	Ministry of Interior (2015b)
Total Debt (***Debt***)	Accumulated debt (long term) per inhabitant.	Ministry of Finance (2015a)
Net Debt Index (***NDI***)	Annual accumulation variation long-term credit operations per inhabitant.	Ministry of Finance (2015b)
Non-financial Budgetary Results (***Budgetbalance***)	Non-financial receivables less non-financial budgetary payables per inhabitant.	
Social Expenditure on Public Services (***Socialexp***)	Social expenditure on public services per inhabitant.	Sielocal (2016)
Investment (***KEI***)	Capital Expenditures per inhabitant.	Ministry of Finance (2015b)
Fiscal Revenue Index (***FRI***)	Fiscal receivables divided by net current budgetary receivables	
Unemployment (***Unemploy***)	Rate of unemployed population of the municipality.	Public Employment Service (2015)
Population (***Population***)	Population expressed in natural logarithms.	National Institutive of Statistics (2015)
Immigration (***Inmigr***)	Percent of immigrants of the municipality.	
Ideology (***Ideology***)	Political ideology of the municipal council for 2012-2014. Dummy variable: 0 - Municipalities governed by right-wing parties. 1 - Municipalities governed by left-wing parties.	Ministry of Interior (2015a)

Methodology and Sample

The analysis is carried out for Spanish local governments with more than 50,000 inhabitants although some entities have been eliminated because of lacking information. In total 103 local governments have been considered each year. In accordance with data from the National Institute of Statistics (2015) the sample used for the analysis includes about 85% of the municipalities with more than 50,000 inhabitants.

Firstly, the relationship between the dependent and the independent variables is checked through the Pearson's correlations. The aim is to check whether the variables included in the models have statistical significant with respect to both the change of political party and to the variation of vote.

Secondly, a logit regression is applied to measure the probability of change of political party in the local government. A logit panel data analysis (model 1) is carried out considering the data of the three years of the period of the political cycle (2012-2014). Model 2 estimates a logit regression for 2014 considering the variables of the pre-election year.

Thirdly, the ordinary least squares (OLS) analysis is carried out to verify the influence of the different variables in the variation in the percentage of votes for the political party that had governed during the previous political cycle. We apply a pooled regression (model 3) for the same period as the logit regression (2012-2014). In this model all the data are grouped, and carried out ordinary regression of least squares. We also check the influence of the different variables for 2014 with an OLS regression (model 4).

The political ideology is included only in the models 1 and 3 because these models are related to the electoral cycle. With this variable it is possible to analyze the direction of the change in political ideology (left to right or right to left).

In summary, in the models 1 and 3 are used the data of three years (2011-2014) and in the models 2 and 4 data of the year 2014.

The models can be defined as follows:

Model 1

$$Changegov_{it} = \alpha + \beta_1 Socialexp_{it} + \beta_2 KEI_{it} + \beta_3 FRI_{it} + \beta_4 Unemploy + \beta_5 Population_{it} + \beta_7 Inmigr_{it} + \beta_8 Ideology_{it} + \varepsilon_{it} \cdot$$

Model 2

$$Changegov = \alpha + \beta_1 Socialexp + \beta_2 KEI + \beta_3 FRI + \beta_4 Unemploy + \beta_5 Population + \beta_6 Inmigr + \varepsilon \cdot$$

Model 3

$$Varvoto_{it} = \alpha + \beta_1 Socialexp_{it} + \beta_2 KEI_{it} + \beta_3 FRI_{it} + \beta_4 Unemploy + \beta_5 Population_{it} + \beta_6 Inmigr_{it} + \beta_7 Ideology_{it} + \varepsilon_{it} \cdot$$

Model 4

$$Varvoto = \alpha + \beta_1 Socialexp + \beta_2 KEI + \beta_3 FRI + \beta_4 Unemploy + \beta_5 Population + \beta_6 Inmigr + \varepsilon$$

Where: α represents the constant term; β is the coefficient; ε_{it} and ε are a random term; *i* is the local government; *t* is the year; *Changegov* is a dummy variable that equals 1 if there is a change of the political party in the government; 0 if there is not a change; *Varvoto* is a continuous variable.

In the models 1 and 2 the sign β_1 is expected positive. It is probably that the local government with higher debt be punished by citizens in the electoral process. The coefficients β_2 and β_3 are expected to be negative. A higher level of social public expenditure and local investment, it is more probably that the same political party can be reelected. Respect to the fiscal pressure, it can be assumed that in the local governments with higher fiscal pressure the citizens would prefer a change of the government. Hence, the expected sign of β_4 is positive. In relation to the socioeconomic variables, the coefficient β_5 is expected positive, because the unemployment situation can affect in the change of the government. By last, there is no expected sign in the coefficients β_6, β_7 and β_8 because the relationship of the variables with the dependent variables is not so clear. On the contrary, in the models 3 and 4 the opposite signs in each of the coefficients are expected.

Finally, in order to detect multicollinearity problems the Variance Inflation Factors (VIF) are analyzed. Multicollinearity occurs when two or more predictors in the model are correlated and provide redundant information. A maximum VIF value in excess of 10 is frequently taken as an indication that multicollinearity may be unduly influencing the least squares estimates (Hutner et al., 2005).

Table 2. Pearson's correlation: non-financial budget balance, debt and variation of debt respect to the change of the political party of the government and percentage of variation of votes

	Changegov	**Varvoto**	**Budgetbalance**	**Debt**
Changegov	1			
Varvoto	-0.2707*	1		
Budgetbalance	0.0597	-0.0716	1	
Debt	0.019	0.0083	-0.3086*	1
NDI	-0.0024	0.031	-0.6306*	0.3510*

*** p<0.01, ** p<0.05, * p<0.1

Table 3. Univariate logit analysis. Relation of debt, variation of debt and non-financial budget balance respect to the change of the political party of the government

	Changegov	*Changegov*	*Changegov*
Debt	0.0000672		
	(0.000201)		
NDI		-0.0000232	
		(0.000552)	
Budgetbalance			0.00103
			(0.000989)
Constant	-0.110	-0.0577	-0.144
	(0.192)	(0.115)	(0.141)
Observations	309	309	309

Standard errors in parentheses
*** p<0.01, ** p<0.05, * p<0.1

Table 4. Univariate OLS regression analysis. Relationship of debt, variation of debt and non-financial budget balance with the percentage of variation of votes of the political party

	Varvoto	*Varvoto*	*Varvoto*
Debt	0.000117		
	(0.000800)		
NDI		0.00120	
		(0.00220)	
Budgetbalance			-0.00486
			(0.00386)
Constant	-11.56***	-11.50***	-11.07***
	(0.765)	(0.457)	(0.553)
Observations	309	309	309
R-squared	0.000	0.001	0.005

Standard errors in parentheses
*** p<0.01, ** p<0.05, * p<0.1

ANALYSIS OF RESULTS

The Influence of Debt and Deficit on Voting Behaviour

Table 2 shows Pearson's correlation coefficients between the variables of debt and deficit and the change of government and the variation in the percentage of votes for the political party in power. It shows that the relationship between the variables is not statistically significant. This evidences that there is no influence of the level of debt that governments have on the electoral outcomes, as citizens do not perceive this as signal of good or bad management. Neither do the deficit of the year or the net variation of debt during the year have a statistical relationship with the percentage of change in the votes or the change of the political party in the government.

The results also show that there is a significant relationship between the independent variables used. Taking into account it, the variables have introduced separately in the logit analysis.

Table 3 shows the results of the univariate logit analysis, which confirms that the variables are not statistically significant to predict the change of government. None of them are statistically significant when the change of government is used as the outcome variable.

Table 5. Pearson's correlation of independent variables and the change of the political party of the government and percentage of variation of votes

	Changegov	Varvoto	Socialexp	KEI	FRI	Unemploy	Population	Inmigr
Changegov	1							
Varvoto	-0.2707***	1						
Socialexp	-0.1291*	0.1884***	1					
KEI	-0.0481	0.1804***	0.2077***	1				
FRI	-0.013**	-0.1374**	-0.2397***	-0.1023*	1			
Unemploy	0.1579***	0.021	-0.0184**	-0.1454**	-0.3113***	1		
Population	0.2145***	-0.1784***	0.1254	0.038	-0.2815***	0.0222	1	
Inmigr	0.1645***	-0.055	-0.1012*	0.0191	0.2478***	-0.2531***	-0.0888	1
Ideology	-0.2780***	0.3561***	0.1319**	0.0797	-0.0396	-0.0537	-0.1401**	-0.0321

*** p<0.01, ** p<0.05, * p<0.1

The univariate OLS regression carried out (Table 4) evidences that the percentage of variation in the votes for the political party in power does not have a linear relationship with anye of the variables included in the regression.

As a consequence, if we focus the research questions on the impact of debt and deficit, the results of the statistical analysis show that citizens do not perceive that the level of debt, the deficit or the variation in the level of debt are relevant to influence their voting decisions. There are no advantages and disadvantages of the governments due to their management in these variables. Regardless of whether they are prudent in their management or whether they use debt the behaviour of citizens is not influenced. Thus, our results do not support Political budget cycles with effects on debt and deficit. Neither do they support the previous literature about the penalization of governments that increase deficit (Pelzman, 1992; Klomp and De Haan, 2013). These results may be due to the relevance of other variables that can be considered more important to citizens in the Spanish framework.

The Influence of Financial Variables and Socioeconomic Factors on Voting Behaviour

Table 5 shows Pearson's correlation coefficient between the variables related with revenues and expenditures management and the change of government and the variation in the percentage of votes of the political party in power. It shows that the relationship of the three variables selected and the percentage of variation in the votes of the political party in the power is statistically significant. The social expenditures and the fiscal revenues index also have a significant relationship with

Table 6. Logit estimation for the change in government

	Model 1	Model 2
	Changegov (2012-2014)	*Changegov (2014)*
Socialexp	-0.00909*	-0.0154*
	(0.00494)	(0.00872)
KEI	0.000396	0.00368
	(0.00234)	(0.00436)
FRI	0.796	1.788
	(1.808)	(3.272)
Unemploy	18.85***	21.76**
	(5.617)	(9.952)
Population	0.720***	0.832**
	(0.195)	(0.334)
Inmigr	5.360***	5.469**
	(1.509)	(2.707)
Ideology	-1.223***	------
	(0.318)	------
Constant	-10.96***	-13.29**
	(3.108)	(5.338)
Observations	309	103
Pseudo R-squared	0.147	0.1182
Log Likelihood	-182.56871	-62.91664

Standard errors in parentheses
*** p<0.01, ** p<0.05, * p<0.1

the change of government, while the capital expenditure is not correlated with the variable of change in government.

It can be seen that all the variables of control used also have a statistical relationship with the variable of change of government, while only the population has relationship with the percentage of variation in the votes of the political party in government. Furthermore, the correlation between the variables used in the analysis can be considered low in all the cases, even if on occasions it is statistically significant. In fact, the VIF of the variables is in all the cases low, evidencing that the variables can be used simultaneously in the analysis without creating a problem of multicollinearity (Appendix 1).

The logit estimation for the dichotomous variable of change in the government (Table 6) shows that only social expenditure has a significant impact for predicting the change in government. The analysis has been carried out considering previous year data and also the total years in government of the political party. It can be seen that the results are very similar considering both models.

The coefficient of the variable is negative in both cases, indicating that those governments that have higher social spending have more probabilities of being re-elected. That is, citizens reward the management of politicians who increase social spending during their governments. This would indicate that in order to have a positive effect of political budget cycles, governments should focus on social expenditures.

However, capital expenditure is not statistically significant to predict the change in the governing party of a municipality, showing that in spite that some studies confirm that this is one of the variables chosen by the politicians to influence the electoral results, the results do not show the relevance of this variable to change the government. Nevertheless, governments with higher capital expenditure in the year previous to the elections do not have more probabilities of being re-elected. Therefore, in relation to our first research question, the results evidence that there are some advantages in elections by governments that increase social expenditure and therefore this should be the targeted variable for those governments that want to be reelected.

The three social and economic variables of control used in the analysis have a significant impact on the binary variable. The municipalities with a higher number of inhabitants, and which also have a higher level of unemployment and a higher immigrant population are more likely to change the political party in the power. These results confirm those obtained by Cunha (2018) for Portuguese local governments, where the level of unemployment, density of population and the proportion of population with higher education influence the electoral outcomes.

The political variable of control introduced, that is the ideology of the political party in power, is statistically significant and negative, which indicates that in the elections of the analyzed year, local governments governed by a conservative party had higher probabilities to be changed while left governments were re-elected. This may be due to the general trend in Spain for a change to left governments in the elections of 2015, because after the deep crisis left governments have increased their power.

Table 7. OLS estimations for the percentage of variation in the votes of the political party in power

	Model 3	**Model 4**
	Varvoto **(2012-2014)**	*Varvoto* **(2014)**
Socialexp	0.0312**	0.0351
	(0.0150)	(0.0269)
KEI	0.0183**	0.0188
	(0.00752)	(0.0147)
FRI	-12.90**	-25.24**
	(5.877)	(11.24)
Unemploy	5.602	-2.682
	(17.97)	(33.26)
Population	-2.118***	-3.121***
	(0.596)	(1.083)
Inmigrat	-1.408	-1.766
	(4.506)	(8.876)
Ideology	5.543***	------
	(0.980)	------
Constant	17.17*	39.43**
	(9.747)	(17.48)
Observations	309	103
R-squared	0.205	0.145

Standard errors in parentheses
*** p<0.01, ** p<0.05, * p<0.1

Table 7 contains the OLS estimations using the data of 2014 and the three years that the political party has been governing. However, in this case there are some differences in the results.

If we focus on the model that considers the data of all the period (model 3), the three financial variables analyzed are statistically significant. This evidences that, in relation to the second research question, those governments that have higher social expenditures, higher capital expenditures and lower fiscal revenues increase the percentage of votes of the political party in the power, while those with lower level of social expenditure and investment and higher own tax collection will have worst results. As a consequence, governments that focus their efforts in manipulating these variables through political budget cycles can have positive effect on electoral outcomes. These results support the findings of Drazen and Eslava (2005), who maintain that capital expenditures are rewarded by voters, and Balaguer-Coll and Brun-Martos (2013), who found that the electorate values capital expenditures in a positive way. Also, Chortareas et al. (2016) support the positive effect that can have increased expenditures and election year opportunistic excesses on incumbents' reelection prospects.

However, considering just the data of the year previous to elections, the results indicate that neither the social expenditure nor the capital expenditure have a significant effect on the electoral outcomes. The comparative analysis evidences that considering just the pre-electoral management, really PBC are not efficient and those governments that change budgetary management during the last year cannot achieve advantage in the elections. The citizens do not perceive the signals of the last year but the management of the expenditure during all the period. They reward governments that have higher social expenditure and higher expenditure on investments for the budget cycle.

The fiscal revenues variable, determined as percentage of the total current revenues, is statistically significant and negative in the two models, indicating that governments with higher fiscal revenues and then higher fiscal pressure will have a decrease in the votes of the political party in power. The citizens perceive fiscal pressure both during the period of government and in the previous year to the elections and penalize this management in elections. They prefer government with less fiscal pressure. In this case, the financial information of own revenues is more determinant than the social expenditure or investment in the previous year to the elections. It seems that the citizens visualize more the fiscal pressure than the expenditure policies in the pre-electoral year. These results do not confirm the situation found in Portugal by Cunha (2018), where there is a positive association between the level of financial independency of governments and the re-election of governments. This means that the context is important in order to understand the influence of financial information in voting behaviours.

The size of the municipality is also significant in this case, evidencing that municipalities with higher number of inhabitants have more probabilities to decrease the percentage of votes of the political party in power. Citizens of larger municipalities lost trust in governments more easily than smaller ones. However, the unemployment level and the percentage of immigrants do not have a statistically significant influence in the electoral outcomes measured by the percentage of change in the votes of the political party in the power.

Finally, the results confirm the influence of the ideology in the elections of 2015, as left parties win votes with independency of financial management of the political party in the power.

CONCLUSION

Democratic systems have an electoral system that increases the efficiency and accountability of governments. Assuming that voters are rational, under the perspective of public choice theory, financial reporting can be useful to inform citizens about the financial management of governments. In this framework it is important to analyze whether voters really perceive financial management and, as a consequence, what role can financial reporting have in voting behaviour? Furthermore, the application of agency theory supports that citizens and voters control the management of politicians and information will influence decisions about who to vote for. Financial reporting reflects the results of public policies and consequently serves as a vehicle for communicating the economic effects of political management. Thus, citizens can perceive financial management and the latter can influence their election decisions.

Previous literature has introduced the relationship between municipal financial management and voting behaviour through political budget cycles. This chapter tries to contribute to this field, with the aim of analyzing whether there is a relationship between financial reporting and electoral outcomes or not.

The results of the empirical study carried out for Spanish municipalities show that electoral outcomes are, effectively, influenced by some variables that reflect financial management, while there are others that do not influence the results of the political party in government.

The results show that the level of debt and deficit are not statically significant to explain the re-election of governments or the percentage of votes obtained by the political party in the government. As a consequence, the level of debt and deficit do not compromise the continuity of the politicians in government.

Nevertheless, our second analysis shows that governments that have higher social spending have more probabilities of being re-elected. That is, citizens reward the management of politicians who increase social spending during their governments. The capital expenditure is not statistically significant to predict the re-election of the governing party of a municipality and the level of capital expenditure in the year previous to the elections does not influence the variation in the votes of the government. The results imply that if governments choose the capital expenditure to impress voters the year before elections, this would not have positive effects on the elections. However, governments with higher capital expenditures during all the government period may be rewarded by citizens.

The analysis shows that citizens penalized governments with higher fiscal pressure, both during the period of government and in the previous year to the elections. They prefer government with less fiscal pressure. A practical implication of these results is that they may encourage governments to search for alternative resources for financing services.

This evidences that voters perceive the consequences of public policies and this information can influence their voting decisions. Financial reporting is a tool to inform about the financial management of governments and can provide citizens information about public policies carried out by the political party in power. An important conclusion is that citizens can benefit from this financial and budgetary reporting, because they can find out the consequences of public policies. This implies that the financial report can be useful for voters and citizens.

To sum up, the results can enrich literature about the effect of financial management of governments in electoral outcomes, and also about the effectiveness of political cycles of governments. Furthermore, they can have practical implications in the financial management of local governments because politicians can have information about what practices are preferred by citizens. In particular, a recommendation derived from the results is that these encourage Spanish local governments to present a financial report to the citizenry, simplifying the format and combining financial data with graphics and discussions of local government activities for the year, so that citizens can know how their taxes have been spent. Popular reports should focus on analysis rather than disclosure, be objective, and user-friendly (GASB, 1992). In addition to comparing actual results to the original budget, the report should explain how significant variations would affect future planning, operations, and financial position. Non-financial measures of service efforts and accomplishments related to expenditures, such as miles of streets paved, police response times or usage of recreational facilities are candidates for additional disclosure.

From the perspective of the citizens, the results show that they should be aware of the importance of financial and budgetary data, because they can explain public policies and the results of public management. Governments must provide incentives to encourage citizens to use the reports.

This study is not without its limitations, such as the sample of entities selected or the use of data of electoral outcomes of only one electoral period. The use of more entities and more periods as well as the application of dynamic models could improve the statistical analysis and increase the robustness of the results.

ACKNOWLEDGMENT

This study was carried out with the financial support of the Spanish Regional Government of Aragon (Research Group 268242- CEMBE).

REFERENCES

Aidt, T. S., Veiga, F. J., & Goncalves Veiga, L. (2011). Election results and opportunistic policies: A new test of the rational political business cycle model. *Public Choice*, *148*(1-2), 21–44. doi:10.100711127-010-9644-3

Akhmedov, A., & Zhuravskaya, E. (2004). Opportunistic political cycles: Test in a young democracy setting. *The Quarterly Journal of Economics*, *119*(4), 1301–1338. doi:10.1162/0033553042476206

Alesina, A., & Paradisi, M. (2017). Political budget cycles: Evidence from Italian cities. *Economics and Politics*, *29*(2), 157–177. doi:10.1111/ecpo.12091

Alesina, A., Perotti, R., Tavares, J., Obstfeld, M., & Eichengreen, B. (1998). The political economy of fiscal adjustments. *Brookings Papers on Economic Activity*, *1998*(1), 197–266. doi:10.2307/2534672

Alvarez, B., & Delgado, M. (2006). Manipulación electoral del gasto público: Evidencia empírica en las provincias argentinas (1983-2002). Anales de la Asociación Argentina de Economía Política.

Arrow, K. J. (1951). Alternative approaches to the theory of choice in risk-taking situations. *Econometrica*, *19*(4), 404–437. doi:10.2307/1907465

Balaguer-Coll, M. T., & Brun-Martos, M. I. (2013). El efecto del gasto público sobre las posibilidades de reelección de los gobiernos locales. *Revista de Contabilidad*, *16*(1), 74–80. doi:10.1016/S1138-4891(13)70008-6

Black, D. (1948). On the rationale of group decision-making. *Journal of Political Economy*, *56*(1), 23–34. doi:10.1086/256633

Blais, A., & Nadeau, R. (1992). The electoral budget cycle. *Public Choice*, *74*(4), 389–403.

Boetti, L., Piacenza, M., & Turati, G. (2012). Decentralization and local governments' performance: How does fiscal autonomy affect spending efficiency? *FinanzArchiv: Public Finance Analysis*, *68*(3), 269–302. doi:10.1628/001522112X653840

Brender, A. (2003). The effect of fiscal performance on local government election results in Israel: 1989–1998. *Journal of Public Economics, 87*(9-10), 2187–2205. doi:10.1016/S0047-2727(02)00045-2

Brusca, I., & Montesinos, V. (2006). Are citizens significant users of government financial information? *Public Money & Management, 26*(4), 205–209. doi:10.1111/j.1467-9302.2006.00526.x

Chan, J. L., & Rubin, M. A. (1987). The role of information in a democracy and in government operations: The public choice methodology. *Research in Governmental and Nonprofit Accounting, 3*(Part B), 3-27.

Chortareas, G., Logothetis, V., & Papandreou, A. A. (2016). Political budget cycles and reelection prospects in Greece's Municipalities. *European Journal of Political Economy, 43*, 1–13. doi:10.1016/j.ejpoleco.2016.02.001

Cioffi, M., Messina, G., & Tommasino, P. (2012). *Parties, institutions and political budget cycles at the municipal level.* Bank of Italy Temi di Discussione (Working Paper) No, 885.

Cunha, A.M. (2018). *Informação Financeira e Fatores Socioeconómicos: Impacto na Reeleição do Autarca* (Tesis Doctoral). Universidad de Aveiro, Portugal.

Drazen, A., & Eslava, M. (2005). *Electoral manipulation via expenditure composition: theory and evidence (No. w11085).* National Bureau of Economic Research. doi:10.3386/w11085

Drazen, A., & Eslava, M. (2010). Electoral manipulation via voter-friendly spending: Theory and evidence. *Journal of Development Economics, 92*(1), 39–52. doi:10.1016/j.jdeveco.2009.01.001

Galli, E., & Rossi, S. P. (2002). Political budget cycles: The case of the Western German Länder. *Public Choice, 110*(3-4), 283–303. doi:10.1023/A:1013089504557

GASB. (1992). *Popular Reporting: Local Government Financial Reports to the Citizenry. Research Report 16*. Norwalk: GASB.

Guillamón, M. D., Bastida, F., & Benito, B. (2013). The electoral budget cycle on municipal police expenditure. *European Journal of Law and Economics, 36*(3), 447–469. doi:10.100710657-011-9271-6

Ingram, R. W., & Copeland, R. M. (1981). Municipal accounting information and voting behaviour. *The Accounting Review, LVI*(4), 830–843.

IPSASB. (2018). *Handbook of International Public Sector Accounting Standards*. Author.

James, O., & Peter, J. (2007). Public Management at the Ballot Box: Performance Information and Electoral Support for Incumbent English Local Governments. *Journal of Public Administration: Research and Theory*, *17*(4), 567–580. doi:10.1093/jopart/mul020

Klein, F. A. (2010). Reelection incentives and political budget cycle: Evidence from Brazil. *Revista de Administração Pública*, *44*(2), 283–337. doi:10.1590/S0034-76122010000200006

Klomp, J., & De Haan, J. (2013). Political budget cycles and election outcomes. *Public Choice*, *157*(1-2), 245–267. doi:10.100711127-012-9943-y

Kutner, M. H., Nachtsheim, C. J., Neter, J., & Li, W. (2005). *Applied linear statistical models* (Vol. 5). Boston: McGraw-Hill Irwin.

Lago-Peñas, I., & Lago-Peñas, S. (2008). Explaining budgetary indiscipline: Evidence from Spanish municipalities. *Public Finance and Managament*, *8*(1), 36–69.

Lopez Uribe, M. D. P. (2013). *Roads or Schools? Political Budget Cycles with different types of voters*. Documento mpra, núm. 50529.

Ministry of Finance. (2015a). *Deuda viva de las entidades locales*. Retrieved from: http://www.hacienda.gob.es/es-ES/CDI/Paginas/SistemasFinanciacionDeuda/InformacionEELLs/DeudaViva.aspx

Ministry of Finance. (2015b). *Datos presupuestarios de las entidades locales: consulta presupuestos y liquidaciones de entidades locales*. Retrieved from: https://serviciostelematicosext.minhap.gob.es/SGCAL/CONPREL

Ministry of Interior. (2015a). *Base de datos de Alcaldes. Elecciones 1979-2015. Listas electorales legislaturas 2011 y 2015*. Retrieved from: https://www.mptfp.gob.es/portal/politica-territorial/local/sistema_de_informacion_local_-SIL-/datos_legislaturas_1979_2015.html

Ministry of Interior. (2015b). *Consulta de resultados electorales. Área de descargas – Datos de municipios 2015 -2011*. Retrieved from: http://www.infoelectoral.mir.es/infoelectoral/min/areaDescarga.html?method=inicio

Mueller, D. (1976). Public Choice: A Survey. *Journal of Economic Literature*, *14*(2), 395–433.

National Institute of Statistics. (2015). *Estadísticas territoriales del padrón municipal continuo.* Retrieved from http://www.ine.es/dynt3/inebase/es/index.html?padre=517&dh=1

Nordhaus, W. (1975). The Political Business Cycle. *The Review of Economic Studies, 42*(2), 169–190. doi:10.2307/2296528

Peltzman, S. (1992). Voters as fiscal conservatives. *The Quarterly Journal of Economics, 107*(2), 327–361. doi:10.2307/2118475

Public Employment Service. (2015). *Datos estadísticos de paro registrado y contratos por municipios.* Retrieved from: https://www.sepe.es/HomeSepe/que-es-el-sepe/estadisticas/datos-estadisticos.html

Repetto, L. (2018). Political budget cycles with informed voters: Evidence from Italy. *Economic Journal (London), 128*(616), 3320–3353. doi:10.1111/ecoj.12570

Rogoff, K. (1990). Equilibrium political budget cycles. *The American Economic Review, 80*, 21–36.

Rogoff, K., & Sibert, A. (1988). Elections and macroeconomic policy cycles. *The Review of Economic Studies, 55*(1), 1–16. doi:10.2307/2297526

Sakurai, S. N., & Menezes-Filho, N. (2011). Opportunistic and partisan election cycles in Brazil: New evidence at the municipal level. *Public Choice, 148*(1-2), 233–247. doi:10.100711127-010-9654-1

Schick, A. (1969). Systems politics and systems budgeting. *Public Administration Review, 29*(2), 137–151. doi:10.2307/973694

Shi, M., & Svensson, J. (2006). Political budget cycles: Do they differ across countries and why? *Journal of Public Economics, 90*(8-9), 1367–1389. doi:10.1016/j.jpubeco.2005.09.009

Sielocal. (2016). *Gastos en los principales servicios públicos.* Retrieved from: http://www.sielocal.com/informe/266/Gastos-en-los-principales-servicios-p%C3%BAblicos

Sjahrir, B. S., Kis-Katos, K., & Schulze, G. G. (2013). Political budget cycles in Indonesia at the district level. *Economics Letters, 120*(2), 342–345. doi:10.1016/j.econlet.2013.05.007

Vicente, C., Ríos, A. M., & Guillamón, M. D. (2013). Voting behaviour and budget stability. *Revista de Contabilidad, 16*(1), 46–52. doi:10.1016/S1138-4891(13)70005-0

Wagner, N. (2012). *No matter who rules! Local elections and fiscal spending in rural Senegal.* International Institute of Social Studies, Working paper.

Wang, W., & Hou, Y. (2012). Do local governments save and spend across budget cycles? Evidence from North Carolina. *American Review of Public Administration, 42*(2), 152–169. doi:10.1177/0275074011398387

Zimmerman, J. L. (1977). The municipal accounting maze. An analysis of political incentives. *Journal of Accounting Research, 15*(supplement), 107–155. doi:10.2307/2490636

APPENDIX 1

Table 8. Variance inflation factors (VIF): period 2011-2014

Variable	*VIF*	*1/VIF*
fri	1.33	0.752995
unemploy	1.21	0.827837
socialexp	1.13	0.884799
population	1.13	0.885015
inmigr	1.11	0.897936
kei	1.08	0.923199
ideology	1.06	0.947402
Mean VIF	1.15	

Table 9. Variance inflation factors (VIF):2014

Variable	*VIF*	*1/VIF*
fri	1.28	0.78163
unemploy	1.18	0.850669
socialexp	1.17	0.856746
kei	1.16	0.858397
inmigr	1.12	0.89112
population	1.11	0.901901
Mean VIF	1.16	

Chapter 2
Financial Indicators as Determinants of Mayoral Elections:
Evidence From Italian Local Governments

Serena Santis
https://orcid.org/0000-0003-0919-2080
University of Campania "Luigi Vanvitelli", Italy

Francesca Citro
https://orcid.org/0000-0003-4132-9091
University of Salerno, Italy

Beatriz Cuadrado-Ballesteros
https://orcid.org/0000-0003-3606-2302
University of Salamanca, Spain

Marco Bisogno
https://orcid.org/0000-0003-3155-2919
University of Salerno, Italy

ABSTRACT

The chapter seeks to contribute to the literature on determinants of local government election by adopting a different perspective focused on the effects of financial indicators on the elections of mayors. Using the agency and the public choice theory, this study implements a model where specific financial indicators—whose selection takes into account the increased autonomy and responsibility of local politicians—have been included to document their effect on mayoral re-election. Focusing on the Italian context, the chapter examines a sample of 129 municipalities during the period 2008-2014, where several elections were held. By using different estimators, findings indicate that the re-election of mayors is affected by the level of indebtedness and the current equilibrium. In addition, current spending is better valued by citizens/voters than capital expenditure, which increases the probability of being re-elected.

DOI: 10.4018/978-1-5225-7820-8.ch002

INTRODUCTION

The electoral results are a representation of the opinion of the citizens, who can gratify or penalize the incumbents in polls. Indeed, incumbency is one the most important determinants of the election success, especially at the local level, determining the re-election of local officials (Krebs, 1998; Kushner, Siegel, & Stanwick, 1997). The period during which politicians hold an office is open to the public scrutiny. Rational citizens will vote regarding the government performance. However, a government has information about its competence more quickly than voters, because of the temporary information asymmetries between the two parts (Rogoff & Sibert, 1988). Therefore, voters have to infer government's competence by observing the outcomes of public policies.

Such outcomes are generally represented in financial reports. Concretely, the economic and financial information can affect the voting behaviour (Brusca & Montesinos, 2006), because that information helps citizens know where and how much resources are being allocated and being used, favouring the understanding of decisions and policies implemented by the government.

Prior research has investigated the impact of economic variables on electoral outcomes as well as re-election chances (Key, 1966; Kramer, 1971, 1978). Empirical evidence highlights that citizens are concerned about the local government (LG) economic performance, and politicians are accountable to the voters for past and current economic outcomes (Nannestad & Paldman, 1994). Other studies have highlighted that politicians try to manipulate fiscal policy, with the primary objective being to increase the likelihood of a government being re-elected (Shi & Svensson, 2003).

These effects are particularly relevant at the LG level, due to higher comparability of institutional settings. Local politicians are more accountable to citizens, and LG outputs have higher visibility. Therefore, citizens can monitor more easily the responses of local politicians to their needs.

In this strand of research, several studies have focused on municipal election, documenting the effects played by financial information and socio-demographic variables on electoral outcomes (Ingram & Copeland, 1981; Feroz & Wilson, 1994; Brusca & Montesinos, 2006; Fernandes, Gomes, & Silva, 2012). Other studies, have investigated the potential influences played by political and economic variables on electoral outcomes (Veiga & Veiga, 2007; Cassette, Farvaque & Héricourt, 2009; Castro & Martins, 2011; Martins & Veiga, 2013), revealing that an increase in investment expenditures during the election years, and changes in the composition of spending, aiming at favouring more visible items, positively affect the vote share of politicians.

However, the effect of both financial information and socio-economic factors on a more specific topic, namely the mayor's re-election, seems to be less investigated. Albeit some recent studies (Cuhna, Ferreira, & Fernandes, 2016, 2018) have investigated the determinants of local government re-election of Portuguese mayors, the literature about this last topic is scarce. Furthermore, the decentralisation of several functions from central to local governments, coupled with the adoption of outsourcing strategies, have largely increased LG autonomy in several countries (Boetti, Piacenza, & Turati, 2012). Therefore, LGs can raise own taxes and manage their own assets, which in turn can affect their performance. However, previous studies seem to have paid less attention to the effects on mayor's re-election of this autonomy, as expressed through several financial variables. Accordingly, adopting the agency theory, combined with the public choice perspective, the primary goal of this chapter is to provide a new insight by identifying financial indicators to be considered as potential determinants of the re-election of mayors. More specifically, the chapter aims to examine to what extent the probability of the mayors' re-election (or the election of their party colleagues as successors) is positively affected by financial indicators expressing both the performance and the financial autonomy of the LG.

As far as the methodological perspective is concerned, this study is based on a sample of 129 Italian LGs, consisting of municipalities with more than 50,000 inhabitants, during the period 2008-2014. The Italian context has been selected because of the reforms introduced in the last decades which have, among other things, increased the financial autonomy of LGs, stimulating politicians and managers to preserve the financial health of the LG. Therefore, bearing in mind that similar processes have occurred in many other countries, we would argue that results from this study could be of interest to international readers.

Findings emerging from the empirical analysis document that the re-election of mayors is affected by the level of indebtedness and the ability of current revenue to cover current expenditures. In addition, current spending is better valued by citizens/voters than capital expenditure. Besides, among control variables, findings indicate that unemployment and the political ideology are determinants of the electoral results.

Our results extend findings from previous literature as this study analyses the effect of additional economic and financial variables. Furthermore, this research contributes to the literature on determinants of LG's mayor re-election, which has been little investigated until now (Cuhna et al., 2016; Cuhna et al., 2018).

The remainder of the chapter is structured as follows. Section 2 describes the Italian context while Section 3 develops the theoretical background of the study. Sections 4 reviews previous studies dealing with the determinants of LG's re-election and develops the research hypotheses. Section 5 presents the methodology, while

Section 6 illustrates the results, which are discussed in the final section, along with the conclusions of the study and future developments of the research.

DESCRIBING THE RESEARCH SETTING: ITALIAN LOCAL GOVERNMENTS

In Italy, there are three levels of public administration: central, regional and local governments. In the last years, significant innovations have been introduced, especially at an LG level. Over the time, many functions have been decentralised from the central government to local governments, aiming at improving efficiency and effectiveness while managing public resources. This process has implied a progressive reduction of central government transfers, affecting the financial autonomy of LGs (Steccolini, 2004). LGs are responsible for a broader range of activities, operating simultaneously at different levels: by setting the local regulatory framework and providing institutional services to citizens (e.g. civil registry), by delivering public services either directly (namely social services) or through private organizations (with specific regard to public utilities, where they often hold shares; Manes-Rossi, 2011). In doing so, LGs are entitled to raise own taxes and manage their own assets, although they still remain markedly dependent on transfers and grants from the central government, and, to a lesser extent, from the regions, especially in low-income areas of the country (Anessi-Pessina, Sicilia & Steccolini, 2012; Mussari & Giordano, 2013).

Furthermore, several innovations have been implemented concerning the accounting systems. Indeed, an accrual basis of accounting was introduced since 1995; a more recent reform (Decree n. 118/2011) has emphasised the role of this system, introducing also consolidated financial statements, although the traditional modified cash-basis system still remains the linchpin of the whole accounting system (Anessi-Pessina, Nasi & Steccolini, 2010; Caperchione, 2003). Besides, the modernisation of the accounting systems has played a key role in public sector reform processes, especially after the economic and financial crisis. In fact, the crisis has enhanced the need for harmonised public-sector accounts, in order to provide information alerting for financial problems, as well as to increase transparency and accountability in public administrations (Mussari, 2014).

In this view, the Italian central government has issued a regulation to fight misuse of public resources, enhancing transparency, introducing widespread forms of control over the pursuit of the institutional functions, at the same time enhancing the efficiency and performance of public administrations. Moreover, reforms implemented in the last decades have strengthened the responsibilities of local politicians (as well as managers) on the use of public resources and the objectives to be achieved. More specifically, politicians and the mayor itself have to guarantee the financial equilibrium of the LG while providing services to citizens. Accordingly, LGs have to respect different thresholds concerning specific financial indicators, such as the level of indebtedness and the current equilibrium, namely the ability of current revenue (mainly local taxes and transfers from both central and regional government) to cover current expenses.

Furthermore, to promote transparency and accountability for the quantity and the quality of the services to be provided to citizens, the Directive 2003/98/EC recommends a broader availability of public sector data. Therefore, Italian LGs have to provide citizens with full information accessibility about their future strategies and activities (Aiello, Bisogno & Nota, 2018).

Regarding the governance systems, it consists of a representative body (the town council) and an executive body, headed by the mayor. Members of the council are elected for a five-year term, and their number depends on the size of the LG, namely the number of inhabitants. The mayor is elected by universal direct suffrage and can exercise a number of powers, such as representation, nomination, designation and administration.

The election of the mayor and the representative body take place every five years; they can be re-elected for a second mandate, even if the mayor in charge for two consecutive times cannot be re-elected. Regarding the political party supporting the mayor, he/she must be supported by a single party in small municipalities (< 15,000 inhabitants), while can be supported by more than one parties, namely, a coalition, in large municipalities (> 150,00 inhabitants).

SCIENTIFIC BACKGROUND

A growing body of research has documented the benefits of transparency for economic and governance outcomes (Bellver & Kaufmann, 2005; Hameed, 2005; Islam, 2003). Empirical studies have found that governments with more transparent public finances are characterized by better fiscal performance (Alt, Lassen & Rose, 2006), lower sovereign borrowing costs (Glennerster & Shin, 2008), and lower levels of corruption (Reinikka & Svensson 2004; Douglas & Meijer, 2016; Grimmelikhuijsen & Meijer, 2014; Hood & Heald, 2006; Meijer, 2012).

Transparent public institutions are characterised by economic growth, democratic consolidation, poverty reduction, manageable debt practices, and improved governance (Alt et al., 2006; Benito & Bastida, 2009).

Therefore, budget transparency can facilitate government accountability, improving the quality of governance and more generally of democracy (Seifert, Carlitz, & Mondo, 2013; Harrison & Sayogo, 2014). Governments promoting budget transparency tend to be more democratic, have free and fair elections, and encourage partisan competitions (Harrison & Sayogo, 2014; Wehner & de Renzio, 2013).

From a theoretical viewpoint, the ideas underlying the democratic accountability perspective have been conceptualized through the agency theory (Bovens, Schillemans, & Hart, 2008), where the principal and the agent are supposed to be rational, acting in a self-interested manner to maximise their utility.

As a consequence, the agent is not always expected to act in the interests of the principal (Jensen & Meckling, 1976; Zimmerman, 1977); therefore, both agent and principal can incur in agency costs.

Ingram and Copeland (1981) evidenced that citizens/voters support the policy maker who is believed to generate high income levels. In this agency relationship, a conflict of interest could emerge. Politicians may try to maximise their interests, namely to be re-elected, to promote career advancements and increase their current and future income, with the consequence being that they might not maximise the needs and desires of voters. To put it differently, politicians may act opportunistically (Rogoff & Sibert, 1988), taking decisions not only to serve the citizens but also to pursue rent-seeking activities. Moreover, the adoption of institutional arrangements is required to reduce their ability to engage in opportunistic activities (e.g. rent-seeking, corruption).

In other words, to achieve their objective, namely to gain re-election, politicians on the one hand could tend to develop public policies to meet the expectations of citizens; on the other hand, they could be prone to manipulate accounting numbers, because accounting information could influence voters (Cohen, Bisogno & Malkogianni, 2019). As a matter of fact, politicians face significant pressure from citizens/voters (as well as other stakeholders, such as the media, investors, and so on) to be accountable for public resources and to manage them adequately. Following Cardoso and Fajardo (2014), these facts are sufficient to boost the manipulation of financial reports reporting a break-even position, in order to show that public services are provided at a reasonable cost or to underline that the entity is not charging excessive taxes (Hodges, 2017). It is worth observing that this aspect can be particularly important when a municipality can take decisions regarding local taxes and the quality/quantity of public service to be delivered to citizens, namely when it has autonomy toward the central government (Boetti Piacenza, & Turati, 2012).

Following this line of thought, the public choice theory offers a useful support, as it investigates the behaviour of the agents interacting on the political markets (Buchanan, 2009). Public choice scholars claim that politicians are expected to remain egoistic, rational, utility maximisers (Mueller, 1989). As a consequence, they are supposed to pursue their own interest, as individuals could do in economic markets, rather than that of the public, in accordance with the so-called "self-interest" axiom. Furthermore, public choice scholars also claim that more reliable and comparable information could stimulate politicians to act in the interest of citizens, according to the "pressure of the competition" axiom (Boyne, 1997). Actually, the election periods can create this kind of pressure, stimulating politicians to act in the public interest instead of their own (Boyne, 1997; Buchanan, 2009). Research on voting behaviour (Holbrook et al., 2001; Capelos, 2010) suggests that reputation and prestige of incumbents affect voters' decisions in polls.

Retaining that citizens/voters (principal) and politicians (agent) aim to maximise their own interest (Watts, 1977) and that politicians could adopt an opportunistic behaviour because of information asymmetries (Rogoff & Sibert, 1988), the agency theory and the public choice theory are appropriate to analyse government management practices and political processes.

Consistently with these theories, the conflict of interest between politicians and citizens and the adoption of opportunistic behaviour can be solved, by reducing the information advantage of the former. Accordingly, voters push politicians to disclose information, in order to be able to monitor their activities, at the same time reducing information asymmetry (Zimmerman, 1977). Ingram and Copeland (1981) argue that accounting information can be considered as "... a vehicle for communicating the economic effects of policy decisions". Politicians steer public policies toward the expectations of citizens/voters, affecting several items such as revenue, expenses and debt (Ingram & Copeland, 1981). Therefore, politicians are aware that information concerning financial condition of the LG can influence the voters and, hence, could affect the re-election.

RESEARCH HYPOTHESES

Several studies (Ingram & Copeland, 1981; Feroz & Wilson, 1994; Brusca & Montesinos, 2006; Fernandes et al., 2012; Cuhna et al., 2016; 2018) have investigated the determinants of the election results of LGs, documenting that both financial and socio-demographic variables are common explanatory factors. The political budget cycle approach (Nordhaus, 1975) indicates that ruling politicians have incentives to manipulate economic or financial variables with the aim of creating favourable conditions in the pre-election period to influence the opinions of voters about their mandate. Favourable conditions refer, among other aspects, to fiscal variables (e.g. public spending, taxation, budgetary balance, etc.). This approach is based on the public choice theory (Downs, 1957), which considers politicians as opportunistic agents who act in their own interest, i.e. gain power or to retain it.

However, as anticipated, a government has information about its performance more quickly than voters, because of the temporary information asymmetries between the two parts (Rogoff and Sibert, 1988). Therefore, voters have to infer government's competence by observing the outcomes of public policies, which are usually represented in financial reports. Such information helps citizens know where and how much resources are being allocated and being used, favouring the understanding of decisions and policies implemented by the government. Accordingly, and following previous literature, we expect that financial indicators may represent the incumbents' competence and affect the election results.

As stated in the second section, the reforms implemented in Italy (as well as in many other countries) under the umbrella of the NPM paradigm, have increased the *financial autonomy* of LGs, which expresses the (relative) freedom to impose local taxes, collect revenue and allocate financial resources without external interference (Turley, Robbins & McNena, 2015), while complying with the general rules defined by the central government. One of the main consequences of LG's financial autonomy is that politicians, on the one hand, can take decisions regarding local taxes; on the other hand, they are responsible for the use of public resources. Therefore, to affect citizens' behaviour, it could be hypothesised that politicians will improve financial autonomy, to demonstrate how efficiently they manage resources collected from citizens. In other words, the mayor and its supporting political parties would use their freedom to impose local taxes to cover citizens' demands without damaging the LG financial condition (Honadle, Costa, & Cigler, 2004). Accordingly, we propose the following hypothesis:

HP1: The re-election is positively affected by LGs financial autonomy.

Previous studies have tested the effect of both current expenses and current revenue, namely the *Current equilibrium*, which expresses the ability of current revenue to cover current expenses (i.e. this is like a working capital indicator). Brusca and Montesinos (2006) found that indicators of a change in expenditure or execution of expenditure had a strong influence on electoral results. According to these findings, the vote share of political party actually in charge could be positively affected by the decisions taken and activities carried out during the last municipal legislative year. Furthermore, other studies (Sakurai & Menezes-Filho, 2008; Balaguer-Call et al., 2014) find evidence that higher expenditure throughout the legislature increases the probability for a mayor (or for a candidate of the same political party) to be re-elected.

Therefore, the mayor could influence the voters by increasing the municipal expenses (Veiga & Veiga, 2007) in order to intensify the provision of the public services, or by manipulating accounting information. Several studies (Veiga & Veiga, 2007; Cuhna et al., 2018) highlighted that in pre-election periods, mayors decrease municipal taxes, increase current expenses (such as those concerning cleaning, paving and maintenance of public roads, rural transport, and so on) and the budget deficit, and increase municipal capital expenses to obtain greater visibility to the citizens/voters. Controlling the balance between current revenue and expenses is essential for preventing future solvency problems. Indeed, a high value of current expenditures exceeding current revenues has been interpreted as a warning signal of financial stress (Bisogno, Manes-Rossi & Tartaglia Polcini, 2013; Manes-Rossi, Zito & Costanzo, 2012), which may be negatively valued by citizens in polls; furthermore, this indicator is of a great momentum in the Italian context, as Italian LGs have to comply with it, in order to avoid negative consequences, with the worst of them being the financial distress. The current equilibrium can represent a sound government, which is able of providing public services while also covering the financial obligations derived from such delivery. Accordingly, the second hypothesis is:

HP2: The re-election is positively affected by the LG's current equilibrium.

Previous studies have also tested the effect of the *level of indebtedness*, which refers to the use of public debt to finance public spending instead of using taxes influencing the voting decision (Copeland, 1981; Feroz & Wilson, 1994). Scholars (Cassette, Farvaque & Héricourt, 2013) have documented that the accumulation of debt during the whole term negatively affects the re-election; but in contrast, pre-election debt accumulation favours the election results of the incumbents.

On the one hand, incumbents can use debt to create fiscal illusion (Puviani, 1897), i.e. current voters are the beneficiaries of more/better public services and/or lower fiscal pressure because politicians use debt-financed spending. The real cost of such spending will be covered by future generations instead of the current voters, although future generations will not benefit from the services (Musgrave & Musgrave, 1989). Accordingly, we may expect that the use of debt is positively valued by citizens/voters, ignoring the breakdown in intergenerational equity (Citro, Lucianelli & Santis, 2018; Lucianelli et al., 2018). On the other hand, however, this approach shortens incumbents' time horizon, and it ignores the future deficits bias. The use of debt-financed spending is currently badly valued by citizens today, especially after the recent financial crisis; furthermore, in Italy as well as in other countries, different measures have been adopted to limit the level of indebtedness of LGs (Manes, Rossi, Zito, & Costanzo, 2012; Bisogno et al., 2018). Austerity programs implemented in several countries to decrease the importance of servicing debt and deficits (Lewis-Beck & Lobo, 2016) have damaged the opinion of citizens about the use of debt and public deficits. Concretely, at a local level, indebtedness is considered as a critical element of the financial condition of public sector entities (Zafra-Gómez, López-Hernández, & Hernández-Bastida, 2009; Rodríguez-Bolívar et al., 2016), and LGs have to maintain a low level of indebtedness to guarantee a good financial health. Therefore, the third hypothesis this study would like to test is:

HP3: The re-election is negatively affected by the LG's level of indebtedness.

Another factor that can affect the election results is the *level of investment*, which refers to the portion of the expenses devoted by a municipality to long-term projects (i.e. capital expenditure). Scholars (Veiga & Veiga, 2007; Akhmedov & Zhuravskaya, 2004; Sakurai & Menezes-Filho, 2008) have highlighted that the value of the investment has a substantial impact on the citizen: a higher value of investments can show the high attention of the mayor towards the provision of the public service. In the same vein, other studies (Castro & Martins, 2011; Martins & Veiga, 2013; Cassette, Farvaque & Héricourt, 2013) have documented that changes in the composition of spending (e.g., an increase in investment expenditures) during the election years, aiming at favouring more visible items, positively affect the probability of re-election of mayors.

However, Rogoff (1990) argued that the more "visible" spending category is current spending because it comes from expenditures on general public services (e.g. lighting, waste and water services, road maintenance, and so on), while capital expenditures refer to investments in infrastructures and long-term projects. Therefore, the effects of capital spending on the electorate could be more difficult to see immediately; they can see the current cost, but cannot enjoy its use. Cuadrado-Ballesteros and Bisogno (2018), who have investigated a large sample of Italian and Spanish municipalities, suggest that financial health is worse in municipalities that better assign capital expenditures, because they are usually financed mainly by borrowing, which has relevant costs that may damage the financial health. Therefore, the fourth hypothesis tested in this study is:

HP4: The re-election is negatively affected by the LG's level of investment.

Table 1. Municipalities that held local elections by year

Year	Municipalities
2008	Afragola; Bitonto; Brescia; Carpi; Casoria; Catania; Fiumicino; Grosseto; Imola; Massa; Messina; Modica; Molfetta; Pisa; Pozzuoli; Roma; Siracusa; Tivoli; Treviso; Udine; Viareggio; Vicenza; Viterbo
2009	Acerra; Acireale; Ancona; Aprilia; Bari; Battipaglia; Bergamo; Bologna; Brindisi; Caltanissetta; Cesena; Cinisello; Balsamo; Cremona; Fano; Ferrara; Firenze; Foggia; Foligno Forli; Guidonia; Montecelio; Livorno; Mazara del Vallo; Modena; Padova; Pavia; Perugia; Pesaro; Pescara ; Portici; Potenza; Prato; Sanremo; Terni; Trento
2010	Altamura; Andria; Bolzano; Castellammare di Stabia; Cava de' Tirreni; Cerignola; Faenza; Lamezia; Terme; Manfredonia; Matera; Moncalieri; Quartu S. Elena; Sassari; Teramo; Tivoli; Venezia; Vigevano
2011	Arezzo; Bagheria; Barletta; Benevento; Bisceglie; Bologna; Busto Arsizio Cagliari; Caserta; Casoria; Catanzaro; Cosenza; Crotone; Gela; Giugliano in Campania; Latina; Marano di Napoli; Milano; Napoli; Olbia; Pomezia; Pozzuoli; Ragusa; Ravenna; Reggio di Calabria; Rimini; Salerno; Savona; Siena; Torino; Trieste; Varese; Vittoria
2012	Acerra; Alessandria; Asti; Aversa; Bitonto; Brindisi; Carrara; Catanzaro; Civitavecchia; Como; Cuneo; Genova; La Spezia; Lecce; Legnano; Lucca; Marsala; Monza; Novara; Palermo; Parma; Piacenza; Pistoia; Pozzuoli; Taranto; Trani; Trapani; Verona
2013	Afragola; Ancona; Aprilia; Barletta; Brescia; Castellammare di Stabia; Catania; Cinisello; Balsamo; Fiumicino; Imola; Marano di Napoli; Massa; Messina; Modica; Molfetta; Pisa; Pomezia; Portici; Ragusa; Roma; Siena; Siracusa; Treviso; Udine; Viareggio; Vicenza; Viterbo
2014	Avellino; Bagheria; Bari; Bergamo; Caltanissetta; Cesena; Civitavecchia; Cremona; Fano; Ferrara; Firenze ; Foggia; Foligno; Forli; Guidonia; Montecelio; Livorno; Mazara del Vallo; Modena; Padova; Pavia; Perugia; Pesaro; Pescara; Potenza; Prato; Reggio di Calabria; Sanremo; Sassari; Teramo; Terni; Tivoli; Vicenza

METHODOLOGY

Sample

The proposed hypotheses will be empirically tested on a sample of 129 Italian LGs, consisting of municipalities with more than 50,000 inhabitants, over the period 2008-2014. This results in a panel dataset of 903 observations. During that period, several elections were held in Italian LGs. Concretely, table 1 shows municipalities that have held local elections in each year.

We focus on larger municipalities (over 50,000 inhabitants) because they are required to provide a substantial part of the infrastructure and essential public services (e.g. urban waste collection and treatment, cleaning, paving and maintenance of public roads, drinking water supply, civil protection and security, social services, etc.). These services affect the citizens' welfare directly, and therefore, voters' opinion on the government and, finally, the results in polls.

The Italian context is highly appropriate because LGs have autonomy to set some specific taxes and to decide how spending their resources by approving their own budget (within specific legal constraints). Therefore, their decisions affect the image that citizens have about governments, and then, the electoral results. Furthermore, reforms implemented in Italy, as well as in many other countries, have introduced different measures to monitor the financial equilibrium of LGs, defining a set of financial indicators to which municipalities have to comply with. The most relevant financial indicators are the current equilibrium, the level of indebtedness and the level of investments. LGs which do not respect the predefined thresholds concerning these variables, and other minor indicators, incur in penalties, with the extreme consequence being the declaration of financial distress (Bisogno, Citro & Tommasetti, 2014).

Information on political issues, financial data, and socioeconomic information has been obtained from an open website (www.openbilanci.it). This website shows both financial statements data and the data concerning the mayors/political parties for every Italian LGs for a broad range of time.

Model and Variables

With the aim of testing the proposed hypotheses, we estimate the following model:

$$Reelection_{it} = \beta_0 + \beta_1 Autonomy_{it} + \beta_2 Balance_{it} + \beta_3 Debt_{it} + \beta_4 Investment_{it} + \beta_5 Population_{it} + \beta_6 Unemployment_{it} + \beta_7 Older_{it} + \beta_8 Ideology_{it} + \eta_i + \mu_{it} \cdot \quad (1)$$

where, i and t refer to each municipality and year, respectively; β are the parameters to be estimated; η_i refers to unobservable heterogeneity (i.e. the characteristics of each municipality, which are different from others, but are invariant over time), and μ_{it} is the classical disturbance term.

The dependent variable, *Reelection*, takes the value 1 if the mayor has been re-elected and 0 otherwise, i.e. 0 if the mayor has not been re-elected after the elections and 0 in the years that there are not elections. For the creation of this variable, we based on previous studies. Cunha et al. (2018) and Balaguer-Coll et al. (2015) used a dummy variable to represent the re-election in Portuguese and Spanish LGs, respectively. For their respective periods of analysis, they took only the elections years, leaving aside those years that there were not elections. That is possible because local elections are held in the same year in all LGs. However, we cannot operationalize the variable "re-election" in that way, because local elections in Italy are not held in the same year all over the LGs. This is the only way to operationalize the "re-election" of mayors in Italian LGs, although this approach might bias the results.

The independent variables refer to financial issues regarding each hypothesis:

1. **Autonomy** refers to financial autonomy that is represented by ratio of revenues obtained from local taxes and other additional local revenue to total current revenue.
2. **Equilibrium:** Current equilibrium expresses the ability of current revenue to cover current expenses, and it is represented by the ratio of current revenues to current expenses.
3. **Debt** indicates the level of indebtedness that is measured as the ratio of total debts to total current cash revenue (Copley, 1991; Bisogno, Citro, & Tommasetti, 2014).
4. **Investment** refers to the part of the expenses for long-term projects (i.e., capital expenditure), and it is represented as a percentage of capital expenditure on total current expenditure on the average for the last three years, understanding that the higher the percentage, the higher the ability to invest in the future.

The results are controlled by some socio-economic factors whose effects on the results of re-election have been documented by previous studies (Cunha et al., 2018; Balaguer-Coll et al., 2015):

- **Population** is the logarithm of number of inhabitants.
- **Unemployment** is the unemployment rate.
- **Older** refers to the proportion of inhabitants aged over 65.

Ideology represents the political orientation, which takes the value 1 for left-wing governments and 0 otherwise.

Analysis Technique

Given the dichotomous nature of the dependent variable (*Reelection*), the technique to estimate the model (1) should be the logistic estimator for panel data. Logistic regression is a quantitative procedure designed to determine the explanatory power that a set of independent variables has for the occurrence of an event, here, the re-election of the local government. Accordingly, the model (1) may be rewritten in terms of odds ratio, in order to represent the probability that the government is re-elected or not:

$$\log\left(\frac{\text{prob}\left(Reelection_{it}=1\right)}{\text{prob}\left(Reelection_{it}=0\right)}\right)=\alpha+\beta_1 Autonomy_{it}+\beta_2 Balance_{it}+\beta_3 Debt_{it}+\beta_4 Investment_{it}+\beta_5 Population_{it}$$
$$+\beta_6 Unemployment_{it}+\beta_7 Older_{it}+\beta_8 Ideology_{it}+\eta_i+\mu_{it}$$

The results obtained by using the logistic estimator are showed on Table 4. However, we should take into account that independent and control variables are not strict exogenous; on the contrary, endogeneity problems arise in the model (1), as a correlation between the explanatory variables and the error term[1]. More concretely, we could expect that not only unemployment, the level of investment, or financial situation affects the probability of re-election, but also the possibilities of being re-elected may affect such features.

The endogeneity problem can be addressed by estimating the model (1) with instrumental variables (IV) methods. However, the conventional IV estimator is inefficient (although consistent) in the presence of heteroscedasticity (Baum, Schaffer, & Stillman, 2003). We check this condition by using the Breusch–Pagan test, and the results lead us to reject the null hypothesis of homoscedastic errors at the 95% confidence level. Therefore, the conventional IV estimator is not appropriate in this case.

In such a situation, we use the two-step *system* estimator of Arellano and Bover (1995). To remove endogeneity, the *system* estimator uses the lagged values of endogenous and predetermined variables as instruments. The lagged values are natural candidates for a valid instrument instead of the outside instruments that other estimators (2SLS, 3SLS, OLS, etc.) use. It is demonstrated that lagged values are uncorrelated with the error term when Arellano and Bond (1991) derived the estimator; and they contain information on the current value of their corresponding variable. The results obtained by using the *system* estimator are showed on Table 5.

Nevertheless, using the *system* estimator may prevent a proliferation of instruments and results could be biased. Instrument validity is tested by two tests: (i) the Arellano-Bond test for AR(2) in first differences, under the null hypothesis of no serial correlation between the error terms; and (ii) the Hansen test of over-identification restrictions, under the null hypothesis that the over-identifying restrictions are valid.

FINDINGS

First of all, we can see the descriptive statistics of dependent, independent and control variables of model (1) in table 2. We can see that 28.23% observation of *Re-election* take the value 1, representing LGs (namely: mayors and the related political parties) that were re-elected in the last elections.

After that, the table shows the mean value of the four financial features, namely financial autonomy, current equilibrium, level of indebtedness, and investment. The results for *Autonomy* indicate that 72.24% of current revenue are obtained from taxes, although there are large differences in the sample. Regarding the current equilibrium, the mean value of *Equilibrium* variable indicates that Italian LGs show

Table 2. Descriptive statistics

Variable	Obs	Mean	Std. Dev.	Min	Max
REELECTION	889	0.28	0.45	0	1
AUTONOMY	896	72.24	16.64	31.24	97.87
EQUILIBRIUM	896	107.72	36.09	49.67	1112.35
DEBT	896	87.5387	54.0159	0	340.42
INVESTMENT	896	25.90	20.59	3.1	320.18
POPULATION	903	11.49	0.70	10.82	14.87
UNEMPLOYMENT	893	11.26	5.70	1.87	27.81
OLDER	903	23.68	15.80	7.84	73.46
IDEOLOGY	888	0.58	0.49	0	1

Table 3. Bivariate correlations

	1	2	3	4	5	6	7	8
1. AUTONOMY	1							
2. EQUILIBRIUM	-0.0233	1						
3. DEBT	0.0673*	-0.0742*	1					
4. INVESTMENT	-0.1649***	0.0845*	0.2514***	1				
5. POPULATION	-0.0595†	-0.0056	0.1191***	0.1445***	1			
6. UNEMPLOYMENT	0.1154***	-0.1055**	-0.0483	-0.2871***	-0.145***	1		
7. OLDER	0.1027**	0.0063	0.0776*	0.0308	0.0135	-0.226***	1	
8. IDEOLOGY	0.0826*	0.0441	0.0458	0.0886**	0.126***	-0.0791*	0.0416	1

Notes:
†, *, **, ***significant at 10, 5, 1, and 0.1 percent level, respectively.

enough current income to cover current expenditure, on average. Differences are also very relevant in the case of the level of indebtedness; the mean value of *Debt* is 87.54% but it ranges from 3.31% in Lamezia Terme to 340.42% in Reggio di Calabria, which is the most indebted LG in the sample. Moreover, the mean value of *Investment* suggests that capital expenditure is 25.9% of current expenditure on average, falling to 3.1% in Trapani and raising to 320.1% in Milano.

Table 4. Determinants of re-election - Logistic estimator

	Coef.	*Std. Err.*	*z*	*P>|z|*
AUTONOMY	-0.0026	0.0074	-0.34	0.73
EQUILIBRIUM	-0.0024	0.0038	-0.63	0.527
DEBT	-0.0004	0.0028	-0.13	0.894
INVESTMENT	0.0051	0.0066	0.78	0.437
POPULATION	-0.1571	0.2654	-0.59	0.554
UNEMPLOYMENT	-0.0785**	0.0290	-2.71	0.007
OLDER	-0.9946	1.1832	-0.84	0.401
IDEOLOGY	0.2495	0.2668	0.94	0.35
_cons	1.6764	3.1360	0.53	0.593
/lnsig2u	1.0376	0.2507		
sigma_u	1.6800	0.2106		
rho	0.4618	0.0623		

Notes:
Dependent variable: REELECTION
All regressions include year fixed effects.
†, *, **, ***significant at 10, 5, 1, and 0.1 percent level, respectively.

Finally, we can see also the mean values of control variables: the logarithm of population (*Population*), the average unemployment rate (*Unemployment*), the proportion of population aged over 65 (*Older*), and the political orientation (*Ideology*). The most interesting results are the high unemployment rate on average (11.26%), which rises to 27.8% in Cosenza. The oldest population is found in Verona, where 73.46% of population is aged over 65, while the youngest is found in Bologna. Regarding the political orientation of the government, 57.88% observations show a left-wing ideology, on average.

Table 3 shows the bivariate correlations between independent and control variables entered into the model (1). In general, coefficients are lower than 0.3, suggesting that there are no multicollinearity problems (Wooldridge, 2010).

Table 4 illustrates the results of model (1) by using the logistic estimator for panel data. The results are not statistically relevant, just *Unemployment* at 99%, affecting negatively on the dependent variable (coef. -0785, p. < 0.1). The reason of their irrelevance is the existence of endogeneity problem, such as we indicated previously, that removes the significance of the most of variables. Accordingly, we have estimated the model (1) by using the system estimator of Arellano and Bover (1995) that solves endogeneity through instrumental variables. The results are showed on table 5.

Table 5. Determinants of re-election - system estimator

	Coef.	*Std. Err.*	*t*	*P>|t|*
AUTONOMY	0.0003	0.0037	0.09	0.926
EQUILIBRIUM	0.0012**	0.0004	3.06	0.003
DEBT	-0.0016***	0.0001	-13.26	0
INVESTMENT	-0.0014***	0.0004	-3.9	0
POPULATION	0.0034	0.0143	0.24	0.809
UNEMPLOYMENT	0.0037**	0.0013	2.94	0.004
OLDER	-0.0524	0.0337	-1.55	0.123
IDEOLOGY	0.0682***	0.0137	4.97	0
_cons	0.0003	0.0037	0.09	0.926
Arellano-Bond test for AR(2) in first differences: Pr > z = 0.382				
Hansen test of overid. restrictions: Prob > chi2 = 0.389				
Notes: Dependent variable: REELECTION All regressions include year fixed effects. †, *, **, ***significant at 10, 5, 1, and 0.1 percent level, respectively.				

Financial autonomy (*Autonomy*) is not statistically relevant in explaining re-election of LGs, but the current equilibrium, the level of indebtedness and investment do it. Concretely, *Equilibrium* impacts positively on the dependent variable, being statistically relevant at 99% confidence level (coef. 0.0012, p. < 0.01), while *Debt* and *Investment* show negative coefficients, being relevant at 99.9% (*Debt* coef. -0.0016, p. < 0.001; Investment coef. = -0.0014, p. < 0.001).

These findings suggest that the public opinion on governments is affected by financial factors, such as the existence of current equilibrium and the use of debt. Italian LGs with enough revenues, that do not need public debt to cover expenditures, are well-evaluated by citizens, affecting their final decision in polls. These findings are according to the hypotheses H2, H3 and H4.

Regarding control variables, *Population* and *Older* variables are not statistically relevant, while *Unemployment* and *Ideology* do it. The former has a negative coefficient, being relevant at 99% (coef. -0.0037, p. < 0.01). These findings suggest that the re-election of mayors is negatively affected by unemployment, because this is one of the issues that most concerns citizens, especially in those countries where the international crisis has greatly affected, as in the case of Italy. Finally, left-wing governments tend to be re-elected in more cases than the rightist, since *Ideology* has a positive coefficient that is relevant at 99.9% (coef. 0.0682, p. < 0.001).

DISCUSSION AND CONCLUSIONS

This study has investigated the effect on the election of mayors of different financial variables, coupled with socio-economic factors. More specifically, focusing on LGs, the chapter has examined a sample of 129 Italian municipalities with more than 50,000 inhabitants, during the period 2008-2014. The aim was to unveil the effect on the re-election of mayors of financial autonomy, the trend of current revenue and expenses and the level of both indebtedness and investments. In so doing, this study has implemented a model based on specific additional variables, which differ from those implemented in other studies. Indeed, the variables included in our model were selected considering their importance in the current scenario: NPM reforms implemented in Italy, as well as in many other countries, are based on the decentralisation of many functions from central to local governments, which has determined an increased autonomy of LGs. Furthermore, these reforms have increased the responsibility of local politicians while managing public resources. Accordingly, this chapter has analysed the effect of the so-called current equilibrium, namely the ability of current revenue to cover current expenses. Actually, while previous studies have investigated the effect played by current expenses and current revenue on political re-election, this research has focused on the *relationship* between current revenue and current expenses, considering it as a key financial indicator through which the financial health of a LG should be interpreted. Finally, it is worth recalling that our study investigates factors affecting the re-elections of mayors, contributing to the scarce literature on the topic.

Findings emerging from the empirical analysis document that the re-election of mayors is affected by the current equilibrium and the level of indebtedness. Furthermore, our results indicate that citizens/voters pay more attention to current spending than to capital expenditure, indirectly confirming findings emerging from previous research on LGs' efficiency (Cuadrado-Ballesteros & Bisogno, 2018). As far as the control variables are concerned, findings also indicate that electoral results are affected by unemployment and the political ideology of the parties supporting the mayor. However, financial autonomy seems to be not so important.

These results can be interpreted in the light of the agency theory and the public choice theory, according to which conflicting interests between the principal (citizens/voters) and the agents (politicians) can affect the decision-making process, and the activities carried out by local politicians. During the election period, politicians have a "pressure of competition", so that they are stimulated to improve the quality of services, increasing current expenses, with their main aim being to gain the re-election. This means that, on the one hand politicians would strengthen their power and gain the re-election; on the other hand, citizens/voters would ask for public services of high quality.

Although the chapter concentrates on the Italian context, we would argue that findings emerging from this study could be of interest to international readers, because NPM principles have largely inspired these reforms around the world. Furthermore, municipalities are characterised by a more direct relationship between politicians and citizens/voters, who (coupled with media, investors and other stakeholders) exert a pressure, so that local politicians are more accountable to them. Indeed, LG outputs have higher visibility and citizens can monitor more easily the responses of local politicians to their needs.

Additionally, politicians are aware that accounting information may influence the voters; more broadly, information concerning the financial condition of a public sector entity may affect the re-election. Accordingly, a clear implication for practitioner emerges from this study: local politicians are advised to pay attention on the financial condition of the LG, as it can affect the decisions taken by citizens/voters.

This chapter is not free of limitations. Firstly, the variable "re-election" takes the value 1 if the mayor has been re-elected and 0 if the mayor has not been re-elected and also in the years that there are not elections. As we indicated previously, this is the only way to operationalize the "re-election" of mayors in Italian LG, even though this approach might bias the results. We cannot take into account only the election years, as Cunha et al. (2018) and Balaguer-Coll et al. (2015), as each LGsz holds the elections in a different moment. We tried initially to create different subsamples, but the number of observations was much reduced and the models were not good. Secondly, the study adopts variables based on a modified-cash accounting system; therefore, it would be interesting implementing a model which includes accrual accounting variables. In doing so, future studies could take into consideration earnings management behaviour of local politicians and managers (Cohen et al., 2019), implementing a more complex model to test additional hypotheses concerning the manipulation of accounting numbers. Thirdly, it would be interesting comparing different countries, especially considering those where local elections take place in the same year (as in Spain or in Greece), in order to assess if having the election which is LG specific could influence the behaviour of politicians.

REFERENCES

Akhmedov, A., & Zhuravskaya, E. (2004). Opportunistic political cycles: Test in a young democracy setting. *The Quarterly Journal of Economics*, *119*(4), 1301–1338. doi:10.1162/0033553042476206

Alt, J. E., Lassen, D. D., & Rose, S. (2006). The causes of fiscal transparency: Evidence from the US states. *IMF Staff Papers*, *53*(1), 30–57.

Anessi-Pessina, E., Nasi, G. & Steccolini, I. (2010). Accounting innovations: a contingent view on Italian local governments. *Journal of Public Budgeting, Accounting & Financial Management, 22*(2), 250-271.

Anessi-Pessina, E., Sicilia, M., & Steccolini, I. (2012). Budgeting and rebudgeting in local governments: Siamese twins? *Public Administration Review*, *72*(6), 875–884. doi:10.1111/j.1540-6210.2012.02590.x

Arellano, M., & Bond, S. (1991). Some tests of specification for panel data: Monte Carlo evidence and an application to employment equations. *The Review of Economic Studies*, *58*(2), 277–297. doi:10.2307/2297968

Arellano, M., & Bover, O. (1995). Another look at the instrumental variables estimation of error components models. *Journal of Econometrics*, *68*(1), 29–51. doi:10.1016/0304-4076(94)01642-D

Balaguer-Coll, M. T., Brun-Martos, M. I., Forte, A., & Tortosa-Ausina, E. (2015). Local governments' re-election and its determinants: New evidence based on a Bayesian approach. *European Journal of Political Economy*, *39*, 94–108. doi:10.1016/j.ejpoleco.2015.04.004

Baum, C. F., Schaffer, M. E., & Stillman, S. (2003). Instrumental variables and GMM: Estimation and testing. *The Stata Journal*, *3*(1), 1–31. doi:10.1177/1536867X0300300101

Benito, B., & Bastida, F. (2009). Budget transparency, fiscal performance, and political turnout: An international approach. *Public Administration Review*, *69*(3), 403–417. doi:10.1111/j.1540-6210.2009.01988.x

Bisogno, M., Citro, F., & Tommasetti, A. (2014). The financial distress of public sector entities. Evidence from Italian public universities. *International Journal of Accounting. Auditing and Performance Evaluation*, *10*(2), 203–227. doi:10.1504/IJAAPE.2014.060221

Bisogno, M., Cuadrado-Ballesteros, B., Santis, S., & Citro, F. (2018). Budgetary solvency of Italian local governments: An assessment. *International Journal of Public Sector Management.*

Bisogno, M., Manes-Rossi, F., & Tartaglia Polcini, P. (2013). Audit quality in Italian Local Governments. *Proceedings in GVW-the 1st Global Virtual Conference-Workshop, 1*, 106-111.

Boetti, L., Piacenza, M., & Turati, G. (2012). Decentralization and local governments' performance: How does fiscal autonomy affect spending efficiency? *FinanzArchiv: Public Finance Analysis, 68*(3), 269–302. doi:10.1628/001522112X653840

Bovens, M., Schillemans, T., & Hart, P. (2008). Does Public Accountability Work? An Assessment Tool. *Public Administration, 86*(1), 225–242. doi:10.1111/j.1467-9299.2008.00716.x

Boyne, G. A. (1997). Public choice theory and local government structure: An evaluation of reorganisation in Scotland and Wales. *Local Government Studies, 23*(3), 56–72. doi:10.1080/03003939708433876

Brusca, I., & Montesinos, V. (2006). Are Citizens Significant Users of Government Financial Information? *Public Money & Management, 26*(4), 205–209. doi:10.1111/j.1467-9302.2006.00526.x

Buchanan, J. M. (2009). Politics without romance: a sketch of positive public choice theory and its normative implications. In J. Buchanan & R. Tollison (Eds.), *The Theory of Public Choice- II*. The University of Michigan Press.

Capelos, T. (2010). Feeling the issue: How citizens' affective reactions and leadership perceptions shape policy evaluations. *Journal of Political Marketing, 9*(1-2), 9–33. doi:10.1080/15377850903583038

Caperchione, E. (2003). Local government accounting system reform in Italy: A critical analysis. *Journal of Public Budgeting, Accounting &. Financial Management, 15*(1), 110–145.

Cardoso, R. L., & Fajardo, B. G. (2014). *Public sector creative accounting: A literature review.* Available at SSRN: https://ssrn.com/abstract=2476593

Cassette, A., Farvaque, E., & Héricourt, J. (2013). Two-round elections, one-round determinants? Evidence from the French municipal elections. *Public Choice, 156*(3), 563–591. doi:10.100711127-012-9913-4

Cassette, A., Farvaque, E., Héricourt, J., & Jean, N. (2009). Budget structure and reelection prospects: Empirical evidence from French local elections. ZEI - Center for European Integration Studies, University of Bonn.

Castro, V., & Martins, R. (2011). *Mayors' Reelection Choice and the Economy: Evidence from Portugal*. Portugal: NIPE - Universidade do Minho.

Citro, F., Lucianelli, G., & Santis, S. (2018). Financial Conditions, Financial Sustainability, and Intergenerational Equity in Local Governments: A Literature Review. In Financial Sustainability and Intergenerational Equity in Local Governments (pp. 101-124). IGI Global.

Cohen, S., Bisogno, M., & Malkogianni, I. (2019). Earnings Management in Local Governments: The Role of Political Factors. *Journal of Applied Accounting Research*, *20*(3), 331–348.

Copley, P. A. (1991). The association between municipal disclosure practices and audit quality. *Journal of Accounting and Public Policy*, *10*(4), 245–266. doi:10.1016/0278-4254(91)90001-Z

Cuadrado-Ballesteros, B., & Bisogno, M. (2018). Efficiency as a Determinant of Financial Condition: An Assessment of Italian and Spanish Local Governments. *International Public Management Journal*, 1–32. doi:10.1080/10967494.2018.1476426

Cunha, A., Ferreira, A. D. C. S., & Fernandes, M. J. (2016). The Influence of Accounting Information in the Re-Election of the Mayors in Portugal. In Global Perspectives on Risk Management and Accounting in the Public Sector (pp. 108-131). IGI Global. doi:10.4018/978-1-4666-9803-1.ch006

Cunha, A. M., Ferreira, A. D. C. S., & Fernandes, M. J. (2018). The Impact of Accounting Information and Socioeconomic Factors in the Re-Election of Portuguese Mayors. In Handbook of Research on Modernization and Accountability in Public Sector Management (406-432). IGI Global. doi:10.4018/978-1-5225-3731-1.ch019

Douglas, S., & Meijer, A. (2016). Transparency and public value—Analyzing the transparency practices and value creation of public utilities. *International Journal of Public Administration*, *39*(12), 940–951. doi:10.1080/01900692.2015.1064133

Downs, A. (1957). An economic theory of political action in a democracy. *Journal of Political Economy*, *65*(2), 135–150. doi:10.1086/257897

Fernandes, M., Gomes, P., & Silva, C. (2012). Accounting Information and Voter's Behaviour: Empirical Research in Portuguese Municipalities. Asociación Española da Contabilidad y Administración de Empresas (AECA). XV *Encuentro AECA Nuevos Caminos para Europa: El Papel de las Empresas y los Gobiernos, 106a.* Retrieved from http://www.aeca.es/pub/on_line/comunicaciones_xvencuentroaeca/cd/106a.pdf

Feroz, E., & Wilson, E. (1994). Financial Accounting Measures and Mayoral Elections. *Financial Accountability & Management*, *10*(3), 161–174. doi:10.1111/j.1468-0408.1994.tb00006.x

Glennerster, R., & Shin, Y. (2008). Does transparency pay? *IMF Staff Papers*, *55*(1), 183–209. doi:10.1057/palgrave.imfsp.9450028

Grimmelikhuijsen, S. G., & Meijer, A. J. (2014). Effects of transparency on the perceived trustworthiness of a government organization: Evidence from an online experiment. *Journal of Public Administration: Research and Theory*, *24*(1), 137–157. doi:10.1093/jopart/mus048

Hameed, F. (2005). *Fiscal transparency and economic outcomes (2005-2225).* International Monetary Fund.

Harrison, T. M., & Sayogo, D. S. (2014). Transparency, participation, and accountability practices in open government: A comparative study. *Government Information Quarterly*, *31*(4), 513–525. doi:10.1016/j.giq.2014.08.002

Hodges, R. (2017). *Public Sector Creative Accounting: Past Reflections and a Future Research Agenda.* Paper presented at CIGAR Conference, Oporto, 8 June 2017. Available at: http://web.ipca.pt/cigar/presentation/2017-06_Creative_Accounting_CIGAR_FINAL-for-website.pdf

Holbrook, A., Krosnick, J. A., Visser, P. S., Gardner, W. L., & Cacioppo, J. T. (2001). Attitudes towards presidential candidates and political parties: Initial optimism, inertial first impressions, and a focus on flaws. *American Journal of Political Science*, *45*(4), 930–950. doi:10.2307/2669333

Honadle, B. W., Costa, J. M., & Cigler, B. A. (2004). *Fiscal Health for Local Governments, An Introduction to Concepts, Practical Analysis and Strategies.* San Diego, CA: Elsevier Academic.

Hood, C., & Heald, D. (Eds.). (2006). *Transparency, the key to good governance?* Oxford, UK: Oxford University Press. doi:10.5871/bacad/9780197263839.001.0001

Ingram, R., & Copeland, R. (1981). Municipal Accounting Information and Voting Behavior. *The Accounting Review*, *56*(4), 830–843.

Islam, R. (2003). *Do more transparent governments govern better?* Policy Research Working Paper.

Jensen, M., & Meckling, W. (1976). Theory of the Firm: Managerial Behavior, Agency Costs and Ownership Structure. *Journal of Financial Economics*, *3*(4), 305–360. doi:10.1016/0304-405X(76)90026-X

Key, V. O. (1966). *The Responsible Electorate*. Cambridge, MA: Harvard University Press. doi:10.4159/harvard.9780674497764

Kramer, G. H. (1971). Short-Term Fluctuations in U.S. Voting Behavior, 1896–1964. *The American Political Science Review*, *71*(1), 131–143. doi:10.2307/1955049

Kramer. (1978). Macroeconomic Determinants of the Vote in Presidential Elections. *Public Finance Review, 6,* 427-438.

Krebs, T. B. (1998). The Determinants of Candidates' Vote Share and the Advantage of Incumbency in City Council Elections. *American Journal of Political Science*, *42*(3), 921–935. doi:10.2307/2991735

Kushner, J., Siegel, D., & Stanwick, H. (1997). Ontario Municipal Elections: Voting trends and determinants of electoral success in a Canadian province. *Canadian Journal of Political Science*, *30*(3), 539–553. doi:10.1017/S0008423900016000

Lewis-Beck, M. S., & Lobo, M. C. (2016). *The economic vote: ordinary vs. extraordinary times. In The Sage Handbook of Electoral Behavior*. London: SAGE.

Lucianelli, G., Citro, F., Santis, S., Tranfaglia, E., & Mazzillo, A. (2018). How to Improve the Financial Conditions of Local Governments in a Period of Crisis: An Explanatory Case Study. *International Journal of Business and Management*, *13*(1), 53–69. doi:10.5539/ijbm.v13n1p53

Manes Rossi, F., Zito, M., & Costanzo, A. (2012). How to prevent distress in local government, a new model applied in Italy. *Proceedings of the Virtual International Conference on Advanced Research in Scientific Fields 2012 Thomson,* 1-5.

Martins, R., & Veiga, F. (2013). Economic voting in Portuguese municipal elections. *Public Choice*, *155*(3), 317–334. doi:10.100711127-011-9849-0

Meijer, A. J. (2012). The do it yourself state: The future of participatory democracy. *Information Polity*, *17*(3–4), 303–314. doi:10.3233/IP-2012-000283

Musgrave, R. A., & Musgrave, P. B. (1989). *Public Finance in Theory and Practice* (International Editions). New York: McGraw-Hill.

Mussari, R. (2014). EPSAS and the unification of public sector accounting across Europe. *Accounting. Economics and Law*, *4*(3), 299–31.

Mussari, R., & Giordano, F. (2013). Emerging issues in Italian fiscal federalism: The case of municipalities. *Making multilevel public management work: Stories of success and failure from Europe and North America, 12.*

Nannestad, P., & Paldam, M. (1994). The VP-Function: A Survey of the Literature on Vote and Popularity Functions after 25 Years. *Public Choice*, *79*(3-4), 213–245. doi:10.1007/BF01047771

Nordhaus, W. D. (1975). The political business cycle. *The Review of Economic Studies*, *42*(2), 169–190. doi:10.2307/2296528

Puviani, A. (1897). Teoria della Illusione nelle Entrate Pubbliche. Annali dell'Università di Perugia, 7.

Reinikka, R., & Svensson, J. (2004). Local capture: Evidence from a central government transfer program in Uganda. *The Quarterly Journal of Economics*, *119*(2), 679–705. doi:10.1162/0033553041382120

Rodríguez-Bolívar, M. P., Navarro-Galera, A., Alcaide-Muñoz, L., & López-Subirés, M. D. (2016). Risk factors and drivers of financial sustainability in local government, An empirical study. *Local Government Studies*, *42*(1), 29–51. doi:10.1080/03003930.2015.1061506

Rogoff, K. (1990). Equilibrium political budget cycles. *The American Economic Review*, *80*(1), 21–36.

Rogoff, K., & Sibert, A. (1988). Elections and macroeconomic policy cycles. *The Review of Economic Studies*, *55*(1), 1–16. doi:10.2307/2297526

Sakurai, S. N., & Menezes-Filho, N. A. (2008). Fiscal policy and reelection in Brazilian municipalities. *Public Choice*, *137*(1-2), 301–314. doi:10.100711127-008-9329-3

Seifert, J., Carlitz, R., & Mondo, E. (2013). The Open Budget Index (OBI) as a comparative statistical tool. *Journal of Comparative Policy Analysis*, *15*(1), 87–101. doi:10.1080/13876988.2012.748586

Shi, M., & Svensson, J. (2003). Political budget cycles: A review of recent developments. *Nordic Journal of Political Economy*, *29*(1), 67–76.

Steccolini, I. (2004). Is the annual report an accountability medium? An empirical investigation into Italian local governments. *Financial Accountability & Management, 20*(3), 327–350. doi:10.1111/j.0267-4424.2004.00389.x

Torres, L., Pina, V., & Yetano, A. (2011). Performance measurement in Spanish Local Governments. A cross case comparison study. *Public Administration, 89*(3), 1081–1109. doi:10.1111/j.1467-9299.2011.01919.x

Turley, G., Robbins, G., & McNena, S. (2015). A Framework to Measure the Financial Performance of Local Governments. *Local Government Studies, 41*(3), 401–420. doi:10.1080/03003930.2014.991865

Veiga, L. G., & Veiga, F. J. (2007). Does opportunism pay off? *Economics Letters, 96*(2), 177–182. doi:10.1016/j.econlet.2006.12.026

Watts, R. (1977). Corporate Financial Statements, a Product of the Market and Political Process. *Australian Journal of Management, 2*(1), 53–75. doi:10.1177/031289627700200104

Wehner, J., & De Renzio, P. (2013). Citizens, legislators, and executive disclosure: The political determinants of fiscal transparency. *World Development, 41*, 96–108. doi:10.1016/j.worlddev.2012.06.005

Wooldridge, J. M. (2010). *Econometric analysis of cross section and panel data.* Cambridge, MA: The MIT Press.

Zafra-Gómez, J. L., López-Hernández, A. M., & Hernández-Bastida, A. (2009). Developing a model to measure financial condition in local government. Evaluating service quality and minimizing the effects of the socioeconomic environment, An application to Spanish municipalities. *American Review of Public Administration, 9*(4), 425–449. doi:10.1177/0275074008320710

Zimmerman, J. (1977). The Municipal Accounting Maze: An Analysis of Political Incentives. *Journal of Accounting Research. Studies on Measurement and Evaluation of the Economic Efficiency of Public and Private Nonprofit Institutions, 15*, 107–144.

KEY TERMS AND DEFINITIONS

Agency Theory: Agency theory postulates that there is a relationship between a principal (shareholder or citizen) and an agent (manager), and the main agent assumes the role of decision making.

Current Equilibrium: The ability of current revenue to cope with current expenses.

Financial Autonomy: Expresses the freedom to impose local taxes, collect revenue and allocate financial resources without external interference.

Financial Variables: Indicators that express the financial health of an entity.

Fiscal Illusion: Financing of public spending with external funding (borrowing or public debt), based on the idea that taxpayers do not realize that current indebtedness must be covered by future taxes.

Investments: Part of the expenses that the municipality decides to devote to long-term projects.

Level of Indebtedness: The incidence of the debts on cashed current revenue.

Public Choice Theory: Public choice theory investigates the behaviour of the agents (manager) interacting on the political markets. Managers (politicians) trying to find how to maximise their own well-being (as individuals could do in economic markets), rather than that of the public ("self-interest axiom").

ENDNOTE

1 Endogeneity appears due to three reasons (Wooldridge, 2010): firstly, the use of proxy variables to represent unobservable or difficult to quantify concepts, such as the probability of re-election, among others, which leads to measurement error; secondly, results could be additionally controlled by other variables, such as population density, education, public debt, financial condition, solvency, etc., but they have been omitted due to multicollinearity problems with other independent and control variables; and thirdly, reverse causality appears theoretically between the probability of re-election and independent and control variables.

Chapter 3
Does It Pay Off for Mayors to Accurately Manage Finance on Municipalities?
The Case of Portugal

Joana Costa
University of Aveiro, Portugal

ABSTRACT

Under the premise of rationality, politicians behave to maximize re-election probability. Favorable macroeconomic contexts, alignment with central governance, and balanced public finance will be rewarded leading to re-election. Logit estimations applied to Portuguese municipalities in the period 2002-2017 fail to empirically support these theoretical effects, providing no incentive-controlled policy actions. Local voters do not punish mayors for the adverse economic performance, staying loyal to ideological voting geographically and over time. Only turnout punishes incumbents over the entire period. The introduction of the law of limitation of terms did not change the incentives towards wise governance; therefore, lack of electoral punishments to undesirable policy actions withstands the potential misconduct of incumbents. Existing evidence points to the need of reforms in what concerns electoral participation as when we compel voters to express their democratic rights, they become more critical to undesirable achievements.

DOI: 10.4018/978-1-5225-7820-8.ch003

INTRODUCTION

Elections are the institutional mechanism to legitimate power and the democratic selection of candidates; in this moment the power of choice is twofold as in one hand it allows the identification of the most consensual candidate and the evaluation of incumbents. As democratic elections assume the existence of multiple candidates, and therefore the existence of opposing parties, it promotes alternance and the replacement of the incumbents. Still, political changeovers and the replacement of governants or of the incumbent party do not always happen, as electors tend to continuously vote for the same political party, regardless the performance in former terms. Under the premise of rationality of voting, this action is non-sense and deviates public management from efficiency trends, perpetuating misconducts and misuse of public resources. Consequently, it is of major relevance, in one hand, to appraise the re-election determinants in municipalities with specific detail on the public management and the economic performance to evaluate voter rationality and incumbent incentives. On the other hand, it is of worth addressing if the Law of Limitation of Terms did bring any change.

During the last 43 years, local governance has been playing a major role in the operation of the political system, being the front office of the political power towards voters, moreover, it serves people providing public services and enrolling citizens in proximity decision-making. So, analysing the determinants of re-election at the municipality level is key to address the multilevel framework of the Portuguese governance.

A milestone of the present research is the introduction, in 2005, of the law of the limit of terms in municipalities (Law 46/2005, from 29th of August). The diploma establishes the limits of successive years in governance in municipalities, setting an upper bound of three consecutive terms. Additionally, it was highlighted the incumbent re-election determinants, relying on three vectors of variables: social, economic and political.

Given that the objective was twofold: address the determinants of re-election, with emphasis on public finance, and assess if the LLT has brought any difference, it was collected information for four electoral moments, two before and another two after considering 2002-2005, 2006-2009, 2010-2013 and 2014-2017. To approach the question two sub-samples were set, expecting to find some sort of a structural break, and the determinants were kept to understand the eventual changes in terms of significance and/or magnitude of the effect. This question deserves major attention of the institutions as more than a half of the incumbents were not allowed to run for mayor in each of the electoral moments after the implementation of the LLT.

The present chapter is organised as follows: section 1 presents the literature review on determinants of re-election, section 2 describes the descriptive analysis of the database and the empirical methodology. Section 3 describes the hypotheses in test and the econometric estimation and section 4 concludes.

1. LITERATURE REVIEW

1.1 Voting Theories and (Re)-Election Determinants

On the representative democracies, periodic elections provide the elector opportunity to participate and express political opinion (Dahl, 1998), when expressing their preferences towards political parties and politicians, their reward and punish political players according to their performance (Manin, 1997).

The political power seeks for conquer and maintenance of power therefore, gaining advantage in the elections is the major target of all political parties. Re-election represents the continuity of political power already conquered (Moreira, 1997). As rational players, politicians want to maximize the time span in which they have political power, and elections provide them the legitimation of being in charge. If voters provide the incumbent the opportunity to be re-elected, political alternance fails to exist and the political cycles are therefore enlarged.

Theoretical literature on re-election highlights the connection to economic cycles, budgetary factors, behavioural theories, in sum, political business cycles (Nordhaus, 1975; Rogoff, 1990; Alesina et al.,1997; Persson & Tabellini, 2003).

According to the social cleavage model, the voter's alignment with political parties is connected to their position in the social pyramid, citizen enrolment and political involvement (Lipset & Rokkan,1967).

After the 2WW the cleavage model has been introduced, encompassing four anchors: urban-rural, core-periphery, governance-religion, labour-capital. Subsequent revolutions did provide democratisations among political systems, thus creating alignments among electors. The heterogeneity of economic activities, religion or even the language did create rivalry among the *core-periphery* which were repressed by the centralised governance. The binomial *Religion-Governance* also describes the fight for control among institutions. The different churches often claimed their dividends over the political power given their control over the population and their determinant role in education, and the diffusion of morality. The modernization of the economic activities and the industrial growth along with the globalized trade did enhance the asymmetries between rural and urban areas the cosmopolitan business man wanted liberalist Governance, promoting trade and free competition with little financial burdens; conversely, the rural tenants did want strong legislation to protect their agricultural interest and property. This economic reorganization also changed the equilibrium in the labour market, with the workforce migrating from small villages to large cities and joining the army of industrial workers, seeking for better working conditions, forcing the organisation in groups and trade unions, enlarging the dispute capital-labour. (Lipset & Rokkan, 1967).

In sum, the model proposes two essential aspects: the first considers that social groups will join the political parties, to whom they empathise, underlining their differences and putting the tonic on conflictual interests. The second reinforces the role of nurture, posing the tonic on the environment as a vehicle of transmission of values, beliefs and behaviours which combined to individual characteristics such as age, occupation and social status will generate the *political socialisation*. According to Elff (2007), being a member of certain social groups and sharing their values makes individuals gain political relevance and reinforces their own identity.

The societal changes since the 60s did affect electoral behaviour. The erosion of the highly stratified social pyramid and the social mobility achieved by job progression and entrepreneurial initiative, combined with increased access to education and information did change the voting intentions of individuals (Dalton, Flanagan & Beck,1984).

The economic prosperity of the second half of the twentieth century and the presence of recent conflicts on the voters' memories allowed the growth of the *Welfare State*, the new paradigm re-explains the voting determinants and stating the obsolescence of the social factors (Inglehart, 1977; Dalton, Flanagan & Beck, 1984). In this vein, Inglehart (1977), proposes a post-materialist approach based on the intergenerational values, which is twofold; stating that in recessive environments voting will be based in material foundations and contrarily, in expansionary contexts, the voter will be immaterially driven. The theory set a hierarchy to the individual needs, stating that after accomplishing material needs individual will focus on the post-materialistic to achieve full welfare.

The lack of deprivations and youth tend to boost the post-materialist values (Inglehart, 2008). This behaviour gave momentum to political parties with post-materialist values in their programs which seem determinant in the short-term voting decision (Kriesi, 1998), and are one of the explanations for electoral volatility.

Partidary identification is the foundation of the psycho-sociological model, in which political identification and enrolment explain voting behaviour (Harrop & Miller, 1988). The feeling of belonging is a *long-term connection* with a party influencing the individual positioning towards the social structure, so, long term factors will determine political identification (Campbell et al., 1960).

The short-term effects such as the candidates' image and his evaluation also influence voting intentions along with the macroeconomic climate. These factors will affect the voter's intention without changing partidary identification (Campbell et al., 1960; Lewis-Beck & Stegmaier, 2000; Costa Lobo, 2006). Such that this theory reinforces the role of partidary identification as a mediator between the short and the long term, as it influences the interpretation is information and evaluation of the political performance, influencing the final choice (Campbell et al., 1960; Dalton, 2016). Given the interchange between the short and the long-term determinants and the different weight among them, electoral results became more unpredictable and political alternance expectable (Dalton, 2016).

The influence of the short term determinants and the economic voting theory proposed by Downs (1957) anchored on the utilitarist model, in which politicians behave rationally, conducing policy actions to maximise re-election probability. Therefore, the voters will appraise the candidate's proposals, and, utilitaristically will elect those who maximise their own utility. This approach strongly ties political governance with economic performance, such that in good economic contexts incumbents tend to be re-elected, and, in adverse contexts, they are naturally punished (Lewis-Beck & Stegmaier, 2000). As the voter's decision is based on perception, it will rely either in the personal finance along with the macroeconomic context.

Voting behaviour will be a punishment or a reward according to the economic performance of incumbents (Lewis-Beck & Paldam, 2000; Lewis-Beck & Stegmaier, 2016). This process is simple in a bi-partidary context, becoming more complex in multi partidary scenarios, and, according to Powell and Whitten, (1993) and Anderson, (2000), the effect of negative performances will become neglectable to the incumbent. Moreover, the nature of the electoral act is differently connected to the economic vote as voters tend to exonerate incumbents for the actions running out of their control; such that, in central elections national conditions are evaluated, and for municipalities only the local are taken into account (Anderson, 2006).

As a result, in a context of multi-level governance, *accountability* has become a central tool in terms of economic voting, which can be used to disentangle the quantification of responsibility share of each governance level. Given that the local governance has enlarged competences, and it tend to disclaim the consequences its actions arguing the lack of control, keeping this record is of major importance to provide the relevant information to voters.

Local governance cannot whitewash responsibilities of the central governance and vice-versa, leaving the authorship of political misconduct to nobody. Accountability is at present central to accommodate the theoretical foundations of the economic voting theory and allowing the maximisation of the voter's utility in all governance levels (Anderson, 2006).

1.2 Electoral Behaviour in the Portuguese Case

The first electoral studies addressing the Portuguese case date from the 80s (Gaspar, André & Honório, 1984) and aimed at depict partidary system based on the territory and the socio-economic determinants of vote. They found evidence of the urban-rural and the religion-governance cleavage. Right wing parties are popular in rural and religious areas placed in the North, while left wing parties are more present in the South. So, north-south, urban-rural, coast-hinterland is persistent traits of the electorate (Gaspar, André & Honório, 1984; Freire, 2000b; Jalali, 2003). Core-periphery, urban-rural and labour-capital cleavages are re-assessed by Freire (2000b), focusing on participation. The results highlight alienation among the urban, educated and younger voters; mobilisation is broader in rural areas, mostly in the South, with a communist tradition. Religion and social class are still relevant among the Portuguese voters, despite the recent partidary dealignment. Scant turnout, and a *marais* electorate strongly influences by short term factors are the traits depicted by Jalali (2003). Freire (2000a) has considered the importance of the economic conditions and the social cleavages with a raising trend, and the left-right cleavage did –not suffer significant changes, contrarily from the religious and the social class cleavage (Freire 2002a). Later, Freire and Costa Lobo (2005) did find that economic performance was considered as more importance than the social class voting.

Additionally, Costa Lobo (2006) also described the decreasing trend of partidary identification among all political parties and the individual characteristics. Hence, short term factors did gain importance, and the profile of the candidate, the evaluation of the candidate is also relevant. The evaluation of the economic performance and the political performance determine the electoral decisions, even though the prevalence of religious, social status and ideology still being weighted in the choice (Freire & Santana Pereira, 2012).

There is still scarce evidence on the determinants of electoral behaviour at the municipality level, the study from Veiga and Veiga (2007a, 2007b) and later Martins and Veiga (2013) shed some light on the topic, stating that incumbents use spending to promote popularity, and visibility gains, this will permit permanence in charge. Sociodemographic and institutional factors still weight more than the economic variables and rise participation in local elections. Hence, they found and increasing punishment for misconduct in policy conduction. Albeit, the argument from local candidates was that the punishment they have received is due to the macroeconomic context, which is out of their control; again, accountability should promote the separation of responsibilities to avoid this argument.

More recently, the LLT brought up studies such as Veiga et al. (2017) on the public finance management and turnout, and the evidence is very interesting as, it evidences that municipalities in which mayors are forbidden to run for elections as a consequence of this rule presented lower expenditure levels and less electoral behaviours. Likewise, it raised participation. It is of worth to understand if this trend persists in the future or if it is a sporadic behaviour.

Sociologic characteristics, partidary identification, macroeconomic context, accuracy of Governance along with the short run factors do determine electoral behaviour. The nature of the electoral act relies on the multilevel framework, and the voter's perception about Governative performance builds up the preferences, so, the influence of the different factors will vary accordingly. Re-election depends on the voter's evaluation, considering structural and conjunctural factors, weighting differently accordingly to the governance level.

2. EMPIRICAL ANALYSIS AND METHODOLOGY

2.1 Hypotheses in Test

The literature review has contextualised (re)election determinants in general, hereafter the empirical analysis is presented along with the hypotheses in test to appraise the question in study.

The database is comprehensive in terms of the Portuguese municipalities, counting with the 308, and the time series covers 4 electoral cycles, from 2002 to 2017, broken down into two elections previous to LLT and two after. The analytical target is to identify the determinants and their time prevalence despite the introduction of limits.

Anchored on the theoretical foundations previously discussed there is a belief that territory provides the arena for action, citizenship enrolment, and representativeness, therefore determinant for public policy design. Urban voters tend to emerge in broader discussion forums being therefore more involved in daily Governance with the awareness of the decisions being taken and their implications in life. So, its vision is more critical being more prone to promote change and short political cycles (Keating, 1998). Thus, we posit:

H1: Urbanity decreases re-election propensity.

The macroeconomic context influences the voter satisfaction, and the responsibility is normally put in Governance. Austerity or contractionary policies tend to be unpopular, and bad economic climate will sacrifice incumbent's reputation, and the other way around. Therefore, the reduction on welfare, by means of a fall in purchasing power, decelerations or falls in growth, rises in unemployment will affect the incumbent reputation. The management of the public finances will be appraised by electors, and misuse of the public resources will be penalized. So, electoral results will encompass this punishment, changing their vote to the opponent candidate (Lewis-Beck & Stegmaier, 2000).

H2: Adverse macroeconomic contexts decrease re-election propensity.

The theory of the collective choices explains that the participation in the electoral act is a matter of incentives. So, the voter decides to vote if the utility of the act if higher than de disutility of the effort put in voting (the opportunity cost is everything he could be making instead). Participation does only payoff if there is a potential gain in the election of the voter's candidate and if there is a strong possibility that he will gain (Enelow & Melvin, 1985). The LLT forbids incumbents to have very long Governance cycles, so we would expect, in one hand participation to rise in the second sub-sample (Downs, 1957; Nalder, 2007).

Participation in elections will give the opportunity to the voter to express the value judgement on the political management made by the incumbent over the last term. So, on the other hand, abstention will favour incumbents still capable of running.

H3: Participation decreases the probability of re-election of incumbents.

The inability to continuously run for the elections will produce different incentives among politicians. To some, it will work as a *carrot*, in the sense that good managerial performance will produce electoral satisfaction, thus re-election while possible. To others, it will work as a *stick*, as the impossibility to continue in governance will decrease the incentive of taking accurate policies when unpopular, or the courage to make cuts, and even the temptation to maximize individual benefits rather than the social benefits.

H4: The LLT will work as a structural break, as the re-election determinants did change.

2.2 Variable Description

To test the previous hypotheses, the operationalization of the proxies and the model construction was performed as follows:

The municipality is the unit of account, therefore, our sample has 308 observations for each time period (N=308). To cover the time span of 2002-2017, we have included four electoral moments: 2005, 2009, 2013 and 2017. The structural break has been put in the middle, such that 2002-2005 and 2006-2009 are the years in the first sub-sample and 2010-2013 and 2014-2017 the second. In doing so, the research question will be addressed by means of running the same regression before and after and understand the differences in the determinants.

Our dependent variable is binary and it measures re-election, taking the value 1 if the incumbent has been re-elected 0 otherwise.

As previously mentioned, the explanatory variables are divided into three categories: social, political and economic. In the first vector we will include: region (NUTS 2), which is a multinomial variable reflect in the region of each municipality. Population density (*d_*), measuring the inhabitants per Km and percentage of seniors in the total population (*pop_s_per*). Concerning the political vector we have included electoral participation (*turnout*).

And the economic performance was appraised by means of two sub-vectors: the first proxying the macroeconomic context - variation of the unemployment rate (*var_unemp*), variation of the purchasing power (*var_pp*); and the second the public finance management, including bugetary variables: average municipality expenditures (*desppreel*), average pre-election investment expenditures (*invpreel*), fiscal revenue in the electoral year (*fisc_ae*), municipality debt in the electoral year (*debt_ae*).

As controls, the political party of the mayor is included as a control (*party_president*), taking the value -2, -1, 1 e 2 (it the politician is affiliated in PCP/PEV or BE, PS, PSD e CDS, e 0, for the case of Groups of Citizens (GCEs) or coalitions; and the political alignment with the central government at the national level is addressed by (*party_pm*), under the use of a binary variable that takes the value 1 if the incumbent belong to the same political party than the national Government and 0 otherwise.

Figure 1. Re-elected and non-re-elected mayors in Portuguese municipalities in the 2005, 2009, 2013 and 2017 elections

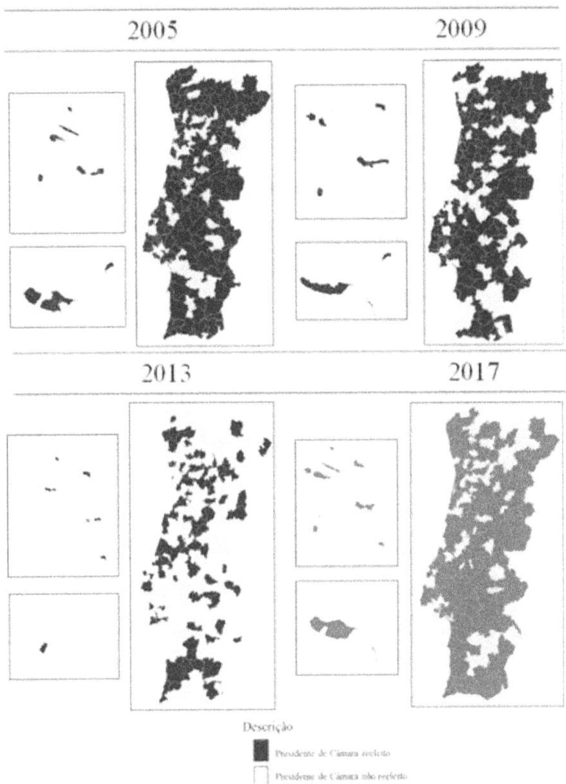

3. EMPIRICAL ANALYSIS AND ECONOMETRIC ESTIMATIONS

3.1 Descriptive Statistics and Diachronic Analysis

The following analysis aims at providing visual information about the time trends of the variables in use and to depict eventual territorial effects to assess the determinants of mayor re-election in Portugal.

It is of worth mentioning that, in general, nearly three quarters of the incumbents are reflected, albeit, in 2013 the proportion significantly fell to one third. So, one can affirm that the introduction of the LLT did affect the length of the political cycle. The LLT has prohibited 160 former mayors to continue running on the elections; forcing political rotation. Among the 308 municipalities, the number of mayors not re-elected is 205, and only one fifth of this figure is due to other reasons rather than the LLT.

Figure 2. Re-elected mayors per political party in Portuguese municipalities in the 2005, 2009, 2013 and 2017 elections

Under the geographic perspective before the LLT, most of the re-elected incumbents were found in the North and Madeira and Azores. On the 2013 elections, there was a significant fall in the number of re-elected candidates, homogeneously affecting the territory. Therefore, the LLT forced the shortening of political cycles and did promote alternance.

Figure 2 presents the distribution of the re-elected incumbents per political party, evidencing the geographic distribution of the incumbents allowed to run and victorious in the election. The overall picture highlights a prevalent preference in theNorth and Center for right wing parties (Partido Social Democrata (PSD) and Partido Popular (CDS/PP)) contrasting with the preference for centre-left and left wing parties in the South (Partido Comunista Português (PCP/PEV), Bloco de Esquerda (BE) and Partido Socialista (PS)). Concerning the municipalities on the islands, for Azores the dominant wing is centre left (PS), and in Madeira, the executive is given to the right-wing candidates from PSD.

Figure 3. Turnout in Portuguese municipalities in the 2005, 2009, 2013 and 2017 election

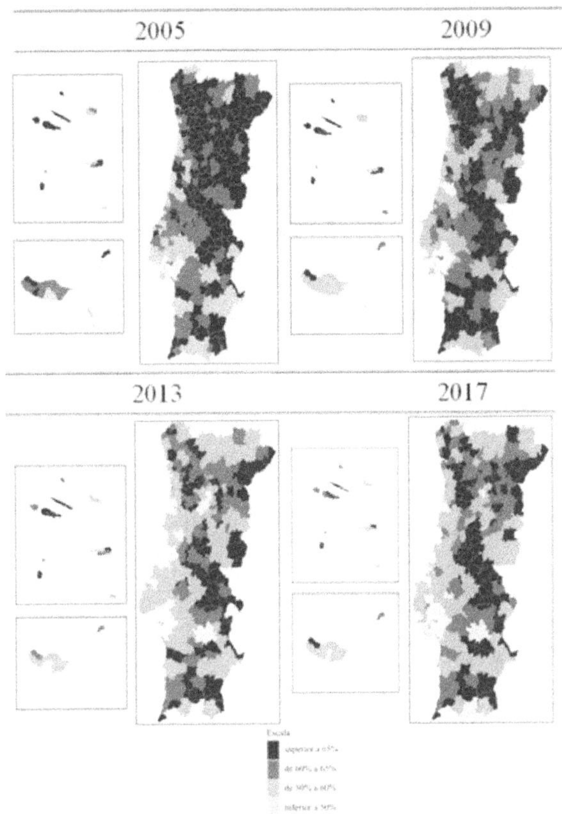

Local governance provided by the centre-right wing is common in rural areas with low density population and a high percentage of seniors; conversely, urban municipalities with higher levels of schooling among the electors, with a higher percentage of young population tend to vote on the left-wing parties. The rural areas on the South (Alentejo) are discrepant from the other Portuguese rural areas, consecutively electing left wing candidates. This picture goes along with what can be found in other studies (Martins & Veiga, 2013).

Under a diachronic perspective, and considering the four electoral cycles, the right-wing parties have assisted to a decrease in the number of mayors (re)-elected, allowing the rising trend of the left-wing mayors. Moreover, it is also increasing the number of candidates arising from coalitions and Groups of Citizens (GCEs).

Figure 4. Unemployment rate change per municipality over the terms 2002-2005, 2006-2009, 2010-2013 and 2014-2017

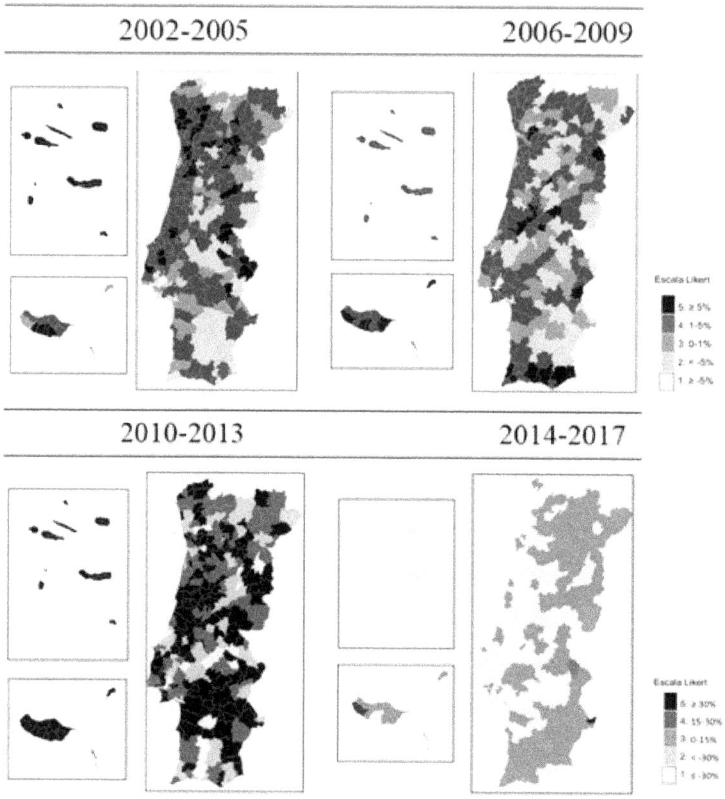

The Portuguese voters present, in general, high levels of abstention, and the electoral moment of 2005 is the period in which the percentage of alienation is higher, with special emphasis in the North. In 2013 and 2017 the turnout is higher, evidencing the utility of the voters in electing a candidate, or in punishing incumbents. It seems evident that the LLT brought new politicians to the arena, and, the electors were involved showing their explicit preferences. Evidence on this can be found in Figure 3.

Concerning the variation of the unemployment rate, the northern coastal line was severely affected by the macroeconomic crisis and an important raise on this indicator was felt. (Figure 4). Rural municipalities in the interior, were statistically less affected by this problem, even though, some misleading information can be evidenced by this indicator as the retired population does not count, along with those who became emigrants. As the analysis is made using the variation, the objective is to appraise the time trend rather than the existing situation.

Figure 5. Purchasing power change per municipality over the terms 2002-2005, 2006-2009, 2010-2013 and 2014-2017

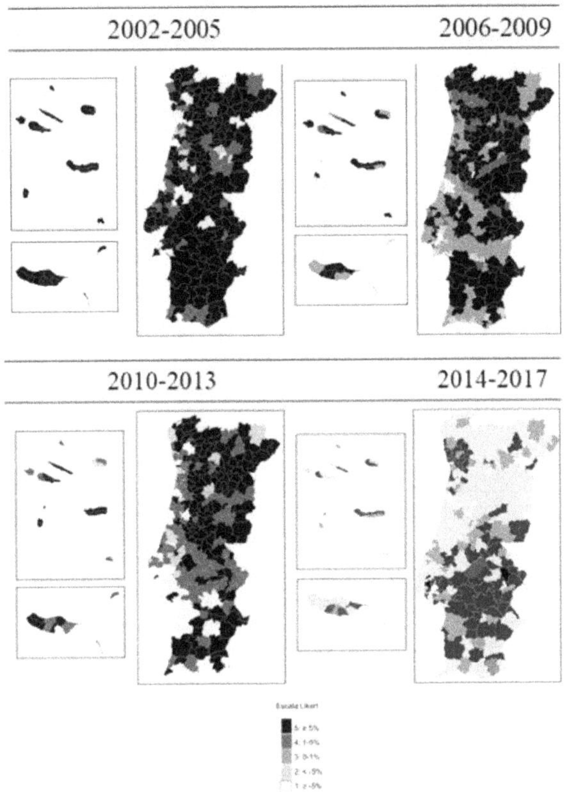

The variation of the purchasing power of the population over the period highlights the interior/coast dichotomy (Figure 5). The ability to generate income of the coastal municipalities is larger, and this time trend promotes regional asymmetries rather than the desired territorial convergence (Faro, Albufeira, Cascais, Oeiras, Lisboa, Alcochete, Porto, Matosinhos, Aveiro, Coimbra and Leiria appear as frontrunners and Armamar, Celorico de Basto, Cinfães, Vila Nova de Paiva, Vinhais, Resende, Ribeira de Pena, can be considered as the lagging behind).

In sum, and considering the indicators in use, one can observe that the asymmetries are evident. Coast and interior are significantly different and the socio-economic characteristics of the municipality vary accordingly. Peripheral municipalities in the interior have low population densities, are populated mainly by seniors and consequently with low proportions of population in working age, their economic activities are connected to the primary sector and the scarcity of resources forces income generation to lower. Conversely, on the coast, municipalities are more urban,

Table 1. Mayor re-election determinants before LLT (2005 & 2009)

Dependent Variable – Re-election		
Variables	**Coefficient (Standard Error)**	**Marginal Effects**
Region NUTS 2	-0,2244494** (0,1034179)	-0,0420401**
Young Population Percentage (*pop_j_per*)	11,92238 (14,28839)	2,233101
Senior Population Percentage (*pop_s_per*)	2,208683 (5,515865)	0,4136937
Mayor's Party	0,1367369 (0,1930394)	0,0256113
Party Alignment	-0,6935703* (0,3806522)	-0,1327001*
Participation Rate *(turnout)*	-7,800911*** (2,412901)	-1,461137***
Variation of the Unemployment Rate (*var_unemp*)	-1,061956* (0,5572056)	-0,1989079*
Variation of the Purchasing Power (*var_pp*)	0,9365732 (1,644845)	0,1754233
Average Municipality Expenditures (*desppreel*)	**0,0009986 (0,0008001)**	**0,000187**
Average Pre-election Investment Expenditures (*invpreel*)	**-0,0021514 (0,0013483)**	**-0,000403**
Fiscal Revenue in the Electoral Year (*fisc_ae*)	**-0,0005631 (0,001369)**	**-0,0001055**
Municipality Debt in the Electoral Year (*debt_ae*)	**-0,0000894 (0,0002824)**	**-0,0000167**
Constant	4,993581 (3,521822)	
Number of observations: 308	*(p≤0,1)**(p≤0,05);***(p≤0,01). Before LLM	

younger, operate in the tertiary sector, and have the most important public and private infrastructures therefore raising welfare and opportunities.

Given the territorial asymmetries, economic variables such as the unemployment rate and the purchasing power are more volatile in these territories during the time span (2002-2017).

The strength of this heterogeneous forces the acknowledgement of its existence when addressing the determinants of the (re)-election, as one previously stated, the socio-economic dimensions do influence the political options.

3.2 Econometric Estimation

In the following section, the hypotheses previously mentioned will be tested to address the research question. The picture described by the descriptive statistics reinforces the territorial asymmetries and the heterogeneity in terms of the economic performance, still, is does not provide correlation or any connection among the variable, this gap will be fulfilled with the econometric estimations.

The results of the econometric estimations using the logit models were presented in tables 1 and 2. The first estimation includes 2005 and 2009, and, the second 2013 and 2017. So the sample is estimated in separate for the period before and after LLT respectively.

The results concerning the time span before the LLT (2005 & 2009) – Table 1, evidence that geography is determinant in terms of the re-election propensity. When moving South, and ceteris paribus, electors prefer shorted political cycles. Which is equivalent to say that voters on the Northern municipalities are more prone to reappraise the incumbent; in Azores and Madeira, re-election probability is smaller. Then, re-election is correlated with the territory.

Concerning the socio-demographic variables included in the model, the estimation puts them as being statistically insignificant, either the coefficient of young population percentage and senior population percentage fail to explain the re-election probability. So, there is no age effect in terms of the candidate choice.

The macro-economic context is appraised by means of the change in the unemployment rate and the change in the purchasing power. For the first one can find statistical significance, observing that worsening conditions in the job market will punish the incumbent. Concerning purchasing power, the effect is statistically insignificant.

To appraise the connectedness between the different layers of Governance a binary variable was included, and, it evidences that voters fail to address accountability, as the local incumbents are less prone to be re-elected if they belong to the same party than the Central power. Being aligned with the central Government is a drawback to incumbents, and perhaps the mayor is an easy prey to evidence unsatisfaction with the central power.

Table 2. Mayor re-election determinants after LLT (2013 & 2017)

Dependent Variable – Re-election		
Variables	**Coefficient (Standard Error)**	**Marginal Effects**
Region NUTS 2	0,103276 (0,1019331)	0,182725
Populational Density	-0,0003657** (0,0001816)	-0,0000647**
Young Population Percentage (*pop_j_per*)	-21,15659 (15,16345)	-3,743568
Senior Population Percentage (*pop_s_per*)	-3,103641 (5,022903)	-0,5491241
Mayor's Party	-0,2564656 (0,218423)	-0,0453762
Party Alignment	-0,5404858 (0,4215352)	-0,0951059
Participation Rate *(turnout)*	-5,367799** (2,352026)	-0,9497194**
Unemployment Rate (*var_unemp*)	0,0064635 (0,5916244)	0,0011436
Variation of the Purchasing Power (*var_pp*)	-2,04927 (1,945681)	-0,3625752
Average Municipality Expenditures (*desppreel*)	**0,0002998 (0,0004941)**	**0,000053**
Average Pre-election Investment Expenditures (*invpreel*)	**-0,0002235 (0,0010641)**	**-0,0000395**
Fiscal Revenue in the Electoral Year (*fisc_ae*)	**-0,0003122 (0,0017208)**	**-0,0000552**
Municipality Debt in the Electoral Year (*debt_ae*).	**-0,0001292 (0,000194)**	**-0,0000229**
Constant	7,871655 (3,559373)	
Number of Observations: 308	*(p≤0,1)**(p≤0,05);***(p≤0,01). After LLM	

The role of ideology, and political socialisation, is evaluated by means of the incumbent's party, which fails to be statistically significant. It seems that there is no prevalent political ideology when choosing weather or not to vote on the incumbent. As a consequence, re-election is not connected to the political party of the incumbent.

Concerning turnout, there is a negative coefficient, strongly significant. Increasing the participation rate decreases the probability of re-election of the incumbents. This is a paradoxal result, as in the Portuguese system participation is not mandatory, and this result evidences that higher participation leads to shorter political cycles.

The evidence reinforces the existence of the *costs of ruling* (Nannested & Paldam, 1994), as the political Governants' popularity erodes over time; as a result, it is expectable a fall in the popularity of incumbents, independent of their party.

All the short-term variables connected to public finance management fail to be statistically significant, which means that our voters do not weight the managerial competences of the mayor when choosing weather or not to reconduct the incumbent. This result deservers further attention as the absence of punishment giver no incentive to local players in the adoption of the accurate policy actions, mostly if they are unpopular and running in the next elections is still possible.

Summarising, before the LLT, geography, job market, party alignment and turnout are the determinants to be considered by incumbents to maximize the re-election probability. The other factors such as age bracket or the managerial accuracy can be reconsidered as electors fail to value them when reappoint the candidate. A perverse correlation is found concerning abstention, as it is interesting for incumbents to promote low levels of participation.

The results concerning the period subsequent to the introduction of the LLT (2013 and 2017), are presented in Table 2. Only slight differences are found as most of the variables did maintain the already found significance.

Concerning geography, the variable fails to be statistically significant. No connection is found among the north south binomial and the political cycles. This result is perhaps due to the introduction of the Law which asymmetrically affected the territory, the existing data highlights the fact that most of the candidates forbidden to run the elections due to the limit of terms were from Northern and Central municipalities.

When trying to appraise the urban-rural cleavage and given the former contingency we measured the impact of the population density and, in the same vein as predicted by the literature, urban centres tend to prefer shorter political cycles. This variable, in the Portuguese case is to some extent a good proxy for Geography as one can find high density territories in the Coastal line and the opposite in the hinterland.

Again, the age of the voters does not influence the re-election of the incumbent. Therefore, it seems that incumbents must not be concerned with the effects of the policies being implemented in the different age brackets. Concerning ideology or political alignment, the effect is statistically insignificant. Given that the party of the mayors does not affect re-election probability along with his political alignment with the Central Government.

In the same vein as formerly to the introduction of the LLT, participation does affect incumbent's re-election. Again, raising the participation rate decreases the incumbents' probability of re-election. This result reinforces the interest of incumbents in low participation rates. Political alternance depends on the opposition mobilization ability.

The proxies for the macroeconomic context continue failing to be statistically significant, which means that the voter does not put accountability over these macroeconomic principals on the mayor. For the first sub-sample the job market was determinant in the re-election, and the loss in terms of significance can be due to the high emigration or the low participation in the electoral act. Or even, the electors can consider other factors rather than the macroeconomic.

In general, one can observe that the LLT, as an operationalization of the institutional reform brought up new determinants of re-election propensity, but, some of them were kept constant. The main change has to do with the territory; even though the empirical evidence is somehow misleading given the asymmetry of the shock produced by the LLT.

Revisiting the hypotheses in test, the empirical evidence provides support to affirm the effect of urbanity in the probability of re-election as in the first sub-sample there is evidence of shorter political cycles is the urban areas. In the second sub-sample, appraising the hypothesis by means of the population density, one can observe that urban areas are less prone to reappoint candidates. Hence, it is of worth mention the fact that the institutional reform did bring changes, not yet consolidated.

The effect of the economic variable, concerning the economic context and the individual itself, fail in general to be statistically significant. Purchasing power was never found as relevant and adverse conditions in the job market are a punishment to the incumbent only for the first sub-sample. Therefore, our second hypothesis fails to be supported, as the voter does not account the local power for the economic performance even in his municipality. Short term effects of the economic performance should not be taken into account by running candidates. Perhaps the LLT has hidden the connection between the fragile economic context and the ruling parties, as the candidate did change compelled by the impossibility to run. Therefore, most of the incumbents which could otherwise be punished were not because of not running.

The participation rate has proved as strongly significant, and a useful tool to reduce political cycles. Higher participation levels bring up new candidates and political alternance. This result holds before and after the LLT.

Finally, there is evidence on the changes of the patterns of re-election that arise with the LLT, and as a consequence it can be seen as a structural break.

4. CONCLUSIONS

Re-election democratically allows the enlargement of the political cycle. Despite the legitimacy of reappointing the candidates, the theoretical and empirical findings do support the need for alternance. Consequently, the institutional reform has reduced the possibility of enlargement of these cycles, promoting the appearance on new candidates and governance. In doing so, policy makers did expect changes in the electoral process and raises in the rational of the voting exercise.

As territory is embedded with tradition and political socialization, geography is key in describing the electoral behaviour. Additionally, there is a strong correlation between the territory with cleavages such as economic occupation, family structure, religion, among others, which deserve being analysed to understand their role in the efficiency of policymaking.

Considering that the voter is self-interested, partidary identification plays a central role. The voter tends to be near to the candidate that better defends his interest or whose proposals are more favourable or empathic. This institutional reform brought significant changes in terms of the party candidates or even in terms of the party in power.

Sadly, citizen enrolment in political activities is weakening over time, and the participation is evidently falling over time. Given the importance of this variable, it is of superlative interest to reduce abstention as it will set aside individuals, weakening the quality of the policies and the politicians. This result is even larger among the municipalities directly affected by the LLT, evidencing alienation. As supported by the empirical results, participation puts pressure on incumbents as voters will evaluate the results of the policy actions. To us, mandatory participation would have a larger effect on the quality of policy rather than the LLT, deserving further attention from central institutions.

The results show that before the introduction of the LLT incumbents were punished by adverse conditions on the job market, and our evidence reinforces that this was not taken into account for re-election after the reform, still, perhaps other factors were taken into account as most of the candidates were not running for re-election and the economic context was retaking from one of the most severe crisis over the last century. Deeper and more detailed analysis should be performed to understand the effective role of the economic variables on voter's choice.

Albeit the importance given in the theory to the public finance management, our evidence is contrary, and the insignificance of the expenditures, the fiscal revenue or the debt deserves to be further appraised. Considering that voters have sufficient financial literacy, their rational behaviour is to penalise misconducts, as a consequence it seems that the information has not been in consideration, and that there is insufficient transparency in terms of the ruling methods. It seems to be a priority to design monitoring methods of Governance, ranking and policy instruments to raise the awareness about these actions and their consequences.

Cross penalisation is not a desirable option, and as a consequence it is positive addressing the fact that political alignment has lost its significance. But, no penalization at all and unaccountability is even worse. The other side of the increased power of municipalities is the increased duties, and the permissiveness of the voters is perhaps due to disinformation. Again, relevant information must be provided to the citizens, promoting a close dialog, civil enrolment and the simple and crystal-clear access to economic information of the municipality.

Broader accountability will promote efficiency gains in terms of policy making, and as a consequence, the vote will be what it is designed to be: rational and enlightened. With the current trends on decentralization of the decision-making processes, the dematerialization and the decrease of bureaucracy municipalities are keys in the promotion of prosperity and sustainable growth. Accordingly, seeking for good political practices among mayors and the promotion of transparency will provide the required quality in the local democracy, involving all citizens and reducing the fiscal burden without reducing the quality and the extent of the state. Fragmentation, voter's alienation at the local level is the first rift in the social contract which cannot be tolerated when aiming at cohesion and inclusion as post-materialistic objectives.

REFERENCES

Alesina, A., Roubini, N., & Cohen, G. (1997). *Political Cycles and the Macroeconomy*. Cambridge, MA: MIT Press. doi:10.7551/mitpress/5437.001.0001

Anderson, C. D. (2006). Economic voting and multilevel governance: A comparative individual-level analysis. *American Journal of Political Science*, *50*(2), 449–463. doi:10.1111/j.1540-5907.2006.00194.x

Anderson, C. J. (2000). Economic voting and political context: A comparative perspective. *Electoral Studies*, *19*(2), 151–170. doi:10.1016/S0261-3794(99)00045-1

Blais, A. (2006). What affects voter turnout? *Annual Review of Political Science*, *9*(1), 111–125. doi:10.1146/annurev.polisci.9.070204.105121

Campbell, A., Converse, P. E., Miller, W. E., & Stokes, E. (1960). *The American voter*. Chicago: University of Chicago Press.

Dahl, R. A. (1998). *On democracy*. Yale University Press.

Dalton, R. (2000). The decline of party identification. In D.J. Russell & M.P. Wattenberg (Orgs.), Parties without partisans (pp.19-36). Nova Iorque: Oxford University Press.

Dalton, R. (2016). Party Identification and Its Implications. *Oxford Research Encyclopedia of Politics*. Consultado de http://politics.oxfordre.com/view/10.1093/acrefore/9780190228637.001.0001/acrefore-9780190228637-e-72

Dalton, R., Flanagan, S., & Beck, P. (1984). Electoral change in advanced democracies: realignment ore dealignment? In *Electoral Change in Advanced Industrial Societies: Realignment or Dealignment?* (pp. 3–22). Princeton, NJ: Princeton University Press.

de Sousa, L. (2015). Constrangimentos ao Pluralismo I: sobre a relação Executivo-Oposição. In *A Reforma do Poder Local em Debate* (pp. 71–79). Lisboa: Imprensa de Ciências Sociais.

Downs, A. (1957). *An Economic Theory of Democracy. Nova Iorque*. Harper Collins Publishers.

Elff, M. (2007). Social Structure and Electoral Behavior in Comparative Perspective: The Decline of Social Cleavages in Western Europe Revisited. *Perspectives on Politics*, *5*(2), 277–294. doi:10.1017/S1537592707070788

Enelow, J., & Melvin, J. (1984). *The Spatial Theory of Voting: An Introduction*. Cambridge University Press.

Freire, A. (2000a). Clivagens, conjuntura económica e comportamento eleitoral em Portugal: uma análise das legislativas de 1995 com dados agregados. *Sociologia, Problemas e Práticas*, (32), 23-54.

Freire, A. (2000b). Participação e abstenção nas eleições legislativas portuguesas, 1975-1995. *Analise Social*, 115–145.

Freire, A. (2001). *Modelos do comportamento eleitoral: uma breve introdução crítica*. Oeiras: Celta Editora.

Freire, A. (2002). Realinhamentos eleitorais, 1983-1999: Estruturas sociais, economia e voto partidário. *Analise Social*, 121–149.

Freire, A., & Lissi, M. (2015). Reformas eleitorais autárquicas (passadas e futuras). In *A Reforma do Poder Local em Debate* (pp. 109–120). Lisboa: Imprensa de Ciências Sociais.

Freire, A., & Lobo, M. C. (2005). Economics, ideology and vote: Southern Europe, 1985–2000. *European Journal of Political Research*, *44*(4), 493–518. doi:10.1111/j.1475-6765.2005.00236.x

Freire, A., & Santana-Pereira, J. (2012). Economic voting in Portugal, 2002–2009. *Electoral Studies*, *31*(3), 506–512. doi:10.1016/j.electstud.2012.02.006

Gaspar, J., André, I., & Honório, F. (1984). As Eleições para a Assembleia da República. In J. Gaspar (Ed.), *Geografia Eleitoral (II) coletânea de artigos* (pp. 83–173). Lisboa: CEG.

Harrop, M., & Miller, W. L. (1988). Models of voting. In *Elections nd voters: a comparative introduction* (pp. 130–172). Basingstoke: Macmillan.

Inglehart, R. F. (1977). *The silent revolution: changing values and political styles among western publics*. Princeton University Press.

Inglehart, R. F. (2008). Changing values among western publics from 1970 to 2006. *West European Politics*, *31*(1-2), 130–146. doi:10.1080/01402380701834747

Jalali, C. (2003). A investigação do comportamento eleitoral em Portugal: História e perspetiva futuras. *Analise Social*, *38*(167), 547–552.

Jalali, C. (2004). As mesmas clivagens de sempre? Velhas clivagens e novos valores no comportamento eleitoral português. In *Portugal a votos – as eleições legislativas de 2002* (pp. 87–119). Lisboa: Imprensa de Ciências Sociais.

Keating, M. (1998). *The New Regionalism in Western Europe: Territorial Restructuring and Political Change*. Aldershot, UK: Edward Elgar.

Kriesi, H. (1998). The transformation of cleavage politics: The 1997 Stein Rokkan lecture. *European Journal of Political Research*, *33*(2), 165–185. doi:10.1111/1475-6765.00379

Lewis-Beck, M. S., & Paldam, M. (2000). Economic voting: An introduction. *Electoral Studies*, *19*(2-3), 113–121. doi:10.1016/S0261-3794(99)00042-6

Lewis-Beck, M. S., & Stegmaier, M. (2000). Economic determinants of electoral outcomes. *Annual Review of Political Science*, *3*(1), 183–219. doi:10.1146/annurev.polisci.3.1.183

Lewis-Beck, M. S., & Stegmaier, M. (2016). Economic Judgment. In *The SAGE Encyclopedia of Political Behavior*. Thousand Oaks, CA: SAGE Publications.

Lipset, S., & Rokkan, S. (1967). Estruturas de clivagem, sistemas partidários e alinhamentos dos eleitores. In *Consenso e Conflito* (pp. 161–259). Lisboa: Gradiva.

Lobo, M. C. (2006). Short-term voting determinants in a young democracy: Leader effects in Portugal in the 2002 legislative elections. *Electoral Studies*, *25*(2), 270–286. doi:10.1016/j.electstud.2005.05.002

Manin, B. (1997). *The principles of representative government.* Cambridge, UK: Cambridge University Press. doi:10.1017/CBO9780511659935

Martins, R., & Veiga, F. J. (2012). Economic performance and turnout at national and local elections. *Public Choice*, *157*(3-4), 429–448. doi:10.100711127-012-0047-5

Martins, R., & Veiga, F. J. (2013). Economic voting in Portuguese municipal elections. *Public Choice*, *155*(3-4), 317–334. doi:10.100711127-011-9849-0

Meirinho, M. M. (2009). Competitividade das eleições e participação política: O caso das eleições autárquicas (1797–2005). In *Eleições e sistemas eleitorais: Perspetivas históricas e políticas* (pp. 263–294). Porto: Universidade do Porto.

Moreira, A. (1997). *Ciência Política.* Coimbra: Almedina.

Mozzicafreddo, J., Guerra, I., Fernandes, M. A., & Quintela, J. (1989). Modelos de gestão e de legitimidade no sistema político local português. *Sociológia*, *6*, 51–80.

Nalder, K. (2007). The effect of state legislative term limits on voter turnout. *State Politics & Policy Quarterly*, *7*(2), 187–210. doi:10.1177/153244000700700207

Nannestad, P., & Paldam, M. (1994). The VP-function: A survey of the literature on vote and popularity functions after 25 years. *Public Choice*, *79*(3-4), 213–245. doi:10.1007/BF01047771

Nordhaus, W. D. (1975). The political business cycle. *The Review of Economic Studies*, *42*(2), 169–190. doi:10.2307/2296528

Persson, T., & Tabellini, G. (2003). *The Economic effects of Constitutions - what do the data say?* Cambridge, MA: MIT Press. doi:10.7551/mitpress/2591.001.0001

Powell, G., & Whitten, G. (1993). A cross-national analysis of economic voting: Taking account of the political context. *American Journal of Political Science*, *37*(2), 391–414. doi:10.2307/2111378

Rogoff, K. (1990). Equilibrium Political Budget Cycles. *The American Economic Review*, *80*(1), 21–36.

Ruel, T. (2015). Constrangimentos ao Pluralismo II: Longevidade no poder e riscos associados. In *A Reforma do Poder Local em Debate* (pp. 81–86). Lisboa: Imprensa de Ciências Sociais.

Veiga, F. J., & Veiga, L. G. (2007a). Does opportunism pay off? *Economics Letters*, *96*(2), 177–182. doi:10.1016/j.econlet.2006.12.026

Veiga, F. J., & Veiga, L. G. (2007b). Political business cycles at the municipal level. *Public Choice*, *131*(1-2), 45–64. doi:10.100711127-006-9104-2

Veiga, F. J., & Veiga, L. G. (2010). The impact of local and national economic conditions on legislative election results. *Applied Economics*, *42*(13), 1727–1734. doi:10.1080/00036840701736107

Veiga, F. J., Veiga, L. G., Fernandes, B., & Martins, J. (2017). *Limitação de mandatos: o impacto nas finanças locais e na participação eleitoral*. Fundação Manuel dos Santos.

APPENDIX 1: Municipalities per NUT2

Table 3.

Alentejo	Alandroal, Alcácer do Sal, Aljustrel Almeirim, Almodôvar, Alpiarça, Alter do Chão, Alvito, Arraiolos, Arronches, Avis, Azambuja, Barrancos, Beja, Benavente, Borba, Campo Maior, Cartaxo, Castelo de Vide, Castro Verde, Chamusca, Coruche, Crato, Cuba, Elvas, Estremoz, Évora, Ferreira do Alentejo, Fronteira, Gavião, Golegã, Grândola, Marvão, Mértola, Monforte, Montemor-o-Novo, Mora, Moura, Mourão, Nisa, Odemira, Ourique, Ponte de Sôr, Portalegre, Portel, Redondo, Reguengos de Monsaraz, Rio Maior, Salvaterra de Magos, Santarém, Santiago do Cacém, Serpa, Sines, Sousel, Vendas Novas, Viana do Alentejo, Vidigueira e Vila Viçosa.
Algarve	Albufeira, Alcoutim, Aljezur, Castro Marim, Faro, Lagoa, Lagos, Loulé, Monchique, Olhão, Portimão, São Brás de Alportel, Silves, Tavira, Vila do Bispo e Vila Real de Santo António.
Região Metropolitana de Lisboa	Alcochete, Alenquer, Almada, Amadora, Barreiro, Cascais, Lisboa, Loures, Mafra, Moita, Montijo, Odivelas, Oeiras, Palmela, Seixal, Sesimbra, Setúbal, Sintra e Vila Franca de Xira.
Centro	Abrantes, Águeda, Aguiar da Beira, Albergaria-a-Velha, Alcanena, Alcobaça, Almeida, Alvaiázere, Anadia, Ansião, Arganil, Arruda dos Vinhos, Aveiro, Batalha, Belmonte, Bombarral, Cadaval, Caldas da Rainha, Cantanhede, Carregal do Sal, Castanheira de Pera, Castelo Branco, Castro Daire, Celorico da Beira, Coimbra, Condeixa-a-Nova, Constância, Covilhã, Entroncamento, Estarreja, Ferreira do Zêzere, Figueira da Foz, Figueira de Castelo Rodrigo, Figueiró dos Vinhos, Fornos de Algodres, Fundão, Góis, Gouveia, Guarda, Idanha-a-Nova, Ílhavo, Leiria, Lourinhã, Lousã, Mação, Mangualde, Manteigas, Marinha Grande, Mealhada, Mêda, Mira, Miranda do Corvo, Montemor-o-Velho, Mortágua, Murtosa, Nazaré, Nelas, Óbidos, Oleiros, Oliveira de Frades, Oliveira do Bairro, Oliveira do Hospital, Ourém, Ovar, Pampilhosa da Serra, Pedrógão Grande, Penacova, Penalva do Castelo, Penamacor, Penela, Peniche, Pinhel, Pombal, Porto de Mós, Proença-a-Nova, Sabugal, Santa Comba Dão, São Pedro do Sul, Sardoal, Sátão, Seia, Sertã, Sever do Vouga, Sobral de Monte Agraço, Soure, Tábua, Tomar, Tondela, Torres Novas, Torres Vedras, Trancoso, Vagos, Vila de Rei, Vila Nova da Barquinha, Vila Nova de Paiva, Vila Nova de Poiares, Vila Velha de Ródão, Viseu e Vouzela.
Norte	Alfândega da Fé, Alijó, Amarante, Amares, Arcos de Valdevez, Armamar, Arouca, Baião, Barcelos, Boticas, Braga, Bragança, Cabeceiras de Basto, Caminha, Carrazeda de Ansiães, Castelo de Paiva, Celorico de Basto, Chaves, Cinfães, Espinho, Esposende, Fafe, Felgueiras, Freixo de Espada à Cinta, Gondomar, Guimarães, Lamego, Lousada, Macedo de Cavaleiros, Maia, Marco de Canaveses, Matosinhos, Melgaço, Mesão Frio, Miranda do Douro, Mirandela, Mogadouro, Moimenta da Beira, Monção, Mondim de Basto, Montalegre, Murça, Oliveira de Azeméis, Paços de Ferreira, Paredes, Paredes de Coura, Penafiel, Penedono, Peso da Régua, Ponte da Barca, Ponte de Lima, Porto, Póvoa de Lanhoso, Póvoa de Varzim, Resende, Ribeira de Pena, Sabrosa, Santa Maria da Feira, Santa Marta de Penaguião, Santo Tirso, São João da Madeira, São João da Pesqueira, Sernancelhe, Tabuaço, Tarouca, Terras de Bouro, Torre de Moncorvo, Trofa, Vale de Cambra, Valença, Valongo, Valpaços, Viana do Castelo, Vieira do Minho, Vila do Conde, Vila Flor, Vila Nova de Cerveira, Vila Nova de Famalicão, Vila Nova de Foz Côa, Vila Nova de Gaia, Vila Pouca de Aguiar, Vila Real, Vila Verde, Vimioso, Vinhais e Vizela.
Região Autónoma dos Açores	Angra do Heroísmo, Calheta, Corvo, Horta, Lagoa, Lajes das Flores, Lajes do Pico, Madalena, Nordeste, Ponta Delgada, Povoação, Praia da Vitória, Ribeira Grande, Santa Cruz da Graciosa, Santa Cruz das Flores, São Roque do Pico, Velas, Vila do Porto e Vila Franca do Campo.
Região Autónoma da Madeira	Calheta, Câmara de Lobos, Funchal, Machico, Ponta do Sol, Porto Moniz, Porto Santo, Ribeira Brava, Santa Cruz, Santana e São Vicente.

Chapter 4
Sustainability Assessment of Portuguese Local Governments (2009 to 2017):
Accounting Information and Public Governance

Paula Gomes dos Santos
https://orcid.org/0000-0003-2192-8855
Lisbon Accounting and Business School, Instituto Politécnico de Lisboa, Portugal

Carla Martinho
https://orcid.org/0000-0001-7675-7390
Lisbon Accounting and Business School, Instituto Politécnico de Lisboa, Portugal

ABSTRACT

Public governance must ensure financial sustainability. This investigation aims to assess Portuguese local governments financial sustainability as the ability to service the upcoming obligations in commercial transactions (under the Late Payment Directive framework) and to study if accounting information enables public local governance with greater transparency and accountability about their financial sustainability. The study will focus on the 308 Portuguese local governments from 2009 to 2017. The number of local governments with average payment periods (PMPs) within 30 days had an increasing tendency. However, their adjusted average payment periods greatly exceed the 30 days, which means limited financial sustainability. In 2017, only 29% of the local governments have an adjusted PMP within 30 days against the 63% if it is used the officials PMPs. Therefore, accounting information does not enable public governance with greater transparency and accountability about Portuguese local government financial sustainability.

DOI: 10.4018/978-1-5225-7820-8.ch004

1. INTRODUCTION

Over the past decade the emphasis in the literature on public sector management reforms has gradually changed from focusing on the management of individual organizations to broader concerns with the governance of complex systems of service provision (Wiesel & Modell, 2014). Values such as accountability and transparency can be perceived in the reforms under the *New Public Management* theory (NPM) (Vigoda-Gadot & Meiri, 2008) and the *New Public Governance theory* (NPG) (Wiesel & Modell, 2014).

Accountability is the relationship between the state and the society in providing – and demanding – better governance (OECD, 2013). Public governance refers to the formal and informal arrangements that determine how public decisions are made and how public actions are carried out, from the perspective of maintaining a country's constitutional values when facing changing problems and environments. The principal elements of good governance refer to accountability, transparency, efficiency, effectiveness, responsiveness and rule of law (OECD, 2013). Hood (2010) stresses the relationship between accountability and transparency as principles of governance. In this context, accounting information enable public governance with greater transparency and accountability. However, this presuppose that accounting information is reliable.

Transparency is in Article 19 of the Lei de Enquadramento Orçamental (Lei 151/2015, September 11th), constituting the provision of reliable, comparable information that allows a precise assessment of the costs and benefits of Public Administration activities, including their current and future economic and social consequences.

One of the challenges faced by public governance, namely as a result of the last international financial crisis, is to ensure financial sustainability. International organizations such as European Parliament (EP) (2009), European Commission (EC) (2011) and International Monetary Fund (IMF) (2014) recommended governments to adopt strategies for the financial sustainability of their public policies.

Financial sustainability can be defined as the ability to service all commitments (CICA, 2009; IFAC, 2013; EC, 2011; Lei 151/2015, September 11th & Lei 73/2013, September 3rd republished by Lei 51/2018, August 16th).

EP (2009) highlighted that late payments have a negative impact on businesses sustainability, particularly on small and medium sized enterprises (SMEs). In response to those concerns, EC has made several efforts over the past years to address this issue. The Directive 2011/7/EU on combating late payments in commercial transactions (within both the public and private sector) committed EU Member States to give effect in their national laws by the 16th of March 2013, date on which it replaced the original Directive 2000/35/EC, which featured the same objectives.

As pointed out by Rodríguez Bolívar, Navarro-Galera, Muñoz and Lopez Subires (2016), the local governments high debt levels and budget deficits have caused a process of policy reforms aimed at promoting their financial sustainability. Estevez and Janowski (2013) conclude that local governments have a key role to play in the sustainability of countries' public services.

Several factors create adverse incentives for subnational governments to overspend, and borrow excessively, thereby jeopardising macroeconomic stability and, possibly, debt sustainability (Ter-Minassian, 2007).

Several authors argues that Portuguese local governments had to resort to credit to finance part of their activity (Carvalho, 1996; Cabral, 2003 & Lobo and Ramos, 2009), which has contributed to their growing indebtedness and to the increase of their expenses (without having the necessary revenues to face them). As Ferreira argues (2011), the resource to credit functioned as a way of providing local authorities with the availability of additional financial means. Thus, excessive and chronic indebtedness represents a significant burden for public entities and, especially, for the next generations (João, 2014).

Given the financial difficulties experienced by the Portuguese Local Governments as a result of the last world crisis, they are the object of study of this research.

Being the financial sustainability a public governance challenge and accounting information a mean of enabling public governance with greater transparency and accountability, this investigation aims the following objectives:

- To assess Portuguese local governments financial sustainability as the ability to service the upcoming obligations in commercial transactions.
- To study if accounting information enables public governance with greater transparency and accountability about Portuguese local governments financial sustainability.

Given its importance to the European and Portuguese economy, financial sustainability will be considered under the Late Payment Directive (LPD) framework. The study will focus on the 308 Portuguese local governments, from 2009 to 2017.

The paper is structured in four sections. The first one presents the theme relevance. On the second one it is presented the literature review about theoretical and legal framework about sustainability and Public Sector payment practices, both in the European Union and in Portugal. Next, in the empirical study section it is explained the methodology and presented and discussed the results. The main conclusions, the study limitations and the future lines of investigation are on section four.

This investigation aims to contribute (1) to the knowledge of financial sustainability of Portuguese local governments in what concerns the ability to service the upcoming obligations in commercial transactions and (2) to the knowledge of the reliability of accounting data and their ability to enable transparency and accountability to local public governance.

2. LITERATURE REVIEW

2.1 Financial Sustainability and Payment Practices at Public Sector

Literature and international agencies recognize that the continued existence of debt and deficit in public administrations implies a risk for sustainability, so they advocate that those aspects should be subject to control measures (Pina, Torres & Royo, 2010; United States Agency for International Development [USAID], 2011; UE, 2013)

Rodríguez Bolívar et al. (2014) analysed 116 local administrations in Spain and found that the annual budget result is a key determinant of local government financial sustainability and highlight the value of controlling the balance of budget expenditures in preventing future problems of viability for these local authority services.

According to Rodríguez Bolívar et al. (2018), the income statement represents a useful measure to assess financial sustainability, showing the effect of political factors on the three dimensions proposed by IFAC (i.e. service, revenue and debt).

For EC (2019, p. 32), "fiscal (or debt) sustainability is broadly understood as the ability of a government to service its debt at any point in time". Historically, fiscal sustainability was meant as 'solvency' of the government. However, recent experience has proven that this definition needed to consider shorter-term or liquidity risks, which entails that a government is able to service all upcoming (short-term) obligations. In fact, liquidity and solvency are interrelated and, therefore, are equally important (EC, 2019).

While frameworks for debt sustainability analysis traditionally focus on 'government debt' (the so-called Maastricht debt in EU countries), government liabilities are (much) wider than what these aggregate captures (EC, 2019). This measure of debt only includes a set of government liabilities, namely currency and deposits, debt securities and loans. Other debt instruments such as other accounts payable are not included in that measure of debt (EC, 2019). However, other definitions of gross debt (IMF, 2013) include all instruments that have a nature of debt liabilities.

Regarding the other accounts payable and recognizing the negative impact that late payments have on the European economy, the European Parliament and Council passed Directive 2011/7, which, among other things, sets maximum payment periods for commercial transactions to reform the payment culture in Europe (Bilotta, 2015).

LPD stipulate that Member States shall ensure that in commercial transactions where the debtor is a public authority, the period for payment the goods and services that they procure is within 30 days, with a possibility of extending it by law to a maximum of 60 days in very specific cases.

According to Bilotta (2015), late payments cause approximately one in four bankruptcies in the EU, leading to the loss of nearly 450,000 jobs every year.

As pointed out by Reynolds and Davis (2015, p. 4), "the executive summary of the Commission's impact assessment for the 2011 directive notably stressed how late payments by public bodies undermine the creation of stable and predictable economic conditions for businesses and policies to drive growth and employment. More recently (September 2014), the European Commission Economic Paper on Late Payments, reveals that "the estimated implicit financial costs associated with payment delays by public administrations observed in 2012 ranged from 0.005% of GDP in Finland to 0.19% of GDP in Greece". Furthermore, a 2015 IMF Working Paper demonstrates, inter alia, that "a standard deviation increase in delayed (government) payments reduces profit growth by 1.5 to 3.4 percentage points". Finally, perhaps the most poignant example of the scale of the problem was recorded in Intrum Justitia's European Payment Index 2012 survey, which identified that written-off debt owing to the non-payment of invoices in the EU had grown to at least 2.8% of total receivables to reach €340 billion, equivalent to the total debt of Greece. In Intrum Justitia's European Payment Report of 2015 this amount has reportedly risen further to 3.1% of total receivables".

At 2015, EU evaluated the impact of the LPD, concluding that it has had limited effect on the average payment duration in Public authorities to business (PA2B) transactions. "While the average payment duration has decreased from 65 days in 2011 to 58 days in 2014, it stays well beyond the terms set out by the Directive" (EU, 2015, p. 47). In some countries the average payment duration greatly exceeds the European average. The detailed country analysis shows that Italy (165 days on average), Greece (155 days), Spain (154 days) and Portugal (129 days) are the slowest payers, while only Finland and Estonia out of all EU Member States comply with the 30-day limit introduced for PA2B transactions by the new Directive (on average) (EU, 2015).

Figure 1. PA2B payments terms and delays from 2015 and 2018
Source: EP (2018, p. 16) (2018 did not cover Luxembourg, Malta and Cyprus)

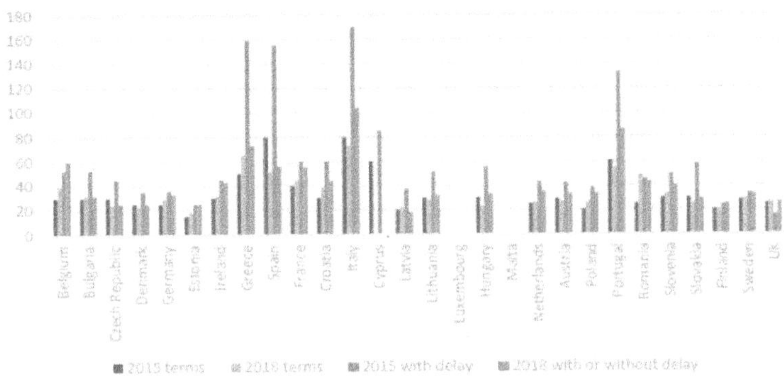

European Parliament assessed the implementation of LPD in 2018. Figure 1 shows the information gathered by the 2018 European Payment Report, showing further improvement in the situation, especially in the southern countries mostly concerned.

LPD do not establishes how to measure late payments. As pointed out by EC (2015, p. 12), "such harmonised measurement would facilitate the provision of up to date statistical data and it would allow cross-country comparison over time". In the LPD implementation assessment, European Parliament (2018, p. 26) highlighted that "in the absence of any provisions of the Late Payment Directive, there is no common methodology for the gathering of data concerning the payment behaviour of public authorities and businesses in Europe". Establishing common indicators for such reporting mechanisms would have the benefit of limiting the risk that obligatory or voluntary monitoring brings different categories of data across the EU (European Parliament, 2018).

2.2 Measures to Assess the Payments Practices of Portuguese Local Governments

In 2011, Portugal requested international financial assistance. The 'Programa de Assistência Económica e Financeira' (PAEF) for Portugal (2011-2014) gave a particular attention on combating late payments of public sector in commercial transactions. The 'Lei dos Compromissos e dos Pagamentos em Atraso' (LCPA) (Lei 8/2012, February 21st, republished by Lei 22/2015, March 17th) has set the objective of reducing late payments (due debts for more than 90 days) in the public sector, stipulating penalties for the entities in case of non-compliance.

Table 1. Average Payment Formula

Average payment (PMP) formula	Legend
$PMP_t = \frac{\sum_{i=t-3}^{t} \frac{DF_i}{4}}{\sum_{i=t-3}^{t} A_i} \times 365$	DF = value of the short-term debt to suppliers observed at the end of a quarter A = purchases of goods and services made in the quarter

Source: Adapted from Despacho 9870/2009

According to Baleiras, Dias and Almeida (2018), the average period that an entity takes to pay (PMP) to suppliers is an indicator commonly used to measure payment difficulties.

Veiga (2014) argues that at the end of 2011 there were 174 Portuguese local governments in a situation of cyclical imbalance, and 50 in a situation of structural imbalance, in other words, more than 70% presented financial problems.

For local governments, it was created the 'Programa de Apoio à Economia Local' (PAEL) (Lei 43/2012, August 31st), with the objective of regularizing the payment of debts due more than 90 days.

The instrument transposing the 2011 LPD into Portuguese law is Decreto-Lei 62/2013, May 10th, which establishes that Public authorities must pay for goods and services within 30 days or, in very exceptional circumstances, within a maximum of 60 days.

It is Direcção-Geral das Autarquias Locais (DGAL) responsibility to publish the average payment period of each local government at the end of the fourth quarter, as well as the list of those entities that, until the first half of the same year, had a PMP higher to ninety days. Subsequently, the budget execution decree-law for 2017 (Decreto-Lei 25/2017, March 3th) determined the quarterly disclosure of local governments with a PMP of more than 60 days.

Regarding the directive implementation, the assessment made in 2015 by the European Parliament conclude "that a high risk of late payments subsists in Portugal despite the new law, with a reported average length of payment by public administrations to SMEs of 129 days (99 days' delay). These figures are still well above the requirements for payment within 30 days for public entities laid down in the directive. Nevertheless, a sustained downward trend in late payments can be observed since 2012, with average payment delays, which the government monitors, now below 2009 levels. The implementation challenge for Portugal is to continue this path" (Reynolds & Davis, 2015, p. 24).

Table 2. Short-term debt to suppliers and goods and services purchases

Sector	Short-term Debt to Suppliers (*DF*)	Goods and Services Purchases (*A*)
Local Governments	Correspond to the sum of the accounts 22, 252, 261, 265, 266 and 267 of the Official Accounting Plan of Local Authorities.	Correspond to the sum of the accounts 31 and 62 and the acquisitions of property, plant and equipment recorded in accounts 42, 442, 445 and 45 of the Official Accounting Plan of Local Authorities.
Public Companies	Correspond to the sum of the accounts 22, 261, 267 and 268 of the Official Accounting Plan.	Correspond to the sum of accounts 31 and 62 and the acquisition of property, plant and equipment recognized in accounts 42 and 442 of the Official Accounting Plan.
Health Units	Correspond to the sum of the accounts 22, 252, 261, 267, 2685, 2686, 2687, 2688 (excluding the 26881 - Other Creditors - Institutions of the Ministry of Health) and 2689 of the Health Sector Accounting Plan.	Correspond to the sum of accounts 31 and 62 (excluding 62181 - Work performed abroad in Entities of the Ministry of Health) and acquisitions of property, plant and equipment recognized in accounts 42, 442, 445 and 45 of the Health Sector Accounting Plan.

Source: Adapted from RCM 34/2008.

LPD has no guidance in respect of calculating methodology. The Portuguese average payment period in PA2B is evaluated according with the indicator established in Resolução do Conselho de Ministros (RCM) 34/2008, February 22th, with the changes made by Despacho 9870/2009, April 13th, which is presented in Table 1.

RCM 34/2008 defines what is considered as short-term debt to suppliers and as purchases of goods and services. There are some sectors of Portuguese Public Administration were the data are collected in a cash basis, so it will be only considered the sectors in which the data are accrual based: local governments, public companies and health units (Table 2).

When comparing what is considered in short-term debts to suppliers (DF) in the various sectors, it can be seen that in local governments the account 268 'Other debts' is not considered in that debt.

According to the Official Plan of Accounting of Local Authorities (POCAL), published by Decreto-Lei 54-A/99, February 22th, in 268 'Other debts' must be accounted the debts derived from "transactions non-classified in the previous debt accounts". The other sectoral plans follow the same framework, so this is a residual account that should recognize other debts that do not fit into any other account.

Baleiras, Dias and Almeida (2018) and Martinho and Santos (2019) point out that in local governments the numerator does not include account 268, which may imply some underestimation of this indicator, particularly in situations where that account is not immaterial.

Table 3. Factors that may distort the PMP data

PMP Formula	Factors
The formula, being quarterly, puts the total purchases of the quarter in the denominator and in the numerator the debts at the end of the quarter.	A municipality that buys on October 1 and pays on December 31, have a PMP of zero, when in fact it paid in 90 days.
The formula puts in the denominator the purchases of goods and services, as well as the acquisitions of fixed assets.	The acquisitions of fixed assets are the increase of the value of class 4 (tangible fixed assets, intangible assets and property, plant and equipment in progress). This variation is, in its majority, an exchange transaction. However, it may also be by revaluation or donation.
The formula considers the debts value.	There are municipalities that register the invoices (debt) near or at the payment date. Such incorrect practice is a decrease factor of PMP.

Source: Adapted from Carvalho, Fernandes and Camões (2018, p. 219)

According to Santos, Martinho and Escudeiro (2019), there is a significant strong correlation between 'commitments' and 'other debts' for large local governments. The authors conclude that this corroborates that account 268 represents debts of commercial transactions and should therefore be considered in the calculation formula of the PMP.

Regarding the Average Payments (PMPs) of the Portuguese local governments, Carvalho, Fernandes and Camões (2018, p. 217) highlight the "drastic reduction in the number of municipalities with an average payment over 90 days, with a preponderance in small and medium-sized local governments". However, these authors warn about the low reliability of the data, although obtained from the site of Direcção-Geral das Autarquias Locais (DGAL), noting that it is verified "that some local governments have average payment of zero or one day. These excessively low values in a bureaucratic public administration may be contaminated by several factors" (Carvalho, Fernandes & Camões, 2018, p. 289). Table 3 presents the factors that may distort the PMP data.

Carvalho, Fernandes and Camões (2018) conclude that the data analysis does not allow us to verify whether the very small PMPs presented by some local governments result from good payment practices, from a failure to comply with accounting rules (recognizing the debt only at the time of payment) or from the formula, which presents some weaknesses.

It should be noted that there are different indicators data depending on the subsector, a cash basis or an accrual basis indicator (Baleiras, Dias & Almeida, 2018). Those authors highlight that the formula does not capture the number of days that each local government takes, on average, to pay the invoices from the day they are issued, because the indicator disregards payments made within the contractual period. So, the indicator measures the debts period of payment and not the acquisitions period of payment.

The Inspeção-Geral de Finanças (IGF) justified the need to amend the PMP methodology, advising the adoption of a common accounting framework for all sub-sectors that minimize, if not even eliminate, comparability problems (IGF, 2012).

Concerns on data quality are not limited to Portugal. Ausloos, Cerqueti and Mir (2017) states that those concerns and the poor auditing procedures being used in Italy have resurfaced vigorously following the bankruptcy of a number of local government bodies during recent financial crisis.

Given the expected transition in 2020 of Portuguese local governments to an accounting system based on IPSAS, it should be noted that Caruana and Grima (2019) defends that IPSAS compliance would neither simplify, nor standardize the conversion exercise that EU member countries have to do to change a governmental accounting deficit to the EC's required statistical deficit, nor would it directly lead to more reliable statistical data.

3. EMPIRICAL STUDY

3.1 Objectives and Methodology

As defended by EC (2019) and IMF (2013), sustainability analysis must focus on all government debt liabilities, such as other accounts payable which are not included in the so-called Maastricht debt.

This investigation aims to assess Portuguese local governments financial sustainability as the ability to service the upcoming obligations in commercial transactions, measured by the payment practices under the LPD and RCM 34/2008 framework.

It will also be studied if accounting information enables public governance with greater transparency and accountability about Portuguese local governments financial sustainability.

The present study focused on the 308 Portuguese local governments in the period from 2009 to 2017, of which 278 are from the mainland, 19 from the autonomous region of Madeira and 11 from the autonomous region of the Azores. The investigation was based on the information on the PMPs and of the Balance sheets presented on the Autarchical Portal of the Direção-Geral das Autarquias Locais (DGAL) for the years 2009 (first year for which data is available) until 2017. As for the Balance Sheets, it was considered on-balance sheet liabilities (direct and explicit) (EC, 2019). So, 'other debts' is the value of account 268, and 'Short-term debt to

Table 4. Local governments by category (2009 to 2017)

Category	Year								
	2009	2010	2011	2012	2013	2014	2015	2016	2017
Large	24	24	24	24	24	24	24	24	24
Medium	105	105	103	103	101	100	100	99	99
Small	179	179	181	181	183	184	184	185	185

suppliers' refers to the accounts 22, 252, 261, 265, 266 and 267 of the POCAL, as recommended by RCM.

The PMPs considered in the study refers to the last quarter of each year. In 2017 the PMP of the fourth quarter of Oeiras was not available, so it was used the PMP of the third quarter. For the analysis, the local governments were grouped according to the criteria followed by Carvalho, Fernandes and Camões (2018), into three categories according to their size, measured by the number of inhabitants:

- **Small Municipalities**: With population less than or equal to 20,000 inhabitants.
- **Medium Municipalities**: With a population of more than 20,000 inhabitants and less than or equal to 100,000 inhabitants.
- **Large Municipalities**: With a population of more than 100,000 inhabitants.

Table 4 shows the evolution of the number of local governments in each category over the study period (inhabitants data came from 'Pordata' site).

It can be observed that the number of large local governments remains constant, with a small variation in the number of the medium and small size (these correspond to most of the Portuguese local governments).

3.2 Results

The average term of payments (PMP) measures the entity ability to service the upcoming obligations in commercial transactions. For the 308 Portuguese local governments, it was studied the variables PMP, 'Other debts', and 'Short-term debt to suppliers', from 2009 to 2017. Their use is supported by the theoretical framework.

Figure 2. PMPs of Portuguese local governments (2009-2017)

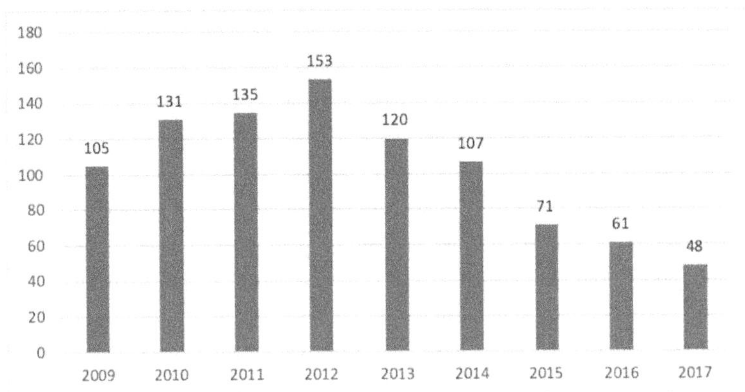

Figure 3. PMPs of Portuguese local governments by category (2009-2017)

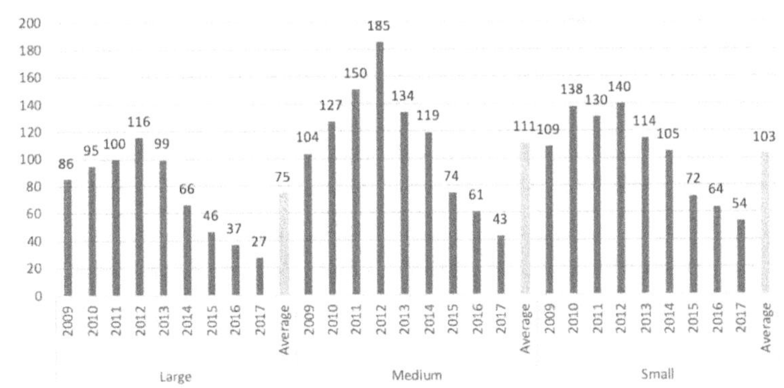

Figure 2 shows the annual averages of the Portuguese local governments PMPs during the period under study.

According to the available data, the PMP of the subnational governments shows a downward trend since 2012 (the year in which the longest terms were observed).

It should be noted that the analysis does not confirm the conclusions of the Conselho das Finanças Públicas (CFP) (2018) about a PMP of 50 days at the end of 2015 and of 38 days at the end of 2017, in line with the objectives outlined in the PAEF and legislated through the LCPA. The available data shows a PMP of 71 days in 2015 and around 48 days at the end of 2017. Although they are in line with the LCPA, they do not, however, comply with Decreto-Lei 62/2013, May 10th that transposed the LPD to the national order.

Figure 4. Adjusted PMPs of Portuguese local governments (2009-2017)

PMPs increased from 2009 to 2012, year in which the highest PMP of the studied period were recorded, in any of the categories analysed. They were higher in medium-sized local governments, as can be seen in Figure 3. Since 2013, these periods have been significantly reduced, with large municipalities reporting the lowest PMPs.

Despite the observed reduction trend, only in 2017 the large municipalities (with 27 days) met the 30 days' objective of LPD. In all the other categories, payment practices still do not comply with LPD (average of 43 and 54 days for the medium and small ones, in 2017).

According to Carvalho, Fernandes and Camões (2018) and Martinho and Santos (2019), the expression for the calculation of the PMP seems to show weaknesses both in the accounts used in the formula, as well as in the reliability of the available data. Given these weaknesses, namely by not considering the 'other debts' (account 268) in its calculation, contrary to what happens in other sectors of the Public Administration, the PMP was calculated for the period under study considering also the value of that account.

So, that indicator was recalculate based on a proportionality ratio between the debts considered by RCM and those added to the account 268. It must be highlighted the existence of local governments with 'short-term debt to suppliers' of 0, or very close, and that have value in the PMP, which is considered unreliable and able to distort the adjusted PMP. In these situations, it was decided to consider an adjusted PMP of 0. The same solution was followed when those debts, considering the RCM framework, were lower than € 10,000, because material 'other debts' would result in very high adjusted PMPs. The evolution of the adjusted PMPs is shown in Figure 4.

Figure 5. Ratio between "other debts" and "short-term debt to suppliers" by category (2009-2017)

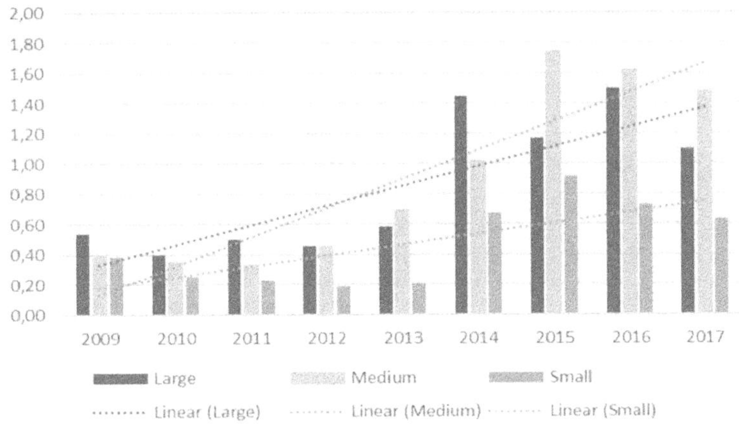

The analysis of the adjusted PMPs also allows to verify a tendency of reduction. However, the year of trend inflection is not 2012, but 2014. It should be noted that these payment practices are not in line with the objectives of PAEF and LCPA, and much less with the LPD. In 2017, the average payment period is if 99 days, three times higher than the 30 days established by the LPD.

The comparison of the Figures 2 and 4, allow us to better understand the variation between the adjusted PMPs and the official PMPs, that is, the impact of considering 'other debts' in that indicator. For example, in 2015, 2016 and 2017 the adjusted PMPs are more than two times higher than the official ones. As can be seen, there is strong evidence that the consideration of account 268 amounts in the PMP formula increases the average payment terms.

This is considered to indicate the relevance of the value considered in 'other debts' (when it should be a residual account compared to the remaining ones).

To better understand the relation between the value of 'other debts' and 'short-term debt to suppliers', in Figure 5 it is presented the ratio between them, which is equal to the ratio between the adjusted PMPs and the PMPs.

A relation between 'other debts' and 'Short-term debt to suppliers' of local governments has become evident. As it can be seen, this relation presents a growing tendency for all the Portuguese local governments, being for the largest ones much more accentuated, even disproportionate, in comparison with the others (medium and small local governments).

Figure 6. Adjusted PMPs of Portuguese local governments by category (2009-2017)

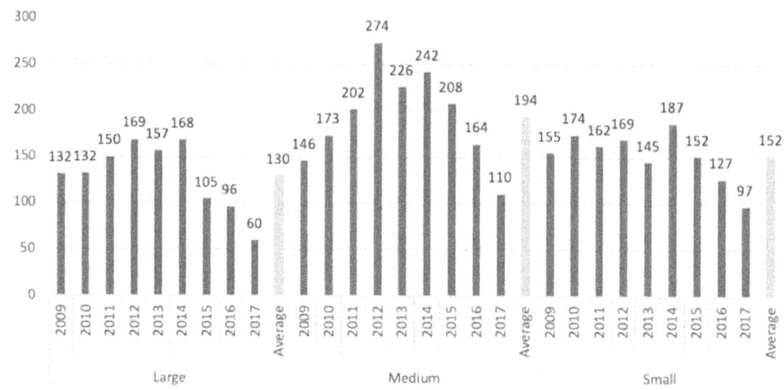

Figure 7. Portuguese local governments, by category, with PMP > 30 days (2009-2017)

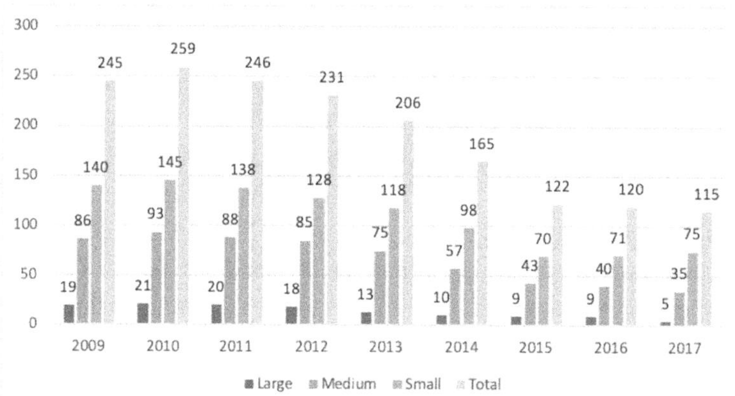

It can be observed the relevance of the 'Other debts' in all categories, and it should be noted that, since 2014, they are higher than the 'Short-term debt to suppliers' in medium and large local governments.

Notice that the tendency to increase the ratio between the value of 'other debts' and the 'short-term debt to suppliers' is accompanied by the trend of reduction of the PMP (as shown in Figure 4). Therefore, the authors believe that there is a strong evidence that local governments are getting smaller PMPs by recognizing relevant debts as 'other debts' (which should probably be considered as 'Short-term debt to suppliers').

Figure 8. Portuguese local governments, by category, with adjusted PMP > 30 days (2009-2017)

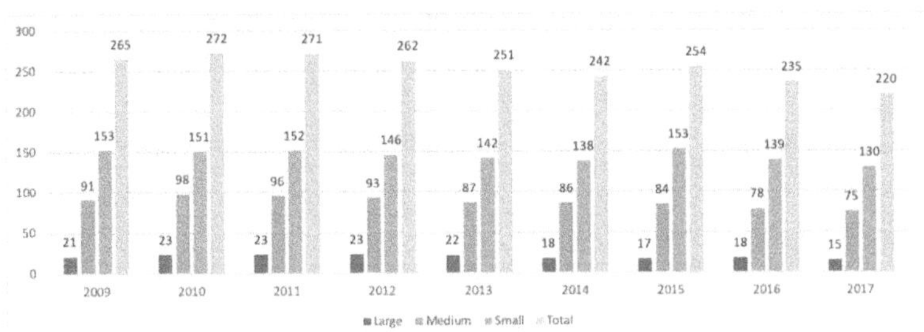

Figure 9. Ratio between "adjusted PMP > 30 days" and "PMP > 30 days", by category, (2009-2017)

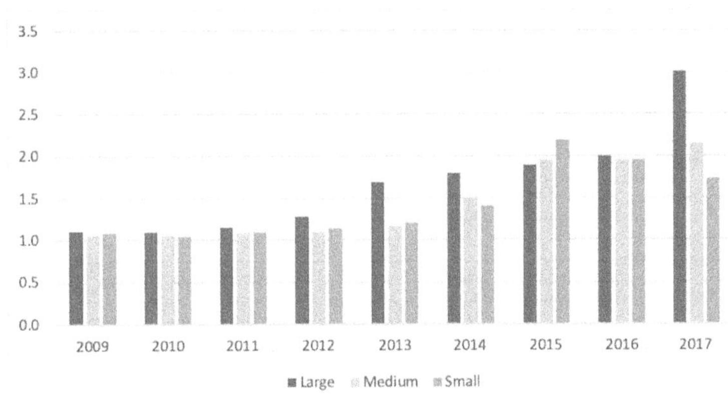

The adjusted PMP by category, presented in Figure 6, allow us to conclude that, using this methodology, the payment practices of the local governments are still far from those defined in the LPD.

Despite the good evolution of the payment practices, none of the categories of local governments have average PMP within 30 days. In fact, it should be noted that the large local governments, that in 2017 showed an average PMP of 27 days, had an adjusted PMP of 60 days (twice of the defined by the LPD).

Table 5. Number of Portuguese local governments by PMP intervals (2009-2017)

PMP	2009	2010	2011	2012	2013	2014	2015	2016	2017
> 1 year	7	19	15	27	21	15	8	9	5
> 6 months and ≤ 1 year	48	50	67	56	29	23	18	15	15
> 90 days and ≤ 6 months	83	91	82	58	58	34	35	23	17
> 60 days and ≤ 90 days	48	43	31	38	36	27	25	19	19
> 30 days and ≤ 60 days	59	56	51	52	62	66	36	54	59
≤ 30 days	63	49	62	77	102	143	186	188	193
Total	**308**	**308**	**308**	**308**	**308**	**308**	**308**	**308**	**308**

Table 6. Number of Portuguese local governments by adjusted PMP intervals (2009-2017)

Adjusted PMP	2009	2010	2011	2012	2013	2014	2015	2016	2017
> 1 year	22	32	29	41	33	32	23	21	13
> 6 months and ≤ 1 year	59	64	83	70	43	34	31	26	25
> 90 days and ≤ 6 months	90	94	85	66	62	65	85	61	44
> 60 days and ≤ 90 days	41	40	31	34	52	48	44	58	48
> 30 days and ≤ 60 days	53	42	43	51	61	63	71	69	90
≤ 30 days	43	36	37	46	57	66	54	73	88
Total	**308**	**308**	**308**	**308**	**308**	**308**	**308**	**308**	**308**

In order to study whether the Portuguese local governments are complying with the LPD, Figure 7 shows those, by size, who have PMPs over 30 days.

It is possible to observe that, since 2010, there is a trend of reducing the number of local governments that present payment terms exceeding 30 days, in all categories. Despite this positive trend, in 2017, there are still 37% of them who have PMPs over 30 days. The most compliant are the large ones, in which only 5 out of 24 (20.8%) have PMPs over 30 days.

In order to understand whether the consideration of the 'other debts' in the calculation of the PMP would have an impact on the previous conclusions, Figure 8 shows the local governments, by size, with adjusted PMPs of more than 30 days.

Although there is still a downward trend, this is more significant since 2011, but there are more local governments with PMPs higher than 30 days. In 2017, 71% of them remain in this situation, with 70% of the small, 75% of the medium and 63% of the largest ones not complying with LPD.

The use of adjusted PMPs leads to significant differences in the number of local governments with payment practices exceeding 30 days, mainly since 2013. In 2017, there are three times more large municipalities in this situation, compared to those considered through the officials PMPs (Figure 9).

In order to have a better knowledge about payments practices, Table 5 shows the number of local governments by PMP intervals.

It can be seen a downward trend of the payment's periods from 2009 to 2017. In this period, local governments with PMPs within 30 days have tripled, with 63% of them complying with the LPD in 2017. Also, those ones with payments exceeding 90 days (LCPA and PAEL) have been significantly reduced, with only 37 local governments (12%) in this situation in 2017.

However, the analysis of the adjusted PMPs (shown in Table 6) leads to a different scenario. Although it is also possible to observe a tendency of reduction of the payment's periods from 2009 to 2017, the number of local governments with adjusted PMPs within 30 days have doubled (but are less than half of the ones with official PMPs within the same period) with only 29% of them complying with the LPD in 2017.

The number of local governments with payments exceeding 90 days in 2017 rise to 82 (27%), more than the double of the ones shown in Table 5.

It should be highlighted that there are 13 local governments with an adjusted PMP that exceeds one year (more than the double of the 5 ones if it is used the officials PMPs).

Table 6 allows to conclude that local governments are recognizing, mainly since 2013, material values in 'other debts' which are not considered as 'short-term debts to suppliers'. Thus, they are getting an official PMP lower than the one they would have if those debts were considered in the PMP calculation (it would be interesting to know if the residual account of 'other debts' would have so material values if it was not excepted of the calculation). Remember that LCPA stipulates penalties for the entities in case of non-compliance with the 90 days' period.

4. CONCLUSIONS

Debts to suppliers and payment delays are not healthy for local economies or local finances. Given its importance to the European and Portuguese economy, it was assessed the ability of Portuguese local governments to service their upcoming obligations in commercial transactions, under the LPD framework.

This study reinforces the conclusions pointed out by Carvalho, Fernandes and Camões (2018), Baleiras, Dias and Almeida (2018) and Martinho and Santos (2019) regarding the weaknesses of the PMP calculation formula. Unlike other sectors of Government, the local governments PMP do not consider 'Other debts' (account 268) in the value of 'short-term debts to suppliers'. This limits the comparability of that information within the Public Sector.

The information disclosed regarding the payment practices of the Portuguese local governments, does not allow us to conclude that they are meeting the 30 days objective imposed by LPD.

In the period from 2009 to 2017, the number of local governments with PMPs within 30 days had an increasing tendency. The official PMPs shows 193 of them (63%) complying with the LPD in 2017, but they are only 88 (29%) if it is used the adjusted PMPs. Also, those ones exceeding the 90 days of the LCPA and PAEL have been significantly reduced in the period studied. The official PMPs shows 37 local governments (12%) in this situation in 2017 and the adjusted PMPs identify 82 (27%).

Given that the adjusted average payment periods of the Portuguese local governments greatly exceeds the terms set out by the Directive, the authors conclude that the ability of them to service the upcoming obligations in commercial transactions is limited what can mean that they are assuming commitments that may put at risk their financial sustainability.

As for the reliability of the accounting information, the trend towards the increase in the value recognized in 'other debts' is accompanied by the trend of reduction of the PMP. Accordingly, it seems that, mainly since 2013, local governments are recognizing 'Short-term debt to suppliers' as 'other debts' (which are getting more material) obtaining smaller PMPs. The use of the adjusted PMPs led to the conclusion that, in 2017, only 29% of the local governments comply with the LPD, against the 63% if it is used the officials PMPs. The non-inclusion of 'Other debts' turns the PMP formula permeable to accounting practices less ethical.

It should be highlighted the recommendation made by EP (2018, p. 12) urging "the Member States to take full responsibility in the exercise of payment on the part of the public administration and to improve their legislation ensuring proper implementation of the Late Payment Directive in all its parts, also by removing any domestic laws, regulations or contractual practices by the public sector that conflict with the aims of the Directive, such as enforcement and assignment bans for public sector receivables; reiterates in parallel that the Commission should do its utmost to try to ensure the full and adequate implementation of existing obligations".

The research led to the conclusion that the PMP indicator considered in Portugal does not allow to obtain reliable information about the payment practices of local governments. Therefore, the available data allows to conclude that accounting information does not enable public governance with greater transparency and accountability about Portuguese local governments financial sustainability.

So, the authors recommend the revision of the RCM 34/2008 in order to harmonize what is considered as short-term debt to suppliers for all the public sector, not allowing different methodologies of calculation and different accounting practices, which result in non-comparable statistical elements.

As a main limitation to the study, the authors point out the lack of reliability of the data even though all the information was obtained from the site of DGAL. Another limitation results from having been considered an adjusted PMP of zero in local governments with 'short-term debt to suppliers' of € 0 and with values in the PMP, and with 'short-term debt to suppliers' lower than € 10,000. However, the researchers consider that this did not have a significant effect on the results and that the exclusion of these entities would only reinforce the findings.

As future research, it is proposed the study about the PMPs of the Portuguese Public Sector, comparing the sectors that have accrual accounting with the cash accounting ones.

REFERENCES

Ausloos, M., Cerqueti, R., & Mir, T. (2017). Data science for assessing possible tax income manipulation: The case of Italy. *Chaos, Solitons, and Fractals, 104*, 238–256. doi:10.1016/j.chaos.2017.08.012

Baleiras, R., Dias, R., & Almeida, M. (2018). *Finanças locais: Princípios económicos, instituições e a experiência portuguesa desde 1987*. Lisboa: Conselho das Finanças Públicas. Available at https://www.cfp.pt/uploads/publicacoes_ficheiros/cfp-2018-livro-financas-locais.pdf

Bilotta, C. (2015). Ending the Commercial Siesta: The Shortcomings of European Union Directive 2011/7 on Combating Late Payments in Commercial Transactions. *Brook. J. Int'l L., 38*. Available at: http://brooklynworks.brooklaw.edu/bjil/vol38/iss2/5

Cabral, N. (2003). *O Recurso ao Crédito Nas Autarquias Locais Portuguesas*. Lisboa: Associação Académica da Faculdade de Direito de Lisboa.

Canadian Institute of Chartered Accountants (CICA). (2009). Indicators of financial condition. In Public Sector Statements of Recommended Practice (SORP). CICA.

Caruana, J., & Grima, L. (2019). IPSAS, ESA and the fiscal deficit—A question of calibration. *Public Money & Management, 39*(2), 113–122. doi:10.1080/09540962.2019.1580897

Carvalho, J. (1996). *O Processo Orçamental das Autarquias das Autarquias Locais*. Coimbra: Almedina.

Carvalho, J., Fernandes, M., & Camões, P. (2018) *Anuário Financeiro dos Municípios Portugueses – 2017*. Lisboa: Ordem dos Contabilistas Certificados. Available at: https://www.occ.pt/pt/a-ordem/publicacoes/anuario-financeiro-dos-municipios-portugueses/

Conselho das Finanças Públicas. (2018). Execução Orçamental da Administração Local 2017. *Relatório do Conselho das Finanças Públicas, 2018*(3). Available at: https://www.cfp.pt/pt/publicacoes/sectores-das-administracoes-publicas/execucao-orcamental-da-administracao-local-2017

Decreto-Lei 25/2017, March 3th. Budget execution decree-law for 2017. Establishes the rules of execution of the Public State Budget for 2017.

Decreto-Lei 62/2013, May 10th. Establishes measures against delays in payment of commercial transactions and transposes Directive 2011/7/EU of the European Parliament and of the Council of 16 February 2011.

Despacho 9870/2009, April 13th. Approves the model of the monitoring report to be used in the quarterly monitoring of the evolution of average payment periods.

Directive 2011/7/EU of the European Parliament and of the Council of 16 February 2011 on combating late payment in commercial transactions. Official Journal of the European Union.

Estevez, E., & Janowski, T. (2013). Electronic Governance for Sustainable Development-Conceptual framework and state of research. *Government Information Quarterly, 30*. Available at: http:// www.sciencedirect.com/science/article/pii/S0740624X12001487

European Commission. (2011). Council Directive 2011/85/EU of 8th November 2011 on Requirements for Budgetary Frameworks of the Member States; EC: Brussels, Belgium.

European Commission. (2012). *Fiscal Sustainability Report 2012*. EU. Available at: http://ec.europa.eu/economy_finance/publications/european_economy/2012/pdf/ee-2012-8_en.pdf

European Commission. (2015). *Ex-post evaluation of Late Payment Directive*. Available at: https://publications.europa.eu/en/publication-detail/-/publication/400ecc74-9a54-11e5-b3b7-01aa75ed71a1

European Commission. (2019). *Fiscal Sustainability Report 2018. Volume 1*. EU. Available at: https://ec.europa.eu/info/business-economy-euro/economy-finance-and-euro-publications_en

European Parliament. (2009). *Proposal for a Directive of the European Parliament and of the Council on combating late payment in commercial transactions*. Available at: http://www.europarl.europa.eu/RegData/docs_autres_institutions/commission_europeenne/com/2009/0126/COM_COM(2009)0126_EN.pdf

European Parliament. (2015). *Transposition and implementation of the Directive on late payment in commercial transactions. Implementation in Action*. Available at: http://www.europarl.europa.eu/RegData/etudes/IDAN/2015/558761/EPRS_IDA(2015)558761_EN.pdf

European Parliament. (2018). *Directive 2011/7/EU on late payments in commercial transactions. European Implementation Assessment*. Available at: http://www.europarl.europa.eu/RegData/etudes/IDAN/2018/621842/EPRS_IDA(2018)621842_EN.pdf

Ferreira, D. (2011). *Determinantes do Endividamento Municipal em Portugal*. Braga: Universidade do Minho. Available at https://comum.rcaap.pt/bitstream/10400.26/6196/1/Disserta%C3%A7%C3%A3o_Meatrado_A.Melo_2013.pdf

Hood, C. (2010). Accountability and Transparency: Siamese Twins, Matching Parts, Awkward Couple? *West European Politics*, *33*(5), 989–1009. doi:10.1080/01402382.2010.486122

IFAC. (2013). *Recommended Practice Guideline. Reporting on the Long-Term Sustainability of an Entity's Finances*. IFAC. Available at: https://www.ifac.org/publications-resources/recommended-practice-guideline-reporting-long-term-sustainability-public-sect

Inspeção-Geral de Finanças, . (2012). *Controlo dos Impactos Financeiros do PPTH e do PREDE nos Municípios: resultados globais e fragilidades do quadro legal. Informação n.º 1949/2012*. Lisboa: Inspeção-Geral de Finanças.

International Monetary Fund. (2013). *Staff Guidance Note for Public Debt Sustainability Analysis in Market-Access Countries*. IMF. Available at: https://www.imf.org/external/np/pp/eng/2013/050913.pdf

International Monetary Fund. (2014). *International Monetary Fund Annual Report 2014: From stabilization to sustainable growth*. IMF. Available at: https://www.imf.org/en/Publications/AREB/Issues/2016/12/31/International-Monetary-Fund-Annual-Report-2014-From-stabilization-to-sustainable-growth-41823

Intrum Justitia. (2012). *European Payment Report*. Author.

Intrum Justitia. (2015). *European Payment Report*. Author.

João, V. (2014). *Estudo comparativo das Leis de Finanças Locais n.os 2/2007 e 73/2013: O endividamento das autarquias locais*. Braga: Universidade do Minho - Escola de Direito da Universidade do Minho. Working papers. Available at:http://tributarium.net/uploads/3/0/9/1/3091332/wp_14_-_vadim_manuel_joo.pdf

Lei 151/2015, September 11th. Lei de Enquadramento Orçamental. Budget framework law.

Lei 73/2013, September 3rd republished by Lei 51/2018, August 16th. Establishes the financial regime of local authorities and inter-municipal entities.

Lei dos Compromissos e dos Pagamentos em Atraso. Lei 8/2012, February 21st, republished by Lei 22/2015, March 17th. Approves the rules applicable to the assumption of commitments and arrears of public entities.

Lobo, F., & Ramos, P. (2009). *Análise do Regime Jurídico do Endividamento dos Municípios em Portugal – A Nova Lei das Finanças Locais.* 15º Congresso da Associação Portuguesa de Desenvolvimento Regional, Cidade da Praia, Cabo Verde. Available at: http://www.apdr.pt/congresso/2009/pdf/Sess%C3%A3o%209/47A.pdf

Martinho, C., & Santos, P. (2019). *Fiabilidade do Indicador PMP para aferir as práticas de pagamento dos municípios portugueses.* Lisboa: OCC. Available at https://www.occ.pt/dtrab/trabalhos/iicicp//finais_site/72.pdf

OECD. (2011). *Policy Framework for Investment User's Toolkit. Chapter 10. Public Governance.* Available at http://www.oecd.org/investment/pfitoolkit

OECD. (2013). *Accountability and democratic governance: Orientations and principles for development. DAC Guidelines and Reference Series.* Available at http://www.oecd.org/dac/accountable-effective-institutions/For%20WEB%20Accountability%20and%20democratic%20governance%20Orientations%20and%20principles%20for%20development.pdf

Plano Oficial de Contabilidade das Autarquias Locais. Decreto-Lei 54-A/99, February 22th. Whith the changes made by Lei 60-A/2005, December 30th, Decreto-Lei 84-A/2002, April 5th, Decreto-Lei 315/2000, December 2nd and Lei 162/99, September 14th.

Programa de Apoio à Economia Local. Lei 43/2012, August 31st. Creates the Program of Support to the Local Economy, with the purpose of proceeding to the regularization of the payment of debts of the municipalities to suppliers due for more than 90 days.

Resolução do Conselho de Ministros, R. C. M. 34/2008, February 22th. Program "Pagar a Tempo e Horas". Approves the program of reduction of payment periods to suppliers of goods and services by the Public State, denominated Program 'Pay in Time and Hours'. Available at: https://data.dre.pt/eli/resolconsmin/34/2008/02/22/p/dre/pt/html

Reynolds, S., & Davis, J. (2015). *Transposition and implementation of the Directive on Late Payments in commercial transactions: Implementation in Action, EPRS, European Parliament.* Available at: http://www.europarl.europa.eu/RegData/etudes/IDAN/2015/558761/EPRS_IDA(2015)558761_EN.pdf

Rodríguez Bolívar, M., Navarro-Galera, A., Lopez Subires, M., & Muñoz, L. (2018). Analysing the accounting measurement of financial sustainability in local governments through political factors. *Accounting, Auditing & Accountability Journal, 31*(8), 2135–2164. doi:10.1108/AAAJ-10-2016-2754

Rodríguez Bolívar, M.; Navarro-Galera, A.; Muñoz, L. & Lopez Subires, M. (2014). Factors Influencing Local Government Financial Sustainability: An Empirical Study. *Lex localis - Journal of Local Self-Government, 12*. doi:10.4335/12.1.31-54(2014)

Rodríguez Bolívar, M., Navarro-Galera, A., Muñoz, L., & Lopez Subires, M. (2016). Analyzing Forces to the Financial Contribution of Local Governments to Sustainable Development. *Sustainability, 8*(9), 925. doi:10.3390u8090925

Santos, P., Martinho, C., & Escudeiro, M. (2019). *(Un)Ethical practices of subnational governments and the sustainability of Portuguese public finances (2010 at 2017)*. 5th Symposium on Ethics and Social Responsibility Research, ISCTE, Lisboa, Portugal.

Ter-Minassian, T. (2007). Fiscal Rules for Subnational Governments: Can They Promote Fiscal Discipline? *OECD Journal on Budgeting, 6*(3). Available at: https://www.oecd.org/gov/budgeting/43469443.pdf

UE. (2013). *Corporate Social Responsibility: Accountable, transparent and responsible business behaviour and sustainable growth*. Available at: http://www.europarl. europa.eu/oeil/popups/ficheprocedure.do?reference=2012/2098(INI)&l=EN

United States Agency for International Development (USAID). (2011). *Fundamentals of NGO Financial Sustainability*. Abt Associates Inc.

Veiga, J. (2014). *Da Lei das Finanças Locais à Recuperação Financeira Municipal*. Braga: Universidade do Minho. Available at http://www.fd.lisboa.ucp.pt/resources/documents/CONFERENCIAS/2014/RecFinanceiraMunicipal_Apresentacao_Francisco%20Veiga.pdf

Vigoda-Gadot, E., & Meiri, S. (2008). New public management values and person-organization fit: A socio-psychological approach and empirical examination among public sector personnel. *Public Administration, 86*(1), 111–131. doi:10.1111/j.1467-9299.2007.00703.x

Wiesel, F., & Modell, S. (2014). From new public management to new public governance? Hybridization and implications for public sector consumerism. *Financial Accountability & Management, 30*(2), 175–205. Available at https://www.researchgate.net/publication/261330877_From_New_Public_Management_to_New_Public_Governance_Hybridization_and_Implications_for_Public_Sector_Consumerism doi:10.1111/faam.12033

Chapter 5
Analysis of the Association Between Political Change in Local Government and Municipal Financial Condition in Spain During the Great Recession

José L. Zafra-Gómez
University of Granada, Spain

Antonio M. López-Hernández
University of Granada, Spain

Juan Montabes
University of Granada, Spain

Ángel Cazorla
University of Granada, Spain

ABSTRACT

The political influence on the financial condition of local government has been examined in various studies in the academic literature. However, no clear relationship has yet been established between such political factors and the constituent elements of financial condition sustainability in the context of the recent Great Recession. The aim of this study is to evaluate the dimensions of electoral size, defined for the chapter's purposes as the effective number of parties, and of transfer (i.e., how electoral gains and losses are related to the configuration of the party system) using a series of aggregate indices. Once these indicators are obtained, they are related to various indicators of financial condition for five Spanish cities. The results obtained show that financial condition either worsened or presented little change in the different cases considered and that various scenarios of aggregate volatility during the study period were detected.

DOI: 10.4018/978-1-5225-7820-8.ch005

1. INTRODUCTION

Various studies have examined the question of political influence on the financial condition of local government (Borges, 1995; Bastida & Benito, 2008; Klomp & De-Haan, 2011). In this respect, Benito et al. (2012) empirically analysed how the characteristics of the governing party impact on the financial activities of the local entity. However, no clear relationship has yet been established between such political factors and the constituent elements of financial condition sustainability in the context of the recent Great Recession (López-Hernández et al., 2012).

Nor has this phenomenon been considered previously with respect to the global economic and financial crisis, although the latter situation may be related to financial sustainability and political change. It has been suggested that financial condition might be modified by ideological political changes, and that a transboundary crisis (Ansell et al., 2010) could affect the relationship (Zafra-Gómez et al., 2013; Zafra-Gómez, López-Hernández, Plata-Díaz & Garrido-Rodríguez, 2016).

From a political standpoint, the present study uses a series of aggregate indices to evaluate the dimensions of electoral *size*, defined for our purposes as the effective number of parties, and of *transfer*, i.e. how electoral gains and losses are related to the configuration of the party system. Once these indicators are obtained, they are related to various indicators of financial condition for five Spanish cities – Barcelona, Madrid, Valencia, Seville and Zaragoza – during the period 2007-2011, which was characterised by the impact of the Great Recession (the transboundary crisis). Each of these cities underwent political changes during this period, either in the ideology of the governing party or as a change of mayor within the same political party.

The results obtained show that financial condition either worsened or presented little change in the different cases considered, and that various scenarios of aggregate volatility during the study period were detected.

The rest of this paper is structured as follows: section 2 presents the theoretical framework used to examine financial condition and its relationship with political characteristics; section 3 then describes the study method employed in this respect, after which section 4 summarises the results of our analysis. Finally, the main conclusions drawn are presented in section 5.

2. THEORETICAL FRAMEWORK: FINANCIAL CONDITION AND POLITICAL CHARACTERISTICS

The concept of financial condition is not a directly observable quantity, and there is no unambiguous way to measure it. Hence, various alternatives have been proposed. According to Groves, Godsey and Shulman (1981), financial condition has four distinct meanings, related to cash solvency, budget solvency, long-run solvency and service-level solvency. Other authors, such as Copeland and Ingram (1983), Berne (1992) and Clark (1990, 1994) have associated the term with the analysis of flows of revenues and expenses and with the determinants that characterise the entities in the acquisition of financial liabilities, within a given time horizon and within a specific economic space or dimension. On the other hand, Berne and Schramm (1986) held that the correct evaluation of financial condition requires us to consider a series of magnitudes concerning the environment, related to the needs and preferences of society, local conditions that affect the provision of public services, the costs of productive factors, activities, the resources available to society and the public policies that affect the local corporation.

In short, financial condition is a complex magnitude that incorporates financial and non-financial factors, both short and long term. In this respect, too, Greenberg and Hiller (1995) and CICA (1997) observed that an entity's financial condition can be measured by three indicators: sustainability, flexibility and vulnerability, defining sustainability as a government's ability to maintain, promote and preserve the social welfare of its citizens through the resources available to it.

In this paper, it is assumed that financial condition should be measured by reference to an appropriate, equitable provision of public services, taking as a starting point for the analysis the establishment of a dimensional structure based on social and economic variables, and performing the analysis within a long-term framework. This view of financial condition is evaluated using the following observable magnitudes:

- Sustainable budgetary policies (sustainability).
- Short-term solvency (cash solvency).
- Level of local government borrowing (flexibility).
- Dependence on other entities (financial independence).

Local government financial condition has been studied using various methods, such as data envelopment analysis (Zafra-Gómez & Múñiz-Pérez, 2010) and survival analysis (Zafra-Gómez et al., 2016a; Zafra-Gómez et al., 2016b; López-Hernández et al., 2017; Plata-Díaz et al., 2017).

The political environment is a factor that may influence the evolution of financial condition, and therefore is fundamental aspect to its understanding. Accordingly, the ideology of the governing party in the local corporation has been included as a variable that can influence its financial condition. Two types of ideologies are traditionally identified with respect to the behaviour of local public managers: conservative (or right-wing) and progressive (or left-wing). The former are expected to have a greater interest in reducing the public deficit (Bastida, Beyaert & Benito, 2012), in view of their preference for the use of market tools and instruments (Bel & Fageda, 2007; Plata-Díaz et al., 2017). Hence conservative governments would seek to improve the corporation's financial situation by enhancing its sustainability, while progressive ones would prefer to increase public spending, rather than rely on market mechanisms, in order to ensure the universal provision of public services (González-Gómez & Guardiola, 2015; Zafra-Gómez et al., 2016a).

3. METHOD

After describing various scenarios of local government, we propose a method to represent the main traits associated with the characteristics of local governments in Spain. This method is based on interrelating financial indicators with electoral indicators, thus creating new analytical dimensions that enhance our understanding of the processes of stability and change in the local entities under study.

The municipalities included in the study sample were selected by performing a cross-segmentation between population characteristics and political criteria, as described below.

The first criterion is that of the size of the city. Five Spanish cities, each of which met a series of composition requirements for the period 2007-11, were selected. The second criterion is that of the centre-periphery cleavage and how this ideological fracture has transcended to the Spanish political system, thus providing space for national and regional parties to flourish.

Under this method, six of the ten largest cities in Spain were within the study scope, with respect to types of national and local government, the re-election of the same candidate from the same political party, the election of a different candidate from the same party, or of a different candidate from a different party, and selecting only cities in regions governed by national or regional parties. The following selection criteria, thus, were applied:

1. Local government with the same candidate from the same political party (PP, or People's Party). Municipality selected: Valencia.
2. Local government without re-election and the same political party (PP). Municipality selected: Madrid.
3. Local government with re-election of candidate from the same political party (PSOE, Socialist Party). Municipality selected: Zaragoza.
4. Local government with no candidate re-election and a change in the political party, between national parties (PSOE to PP). Municipality selected: Sevilla.
5. Local government with no candidate re-election and a change in the political party from a national party to a regional party (PSOE to CiU). Municipality selected: Barcelona.

The composition of this sample group enabled us to describe the continuities and the changes resulting from governments with different political ideologies according to the segmentation of political parties. In addition, we measured the components of voting in each case.

An essential aspect of the analysis was the focus on the interconnections among the political components associated with the main cleavages, and the morphology of the party system in relation to the economic system. This focus enhanced our understanding of the relationship between financial condition and election outcomes.

For the variables related to the party system and the electoral arena (Oñate, 2007), we considered certain electoral indices, to determine two analytical and conceptual dimensions that provide information regarding the size of the electoral space and the changes produced in terms of vote transfers between the political formations that competed in the 2007 and 2011 municipal elections.

The *size* dimension was expressed according to the effective number of political parties, ENP[1]. This indicator describes the number of parties that really occupy the electoral space in an election. Also relevant in this respect is the fragmentation index proposed by Rae[2], which informs us about the relationship between the parties and the system, in terms of the concentration or otherwise of power. Moreover, it provides information about the number of parties and their size, rather than merely acknowledging their existence (Ocaña & Oñate, 1999).

In relation to the *size* dimension, we obtained indexes of electoral concentration and competitiveness, calculated by determining the sum and the difference, respectively, of the percentages of votes obtained by each of the two main political parties, in each election. This analysis of the dimension of size provides valuable information on the changes in the morphology of electoral arenas arising from the interrelations of new spaces, political parties and the balance of forces between them, resulting in turn from voters' reactions to the economic crisis.

For the *transfer* dimension, we must examine how electoral gains and losses are related to the configuration of the party system, according to: a) The support maintained between successive elections for the same political formations; b) Common ideological blocs or differing ones, according to ideology or cleavage. This perspective reveals the volatility of the electoral space in each election, allowing us to determine where votes are won or lost. To perform this analysis, we produced a set of indexes derived from Petersen's aggregate volatility index[3], either for the total of each electoral process (VT), or between ideological blocs (VE) or within the same ideological spaces (VI).

The index of aggregate volatility provides information about the changes in electoral behaviour between consecutive elections, revealing the stability or otherwise of the party system at the aggregate level, by taking into consideration the differences in the votes obtained by the parties from one election to the next. Although these indexes cannot be interpreted as an indicator of individual changes in behaviour, they reflect variations in the inter-election performance of the parties, and so provide a generic idea of the changes in behaviour during this period.

Our analysis of financial condition takes into account four variables related to financial flexibility, which is defined as the municipality's capacity to respond to changes in the economy or in financial circumstances. This may take place through changes in public borrowing (Greenberg & Hillier, 1995; CICA, 1997), which can be determined by determining net savings and the difference between 110% of current income and long-term debt. The variables considered are those of solvency, defined as an entity's capacity to generate sufficient liquidity to pay its short-term debt (Groves, Godsey & Shulman, 2003) and liquidity, i.e. the ratio between liquid funds and obligations. The next block is financial independence, or the level of dependence on external funding received through transfers and grants (Honadle, 2003). The fourth and final variable is financial sustainability, defined as the ability to maintain, promote and protect the welfare of citizens, using available resources (Greenberg & Hillier, 1995; CICA, 1997; Groves, Godsey & Schulman, 2003; Hendrick, 2011). In this respect, too, we determine the limit of non-financial expenditure.

In our analysis, the following elements of financial condition are considered:

Table 1. Components of financial condition

Variable		Description	Source
Short-run solvency	*Cash Surplus Index*	Difference between net short-term receivables, liquidity and net short-term liabilities	Directorate General for Financial Coordination with Regional and Local Authorities (DGCFCAEL, Ministry of Finance and Public Administration)
	Liquidity	Liquidity divided by net short-term liabilities	
Flexibility	*Taxable value divided by Financial Charge Index*	Fiscal receivables divided by annual amortisation payment –interest and principal	
	Net savings index	Difference between the receivables from current budget resources and the budget obligations from non-financial current expenditure, reduced by annual amortisation payment – including interest and principal	
	Fiscal Revenues Index	Fiscal receivables divided by current receivables	
Sustainability	*Non-financial Budgetary Result Index*	Non-financial current budgetary receivables and non-financial capital budgetary receivables divided by current budgetary payables and non-financial capital budgetary payables	
Independence	*Financial Independence Index*	Budgetary payables divided by budgetary receivables except grants	

4. RESULTS

To enhance our understanding of the interaction between financial condition and political stability in local government, we analyse the main financial and political-electoral characteristics of the municipalities selected, isolating the factors that highlight this relationship.

First, we describe some generic characteristics of the Spanish party system (in the corresponding time and space), to contextualise and frame the analysis of each of the five cities examined.

The 2007 municipal elections presented reasonable continuity with the mean values of the basic electoral indexes in Spain, i.e. limited electoral space and very few effective parties in contention. Although second-level elections, such as local elections, represent a greater opportunity for electoral experimentation (Reif & Schmitt, 1970), the fact is that since the 1990s there has been a sustained tendency in Spain for the vote to be concentrated in the two major national parties, PP and PSOE. The outcome, a reduced electoral space and a bipartisan tendency, was one of the most stable features of the latter phase of the party system in Spain until the

Table 2. Evolution of the electoral results obtained by the main parties in the 2007-2011 municipal elections in the five cities considered

	Barcelona		Madrid		Valencia		Sevilla		Zaragoza		Spain	
	2007	2011	2007	2011	2007	2011	2007	2011	2007	2011	2007	2011
PSOE/PSC	31.2%	23.2%	31.6%	24.6%	34.3%	21.8%	41.3%	30.3%	39.1%	28.2%	34.9%	27.8%
PP	16.3%	18.1%	56.8%	51.1%	57.5%	52.5%	42.7%	50.7%	34.9%	42.8%	35.6%	37.5%
IU	9.8%	10.9%	8.9%	11.1%	4.8%	7.2%	8.5%	7.4%	5.5%	8.2%	5.48%	6.6%
UPyD			0.0%	8.1%	0.0%	2.8%	0.0%	3.3%	0.0%	3.7%		2.1%
Ciudadanos	4.0%	2.0%										
ERC	9.2%	5.9%									1.5%	1.2%
CIU	26.5%	30.1%									3.2%	3.5%
UV					0.8%	0.0%						
BLOC					1.4%	0.6%					0.5%	
Compromís					0.0%	9.0%						0.8%
PA							4.6%	4.9%			1.1%	
CHA									9.9%	9.6%	0.3%	0.2%
PAR									8.6%	4.7%	0.4%	0.3%
Others	3.0%	9.9%	2.7%	5.1%	1.4%	4.6%	2.9%	3.4%	2.0%	2.8%	17.2%	20%

Source: Compiled by the authors from data published by the Ministry of the Interior

December 2015 elections. This tendency was nuanced in the regions that contained significant non-national parties, where the effective number of parties and the degree of political fragmentation has always been greater. The 2007 elections were non-volatile, reflecting a perfectly crystallised party system in which few transfers of votes took place between or within ideological blocs.

In contrast, the 2011 municipal elections presented a new electoral situation, in which the above-described situation was modified considerably. The previous bipartisanship, focused on the two major national political forces, was now significantly eroded, a change that mainly affected the PSOE, which was severely punished in these elections, and again in the general elections held in November of the same year. These elections were the first to be called when the economic and financial crisis was exerting its full effect. The subsequent municipal elections of 24 May 2015 provided another nationwide opportunity to punish the government that had managed the response to the crisis; thus, the left-wing PSOE was held responsible for the financial and economic adjustment policies carried out, and lost many mayorships. This situation increased the degree of political fragmentation and the effective number of parties. New figures emerged, such as UpyD and *Ciudadanos* (Citizens) in Catalonia, and many independent formations held the balance of power,

Table 3. Electoral indices 2007-2011 for Barcelona

Indices	2007	2011
Fragmentation	0.785	0.798
Effective Number of Parties	4.7	4.9
Concentration	57.7%	53.3%
Competitiveness	4.6%	6.9%
Aggregate Volatility	9.1	9.9
Volatility Between Blocs	9.0	6.8
Volatility Within Blocs	0.1	3.1

Source: Compiled by the authors from data published by the Ministry of the Interior

determining mayors and entering into local pacts of government. Levels of electoral concentration and of average competitiveness both decreased. However, the most significant event was the increase in the index of volatility, reflecting the climate of political change and the greater probability of a transfer of votes, either between blocs or, and what is most significant, within them.

The following sections present the electoral results recorded in each of the five cities analysed (Table 1), together with the corresponding political and financial analysis for each case, during the period 2007-2011. These elements are inter-related in order to determine the local effects of municipal management policies (whether conservative or progressive), in a context of global crisis during the central years of the Great Recession.

4.1. Barcelona

The first of the cities studied, Barcelona is perhaps the most idiosyncratic of all those selected for analysis, and chief among its singularities is the weight and role played by traditional political cleavages in its political space, which is fundamentally territorial. However, in recent years, a new scenario has emerged. The disintegration of major political structures in Catalonia shows that a sense of identity can be reconstructed from the combination of certain essentialist elements with others that are purely constructivist (Rivera & Cazorla, 2017). This reshuffle of the political map arose in the economic sphere in response to the austerity measures imposed by different levels of government during the Great Recession.

The superposition of the territorial cleavage over the ideological components that have traditionally defined the political space in Catalonia created a wholly new political situation, which first took material shape in the local elections of 2011.

Table 4. Variation in the elements of financial condition, 2007-2011, in Barcelona

Indices	Variation 2007-2010	Variation 2010-2011
Net Savings	-46.0%	5.2%
Fiscal Revenues	6.9%	-1.9%
Financial Independence	-16.3%	16.7%
Flexibility	-38.8%	26.1%
Non-financial Budget Surplus/Deficit	-15.0%	6.2%
Cash Solvency	5.5%	4.4%
Liquidity	5.0%	-42.3%

Source: Compiled by the authors from data published by the Ministry of Finance and Public Administration

These elections represented a milestone in the evolution of the political scene in Catalonia. This was the first vote held after the Constitutional Court issued its ruling on the Catalan Statute of Autonomy[4], and brought to an end a 32-year domination of the mayorality by the Socialist Party of Catalonia (PSC). In 2011, the voters elected Xavier Trías, of the CiU, one of the central political forces in the region since the re-establishment of democracy, but which had never won Barcelona, one of the main socialist fiefdoms in Spain. The outgoing mayor, Jordi Hereu, was defeated after a legislature marked by the beginning of the economic recession and the initial implementation of austerity policies by the socialist government in Madrid, under prime minister Rodríguez-Zapatero.

Our analysis of the electoral data shows that the main characteristic of this change of cycle is that, despite the enormous impact of the loss of this socialist bastion, the general configuration of political spaces in Barcelona was not greatly altered.

Analysis of the first dimension, related to the electoral space, revealed a slight increase in electoral fragmentation and in the effective number of parties (although the latter was insignificant, since *Ciudadanos* was present in both electoral years), while concentration fell slightly and competitiveness also decreased, which corroborates previous observations on the presence of a dual vote in Catalonia (Montero & Font, 1991).

With respect to voting shifts, the most significant data are provided by the indicator of aggregate volatility. In general, this index is not very high (around 9%). Although in general terms it increased slightly between 2007 and 2011, presenting a larger component of between-bloc volatility, as the PSC results worsened from 31.2% to 23.2%, with the governing party being punished by voters hit by austerity policies. This shift in voting patterns marked the trend for subsequent between-bloc territorial movements in the political scene in Catalonia.

Table 5. Electoral indices 2007-2011 for Madrid

Indices	2007	2011
Fragmentation	0.569	0.656
Effective Number of Parties	2.3	2.9
Concentration	88.4%	75.8%
Competitiveness	25.2%	26.5%
Aggregate Volatility	6.2	12.6
Volatility Between Blocs	4.4	3.6
Volatility Within Blocs	1.8	9.0

Source: Compiled by the authors from data published by the Ministry of the Interior

Table 6. Variation in the elements of financial condition, 2007-2011, in Madrid

Indices	Variation 2007-2010	Variation 2010-2011
Net Savings	-181.5%	-239.4%
Fiscal Revenues	15.0%	-3.2%
Financial Independence	13.9%	-15.7%
Flexibility	15.3%	52.1%
Non-financial Budget Surplus/Deficit	-2.8%	13.1%
Cash Solvency	-36.8%	-4.6%
Liquidity	-77.2%	-22.3%

Source: Compiled by the authors from data published by the Ministry of Finance and Public Administration

From the financial standpoint, nearly all of the financial indicators worsened between 2007 and 2010. The only exceptions were the indices of fiscal revenues, of cash solvency and of liquidity. Hence, the proportion of budget debtors pending collection increased during this period. With the change of mayor, the financial indicators for 2010-11 reflected improvements in net savings, financial independence, non-financial deficit and short-term solvency. The only negative aspect was the decrease in liquidity in this period.

This change of scenario presaged future movements of greater importance, and highlighted voters' punishment-reward reactions to the economic situation in elections held during a period of severe economic recession.

4.2. Madrid

The electoral context in Madrid has been less volatile, especially since the early 1990s, when the PP (People's Party) won the mayorality, in the first of a succession of terms of office that continued until the end of the election cycle analysed in this paper. Both in 2007 and in 2011, the PP won a sweeping electoral victory, with over 50% of the votes on each occasion, although in the 2011 election the PP vote decreased from 58.6% to 51.1%. It is important to note that a new mayor was in fact elected, but due to non-electoral factors. Ana María Botella took over at city hall following the resignation of Alberto Ruiz Gallardón, who had been appointed Justice Minister in the first PP government led by Mariano Rajoy. Accordingly, a change took place in the incumbent mayor, but not in the political party that came out ahead in the elections; the PP remained the most voted party in both municipal elections, well ahead of its main adversary, the PSOE.

The political dimensions in Madrid presented certain changes that were becoming more substantive, resembling those observed elsewhere in electoral responses to the impact of the Great Recession on Spanish society. Thus, novel political spaces appeared and were occupied by newly-emerging political parties. In addition, there was increased political volatility, both between blocs and, especially, within them.

With respect to the first dimension concerning political spaces, there was an increase in electoral fragmentation and a slight increase in the effective number of parties, mainly due to the arrival on the electoral scene of the UPyD (Union for Progress and Democracy), a party with no very clear ideological identification that situated itself according to another axis, that of the centre-periphery, as the main element of its discursive and programmatic identification. For the same reason, electoral concentration fell slightly, although the level of competitiveness between the two main political forces in Madrid (PP and PSOE) remained unchanged, due to the comfortable electoral advantage of the PP.

Regarding voting shifts, there was a marked increase in volatility between the two elections. The total value doubled, and most of this change was due to within-bloc volatility, that is, between political parties occupying the same ideological space, as was the case with votes transferred from PP to UPyD or from PSOE to IU (United Left).

The financial indicators presented diverse changes. For the period 2007-2010, corresponding to the political management of the outgoing mayor, the indicators of fiscal revenues, financial independence and flexibility (i.e., the capacity to meet borrowing obligations) improved significantly, while those of short-term solvency

Table 7. Electoral indices 2007-2011 for Valencia

Indices	2007	2011
Fragmentation	0.550	0.671
Effective Number of Parties	2.2	3.0
Concentration	91.7%	74.3%
Competitiveness	23.2%	30.8%
Aggregate Volatility	8.3	18.2
Volatility Between Blocs	2.3	2.0
Volatility Within Blocs	6.1	16.2

Source: Compiled by the authors from data published by the Ministry of the Interior

Table 8. Variation in the elements of financial condition, 2007-2011, in Valencia

Indices	Variation 2007-2010	Variation 2010-2011
Net Savings	-391.0%	-100.1%
Fiscal Revenues	8.3%	-2.3%
Financial Independence	-9.6%	16.5%
Flexibility	166.2%	-59.0%
Non-financial Budget Surplus/Deficit	5.7%	-9.7%
Cash Solvency	7.5%	-29.2%
Liquidity	84.8%	-59.6%

Source: Compiled by the authors from data published by the Ministry of Finance and Public Administration

and net savings worsened to an important degree, and that of non-financial budget deficit/surplus worsened slightly. Between 2010 and 2011, the change of mayor was accompanied by a worsening of the fiscal revenues index and that of financial independence. The only one that improved was the budget deficit/surplus.

In summary, the political situation analysed in this city reflected a climate of continuity in institutional politics. The governing party suffered a slight loss of voter popularity, and the electoral spaces expanded with the arrival of new political formations, giving rise to voting gains and losses, with most voting shifts taking place within the same ideological bloc.

4.3. Valencia

The city of Valencia, like Madrid, was one of the main strongholds of the PP during the electoral cycle that began in 1991, during which the party retained the mayor's office in seven consecutive municipal elections. In Valencia, the same person, Rita Barberá, remained mayor of the city until 2015.

As in the capital, Valencia gave majority support to the PP, with over 50% of the vote and well ahead of its main competitor, the PSOE. The major differentiating characteristic between the two cities is that in Valencia the 2011 elections were marked by a split in the traditional space of partisan crystallisation. This change in the pattern occurred with the entry into the scene of *Compromis* (Commitment), a new political formation that arose from the coalition between *Nationalist Bloc Valenciá* and other formations with a green-ecologist ideology, and embodied a sector of the left-wing electorate that was highly critical of the traditional, majority parties and their attitude towards the economic crisis, based on spending cuts and other austerity measures. Another party, UpyD, also took part in the Valencia elections for the first time, together with a number of small formations.

This alteration in the electoral scenario is clearly reflected in the dimensions studied, both the electoral spaces and the gains and losses of each political formation. Thus, we observe a considerable increase in electoral fragmentation, with the indicator 'Effective number of parties' rising from 2.2 in 2007 to 3.0 in 2011. Electoral concentration, although still relatively high, decreased by a third, and competitiveness also fell. The PSOE was the most obviously affected by this greater degree of electoral competition, and in the 2011 elections lost 12.5% of its votes to *Compromis* and the IU (United Left).

The 2011 elections, thus, were marked by changes in the second study dimension, that of voting shifts between electoral formations and/or ideological blocs. In the Valencia elections of 2011, total volatility rose very significantly, from 8.3% to 18.2%. Moreover, practically all of this volatility corresponded to voting flows within the same bloc, especially among the left-wing parties. The overall pattern was one of punishing the party considered responsible for the financial crisis; the PSOE had governed Spain during the first phase of the recession and was widely blamed for this economic and financial situation.

In relation to the indicators of financial condition during the electoral period 2007-2010, net savings and flexibility worsened just before the elections, while the other indicators presented positive changes. Tax revenues increased and debt ratios

Table 9. Electoral indices 2007-2011 for Sevilla

Indices	2007	2011
Fragmentation	0.638	0.642
Effective Number of Parties	2.8	2.8
Concentration	83.9%	81.1%
Competitiveness	1.4%	20.4%
Aggregate Volatility	8.7	12.2
Volatility Between Blocs	0.7	5.9
Volatility Within Blocs	8.0	6.3

Source: Compiled by the authors from data published by the Ministry of the Interior

Table 10. Variation in the elements of financial condition, 2007-2011, in Sevilla

Indices	Variation 2007-2010	Variation 2010-2011
Net Savings	6.5%	-4.1%
Fiscal Revenues	11.4%	-4.7%
Financial Independence	-4.8%	-5.9%
Flexibility	-50.5%	-29.9%
Non-financial Budget Surplus/Deficit	-7.7%	-4.6%
Cash Solvency	-2.7%	-10.4%
Liquidity	-43.0%	-46.7%

Source: Compiled by the authors from data published by the Ministry of Finance and Public Administration

eased. In the municipal elections, the PP candidate Rita Barberá was re-elected, and most financial indicators continue to worsen during the next year.

In summary, the spaces of electoral competition altered significantly in Valencia during the study period. The weakened position of the PSOE, the governing party at the national level, together with the emergence of new formations that channelled expressions of discontent among the population, were the main factors accounting for the PP retaining its predominant position in the local government of Valencia. The poor economic outlook did not affect the level of support for the PP in the municipal government, which was exonerated of responsibility and, albeit with a slight decrease, broadly maintained its voter base, within a much more fragmented political and electoral space.

4.4. Sevilla

Sevilla is one of the cities presenting most diversity of political options in its city hall. During the modern democratic period (since 1977), the mayor's office has been occupied by three different formations: the PA or Andalusian Party (in two non-continuous terms), the PP (in two non-continuous terms) and the PSOE (in three continuous terms).

The study period represents a moment of inflection, with the PSOE losing the mayoralty to the PP. The socialists had enjoyed three consecutive terms under the mayorship of Alfredo Sanchez de Monteseirín, although the 2007 elections were closely competed with the PP. In fact, the PP candidate won most votes, but Monteseirín obtained the support of IU and so was able to stay in power. In the elections, the socialists lost 12.5% of their votes, with their share of support falling from 41.2% in 2007 to 30.3% in 2011. Support for the PP, on the other hand, rose by eight points, 42.7% to 50.7%. These two electoral processes marked a decline in the fortunes of the PA, a regional nationalist force that was eventually dissolved in October 2015.

Our analysis of the electoral dimensions in Sevilla shows that the interparty space remained virtually unchanged in this city, with almost identical rates of political fragmentation and effective numbers of parties. Nevertheless, there was significant alteration in the political scene, with the inclusion of a new political force (UPyD) and the progressive weakening of the PA. Similarly, levels of political concentration remained very similar between the two elections; in both cases, the two leading political forces obtained over 80% of the votes, although the degree of competitiveness decreased in the 2011 elections. Thus, in the 2007 elections, competitiveness was at a peak, with the two formations separated by only 1.4%, while in the next elections this difference had widened to more than 20%.

With regard to the transfer of votes, the outstanding feature observed was the increased political volatility in the 2011 elections. Patterns of voting gains and losses changed, both within and between ideological blocs, and the loss of prominence of the PSOE was especially significant. The latter party, which in 2007 held the reins of power in Sevilla at all levels of government – national, regional and local – began to suffer an evident erosion in its electoral appeal in the municipal elections of 2011.

The financial indicators worsened during the period 2007-2010, for budget surplus/deficit and short-term solvency, while the proportion of tax revenues to current revenues increased. The municipal elections for Sevilla produced a change of mayor and also a change of political sign in city hall, following the worsening of the financial indicators for the period 2010-2011, including the index of net savings, although the fiscal revenues index improved just before the elections.

Table 11. Electoral indices 2007-2011 for Zaragoza

Indices	2007	2011
Fragmentation	0.705	0.720
Effective Number of Parties	3.4	3.5
Concentration	74.1%	70.9%
Competitiveness	4.2%	14.6%
Aggregate Volatility	8.9	15.2
Volatility Between Blocs	3.0	8.1
Volatility Within Blocs	5.9	7.1

Source: Compiled by the authors from data published by the Ministry of the Interior

Table 12. Variation in the elements of financial condition, 2007-2011, Zaragoza

Indices	Variation 2007-2010	Variation 2010-2011
Net Savings	-77.0%	30.3%
Fiscal Revenues	1.3%	1.7%
Financial Independence	10.7%	-2.4%
Flexibility	14.7%	36.0%
Non-financial Budget Surplus/Deficit	3.0%	-0.9%
Cash Solvency	-14.9%	-7.0%
Liquidity	-90.6%	-49.5%

Source: Compiled by the authors from data published by the Ministry of Finance and Public Administration

The city of Sevilla is paradigmatic of voters' punishment of the government (i.e. the PSOE), blamed for the impact of the crisis and recession. The alterations in the electoral spaces were all in favour of the PP, while the PSOE, the newly-elected party in the municipal government, had to tackle an increasingly adverse economic and political context in the run-up to the forthcoming general elections, in which the party suffered major losses.

4.5. Zaragoza

Finally, Zaragoza presents a situation that is very different from the other cities examined in this study. Here, the mayor's office was won, in both of the elections considered, by the socialist Juan Alberto Belloch, although always with the support of non-national parties, the conservative PAR (Aragonese Party) in 2007 and the CHA (Aragonese Front) and the IU in 2011. In fact, only this alliance enabled Belloch to retain the mayorality, as the PP had won the largest share of the vote. From 2007 to 2011, support for the PSOE fell from 39.1% to 28.2%, continuing the general trend of attrition in votes, at all levels of government. In contrast, the PP rose in the polls, and was the most voted party in the municipal elections of 2007 and of 2011. In the latter, support for the PP rose by 8 points, from 34.9% to 42.8%. Among the non-national parties, support for the CHA remained constant at 9%, while that for the PAR decreased by almost half, from 8.6% to 4.7% .

As commented above, the electoral space in Zaragoza presented greater fragmentation than in the country as a whole, for the period analysed, due to the greater weight of regional parties (PAR and CHA), as well as the participation of UPyD in the 2011 election. In terms of fragmentation, ENP and concentration, this scenario remained virtually unchanged between the two elections, with a slight decline in electoral concentration in 2011, as voters punished the PSOE. For the same reason, the high level of competitiveness observed in 2007 decreased significantly in 2011.

The pattern and degree of voter transfer recorded elsewhere were broadly the same in Zaragoza. Thus, we recorded a significant increase in overall volatility in 2011, with a generally equal distribution of within and between-bloc volatility. However, the latter was slightly greater, as the result of voting shifts away from the PSOE, together with variations in the national vs. non-national party vote.

With respect to the financial indicators, levels of cash solvency worsened from 2007 to 2010, but the other factors improved. After Belloch's re-election as mayor, short-term solvency continued to worsen, and was accompanied by poorer figures for financial independence and budget deficit/surplus. On the other hand, the level of net savings rose.

The political scenario in Zaragoza reflected the marked attrition of the governing party, in power for 12 years, with the mayor only able to stay in office through pacts with regional parties. This support, from all sides of the ideological spectrum, contrasted with the concentrated appeal of the PP, which was the most voted party in 2007 and 2011 but was kept out of power until the next elections, in 2015. Again, we emphasise that this situation was largely caused by a very significant erosion in support for the governing PSOE, but was also due to voters' reaction to the economic policies being applied (Del Águila, 2002), in view of the impact of the economic crisis that broke out in 2008.

Table 13. Summary of the main results obtained

City	Political Changes			Financial Condition 2007-2010	Financial Condition 2010-2011
Madrid	Increased aggregate volatility	Within bloc	Change of mayor, same political sign	57% of indicators worsened	71% of indicators worsened
Barcelona	Increased aggregate volatility	Within bloc	Change of mayor, same political sign	57% of indicators worsened	71% of indicators improved
Valencia	Increased aggregate volatility	Within bloc	Re-election of mayor	57% of indicators improved	86% of indicators worsened
Sevilla	Increased aggregate volatility	Between blocs	Change of mayor, different political sign	57% of indicators worsened	100% of indicators worsened
Zaragoza	Increased aggregate volatility	Within bloc and between blocs	Re-election of mayor	57% of indicators improved	57% of indicators worsened

5. CONCLUSIONS

In general, the financial condition associated with the electoral cycle in the first stage of the Great Recession worsened, or in some cases varied only slightly. Diverse scenarios of aggregate volatility can be distinguished. Thus, in Valencia, within-bloc volatility increased significantly, while in Sevilla the overall increase was due to between-bloc volatility, and in Zaragoza both types were present. When the mayor was re-elected (in Zaragoza and Valencia) in 2011, the financial condition had worsened slightly in each case. We conclude, therefore, that the expectation of re-election was not associated with an improving financial situation in the municipality in question. When there was no re-election and the incoming mayor was of a different political sign, the financial indicators reflected a financial deterioration both during the period managed by the outgoing mayor, and also under the incoming represetnative of the PP.

In Barcelona, the aggregate volatility increased throughout the study period, and the change of mayor was accompanied by a slight improvement in the city's financial condition.

These results suggest that further analysis is needed of financial condition in a volatile political environment, especially when it is subject to a transboundary crisis. Future lines of research should include a greater number of cities, characterised by the political variations we describe, and determine the association between these variables and changes in levels of efficiency.

REFERENCES

Ansell, C., Boin, A., & Keller, A. (2010). Managing transboundary crises: Identifying the building blocks of an effective response system. *Journal of Contingencies and Crisis Management, 18*(4), 195–207. doi:10.1111/j.1468-5973.2010.00620.x

Bartolini, S. (1999). Collusion, competition and democracy: Part I. *Journal of Theoretical Politics, 11*(4), 435–470. doi:10.1177/0951692899011004001

Bastida, F., Beyaert, A., & Benito, B. (2013). Electoral Cycles and Local Government Debt Management. *Local Government Studies, 39*(1), 107–132. doi:10.1080/0300 3930.2012.683861

Bateman, K. R., & Clark, T. N. (1990). *Monitoring local governments: how personal computers can help systematize municipal fiscal analysis*. Dubuque, IA: Kendall/ Hunt Pub. Co.

Bel, G., & Fageda, X. (2007). Why do local governments privatize public services? A survey of empirical studies. *Local Government Studies, 33*(4), 517–534. doi:10.1080/03003930701417528

Benito, B., Bastida, F., & Vicente, C. (2012). Political Budget Cycles in Local Governments. *Lex Localis - Journal of Local Self-Government, 10*(4), 341-361. Retrieved from http://pub.lex-localis.info/index.php/LexLocalis

Benito López, B., & Bastida Albaladejo, F. J. (2008). Política y gestión financiera municipal. *Revista de Contabilidad-Spanish Accounting Review, 11*(2), 55-78. Retrieved from http://www.rc-sar.es/verPdf.php?articleId=178

Berne, R. (1992). *The Relationships Between Financial Reporting And The Measurement Of Financial Condition. Government Accounting Standard Board, Research Report, Nº 18.*

Berne, R. & Scharamm, R. (1986). *The Financial Analysis Of Government*. Prentice Hall.

Canadian Institute Of Chartered Accountants (CICA). (1997). *Indicators Of Government Financial Condition*. Toronto: Author.

Cazorla, Á., Rivera, X. M., & Gulías, E. J. (2017). La abstención electoral en las elecciones al Parlamento Europeo de 2014: Análisis estructural de sus componentes. Reis. *Revista Espanola de Investigaciones Sociologicas*, (159): 31–50.

Clark, T. (1977). Fiscal Management of American cities: Funds Flow Indicators. *Journal of Accounting Research*, *15*(supplement), 54–94. doi:10.2307/2490632

Copeland, R., & Ingram, R. (1983). Municipal Financial Reporting And Disclosure Quality. Addison-Wesley.

Del Aguila Tejerina, R. (2002). De nuevo el fin de las ideologías? In *Las ideas políticas en el siglo XXI* (pp. 59–67). Ariel.

Gibert, J. R. M., & Fabregas, J. F. (1991). El voto dual en Cataluña: Lealtad y transferencia de votos en las elecciones autonómicas. *Revista de Estudios Políticos*, (73), 7–34.

González-Gómez, F., & Guardiola, J. (2009). A duration model for the estimation of the contracting-out of urban water management in southern Spain. *Urban Affairs Review*, *44*(6), 886–906. doi:10.1177/1078087408329274

Greenberg, J., & Hillier, D. (1995). *Indicators Of Financial Condition For Governments*. 5th Conference Of Comparative International Governmental Accounting Research (CIGAR), Paris, France.

Groves, S. M., & Godsey, W. M. (2003). *Evaluating financial condition:A handbook of local government*. Washington, DC: International City/County Management Association.

Hendrick, R. M. (2011). *Managing the fiscal metropolis: The financial policies, practices, and health of suburban municipalities*. Washington, DC: Georgetown University Press.

Laakso, M., & Taagepera, R. (1979). "Effective" number of parties: A measure with application to West Europe. *Comparative Political Studies*, *12*(1), 3–27. doi:10.1177/001041407901200101

López-Hernández, Zafra-Gómez, Plata-Díaz, & de la Higuera-Molina. (n.d.). *Modeling Fiscal Stress and Contracting Out in Local Government: The Influence of Time, Financial Condition, and the Great Recession*. Academic Press.

López-Hernández, A. M., Zafra-Gómez, J. L., & Ortíz-Rodríguez, D. (2012). Effects of the crisis in Spanish municipalities financial condition: An empirical evidence (2005-2008). *International Journal of Critical Accounting*, *4*(5/6), 631–645. doi:10.1504/IJCA.2012.051457

Municipal fiscal strain: indicators and causes. (1994). Retrieved from https://www.thefreelibrary.com/Municipalfiscalstrain:indicatorsandcauses.-a016086840

Oñate, P., & Ocaña, F. (2007). Las elecciones autonómicas de 2007 y los sistemas de partidos autonómicos en la España multinivel. *Elecciones autonómicas y municipales de*, 133-64.

Oñate, P., & Ocaña, F. A. (1999). *Análisis de datos electorales* (Vol. 27). Cis.

Pedersen, M. N. (1983). Changing patterns of electoral volatility in European party systems, 1948-1977: Explorations in explanation. Western European party systems. *Continuity and Change*, 29–66.

Plata-Díaz, de la Higuera-Molina, Garrido-Rodríguez, & Zafra-Gómez. (2018). Contracting Out and Social Services: Responses to the Austerity Machine, Financial Condition and Political Parties. doi:10.1177/0095399717713797

Rae, D., Hanby, V., & Loosemore, J. (1971). Thresholds of representation and thresholds of exclusion: An analytic note on electoral systems. *Comparative Political Studies*, *3*(4), 479–488. doi:10.1177/001041407100300406

Shugart, M. S. (1995). The electoral cycle and institutional sources of divided presidential government. *The American Political Science Review*, *89*(2), 327–343. doi:10.2307/2082428

Zafra-Gómez, López-Hernández, Plata-Díaz, & Garrido-Rodríguez. (2015). Financial and Political Factors Motivating the Privatisation of Municipal Water Services. *Local Government Studies*. doi:10.1080/03003930.2015.1096268

Zafra-Gómez, J. L., López-Hernández, A. M., & Hernández-Bastida, A. (2009a). Evaluating Financial Performance in Local Government. Maximising the Benchmarking Value. *International Review of Administrative Sciences*, *75*(1), 151–167. doi:10.1177/0020852308099510

Zafra-Gómez, J. L., López-Hernández, A. M., & Hernández-Bastida, A. (2009b). Developing a Model to Measure Financial Condition in Local Government. Evaluating Service Quality and Minimizing the Effects of the Socioeconomic Environment: An Application to Spanish Municipalities. *American Review of Public Administration*, *39*(4), 425–449. doi:10.1177/0275074008320710

Zafra-Gómez, J. L., López-Hernández, A. M., & Hernández-Bastida, A. (2009c). Developing an Alert System for Local Governments in Financial Crisis. *Public Money & Management*, *29*(3), 175–181. doi:10.1080/09540960902891731

Zafra-Gómez, J. L., & Muñiz, M. (2010). Overcoming Cost Inefficiencies within Small Municipalities: Improve Financial Condition or Reduce the Quality of Public Services? *Environment and Planning. C, Government & Policy*, *28*(4), 609–629. doi:10.1068/c09118

Zafra-Gómez, J. L., Prior, D., Ana, M. P. D., & López-Hernández, A. M. (2013). Reducing Costs in Times of Crisis: Delivery Forms in Small and Medium Sized Local Governments' Waste Management Services. *Public Administration*, *91*(1), 51–68. doi:10.1111/j.1467-9299.2011.02012.x

ENDNOTES

1 The ENP, first presented by Laakso and Taagepera (1979) and later reformulated by Taagepera and Shugart (1988), is calculated as follows:
ENP = 1 / (A2 + B2 + C2 +.... + n2)
i.e. one divided by the sum of the proportions of votes obtained by the candidates, squared. This indicator summarises the number of parties that compete electorally, taking into account their relative size.

2 Rae (1971) proposed the following formula for its calculation:
F = 1 - (A2 + B2 + C2 +.... + n2)
i.e., one minus the sum of the proportions of votes obtained by the candidates, squared. Its value ranges from 0.000 - for a single-party system - to 1,000 - for an unlimited fragmentation system.

3 Pedersen (1983); Bartolini (1986)

$$VT = \frac{|A1-A2|+|B1-B2|+......|n1-n2|}{2}$$

This is calculated by adding the net change in percentage of votes won or lost by each party from one election to the next, and dividing it by two. From its calculation formula, the index always shows absolute values, and therefore the result will always be positive, showing the degree of variation of the vote, but not the increase or decrease in the number of votes. This measurement reveals the degree to which the party system is fractured, whether it is stable and whether the dimensions around which it is constructed remain relevant.

4 . On 28 June 2010, the Constitutional Court ruled that the reform of the Catalan Statute of Autonomy was unconstitutional, in 14 of its 144 articles, following an appeal to this effect by the PP party.

Chapter 6
Popular Financial Reporting: A New Information Tool for Local Public Groups

Paolo Pietro Biancone
Department of Management, University of Turin, Italy

Silvana Secinaro
Department of Management, University of Turin, Italy

Valerio Brescia
https://orcid.org/0000-0001-7919-5370
Department of Management, University of Turin, Italy

ABSTRACT

The study intends to investigate the possibility of adopting popular financial reporting with a view to greater transparency, accountability, and sharing of results with stakeholders, and responding with this tool to requests for non-financial information. Governance and stakeholders often see a close correlation, and this is what gives rise to the need for non-financial information introduced by Directive 2014/95/EU. The answer to this need for transparency towards stakeholders arises first with the corporatization of public bodies, companies, and social utility bodies; then with the introduction of accounting harmonization within a rational accounting process. The research highlights the relevant aspects and approaches of popular financial reporting, assessing their compliance with the needs of the company, the needs of the stakeholders, and the needs of non-financial information to be considered quality after having analysed the other social reporting tools through the case study of the city of Turin.

DOI: 10.4018/978-1-5225-7820-8.ch006

1. INTRODUCTION

The approach to New Public Management and New Public Governance (Klijn, 2008; Osborne, 2010; Osborne et al., 2013) has placed emphasis on the relationship between the reference stakeholders and public administration with the introduction of new tools and new levers (Biancone et al., 2018). It becomes urgent to understand and identify the priority stakeholders (Clarkson, 1995; Donaldson & Preston, 1995; Carroll, 1996) defining the main ones in terms of power, legitimacy and urgency (Mitchel et al., 1997). Investors and citizens are the two main stakeholders of interest to public groups. It is emphasized how the reports and disclosures normally realized for a few providers including investors (Jones, 1992) supply information that is often too technical and complex to be available and accessible to the citizens (Jones et al., 1985; IPSASB, 2013). From this perspective, the growing need for accountability towards stakeholders (Sternberg, 1997; Belal, 2002; Bäckstrand, 2006; Collier, 2008; Caperchione, 2003) is a particular feature of the environment of local bodies; as is the evolution of the concept of citizenship, from customer and user of services to active stakeholder and co-producer (Doh & Guay, 2006; Chess & Purcell, 1999; Bovaird, 2006) with a say in how business is conducted. In recent years the significant step in the public sector has been to provide more understandable and easy information to a greater number of users (Christiaens et al., 2010). The creation of accessible and transparent financial documents is a starting point for the involvement of citizens, popular financial reporting has gained increasing attention from both scholars, managers and politicians. several finance professional associations including the Government Finance Officers Association (GFOA), the finance professional association have been promoted the Popular Reporting as a reporting tool. Both the Governmental Accounting Standards Board (GASB) and the Association for Governmental Accountants (AGA) promote the diffusion of popular reporting differently with their own guidelines, also proposing prizes (Harris, McKenzie, & Rentfro, 2008). Popular Reporting is a communication tool that is placed at the highest level of the "Pyramid of Accountability" prepared by the Association of Government Accountants (AGA), as it is able to provide aggregated data that meet the needs of public administrations. to account for the use of public resources (AGA, 2010). According to GASB the Popular Financial Reporting could be subjected to a comprehensive and easy-going availability of other potential users such as politicians, public sector employees, the media, community groups, etc. (GASB, 1992). Popular Financial Reportings (PFRs) are defined as financial reports targeted at public stakeholders (e.g. citizens, businesses and community group) who lack a background in public finance but who need or desire a less detailed overview of the government's financial activities (Yusuf & Jordan, 2012). The Popular Financial Reporting purpose is to facilitate public stakeholders understanding of their government's financial activities (Clay, 2008). The Government Finance Officers Association (GFOA) too offers a different approach to the financial statement in generally accepted accounting principles (GAAP). The GAAP are a common set of accounting principles, standards and procedures used by companies to compile their financial statement. GAAP are a combination of authoritative standards (set by policy board) and simply the commonly accepted ways of recording and reporting accounting information. While the Conceptual Framework for General Purpose Financial Report (GPFR) by Public Sector Entities (2008), The International Public Sector Accounting Standards Board (IPSASB) identifies three major groups of potential users: recipients of services or their representatives, providers of resources or their representatives, other parties, including special interest groups and their representatives. The IPSASB particularly emphasizes that the legislature, which acts in the interests of members of the community, is a major user of Popular Financial Report. Thus, since 2010, according the Conceptual Framework for General Purpose Financial Reporting by Public Sector Entities, the IPSAS identified citizens as primary users of Popular Financial Report. This paper analyses what types of information the citizen wants and how, and what communication tools and forms the citizen wants to receive information. The questions answer to the research perspectives highlighted in previous research activities on the popular financial reporting (Yusuf et al., 2013). The analysis conducted analyses the theoretical approach underlying the implementation of popular financial reporting, the legislation and standards in which the model is developed. In the literature review, the characteristics of the Popular Financial Reporting are briefly analysed in afford to the others social reporting tools. The presentation of the first case carried out in a European context makes it possible to identify the model and characteristics of the new instrument linked to transparency and accountability.

2. LITERATURE REVIEW

2.1. New Public Management and New Public Governance, Evolution of Public Companies Towards Citizen Involvement

The theme of renewal of the Public Administration is a sort of constant in the history of modern states and it has undoubtedly received attention in the last forty years. This is still happening both in Western countries and in lower developed countries thanks to the propulsive role of some international institutions (European Union, World Bank and Organisation for Economic Co-operation and Development). The phenomenon presents itself with different characteristics according to the considered realities. The season of reforms initiated in several countries has not yet ended and it is trying to face the challenge of the conditions in which public finance is located. The break point with the previous consideration of public administration finds its origins in the literature distinguished by the following elements (Denhardt & Denhardt, 2000):

- Neutral conception of the administrative machine, seen according to the aims of the political class.
- An excessively bureaucratized and centralized organizational structure.
- The almost exclusive recourse to top-down control instruments, with a low degree of discretion on the part of the bureaucrats.
- The consequent underestimation of the management seen as the executive instrument of political objectives.
- The focus on production and direct provision of public services by citizens.

This type of setting can be traced to the vision of the organization (O'Flynn, 2007) promoted by Weber (1922), to the division between political and administrative levels previously theorized by Wilson (1887), to the model of work organization of the scientific approach, to the study of widespread management. from Taylor of (1911). In this public administration vision, the exercise of decision-making power is strongly conditioned by the formal characteristics of the organizational structure system. This results in closed modes of governance with little recourse to inclusive processes for the definition of political and strategic choices. The emphasis in carrying out internal processes is placed above all on regulatory instruments, leading to widespread irresponsibility and underestimation of the human factor (Mussari, 1997). Many historical authors have focused on the analysis of critical issues of the model (Rebora, 1999; Borgonovi, 2005; Farneti & Pozzoli, 2005). Starting from the 80s, dealing with inefficiencies in the sector, a cultural movement of corporatization that has led to international reform of the public sector has begun to take shape and to spread. The idea was an innovative propulsion with the adoption of principles, logic and tools of private management with the ability to renew the public administration, modifying the organization and behaviours and contributing to raise the degree of efficiency and effectiveness. Corporatization takes the name of New Public Management (NPM). NPM is a broad term for a variety of management ideas, often borrowed from the private sector, introducing ideas and tools like competition, privatization, management by objectives, decentralizations, etc., in the public sector (Hood, 1991, 1995). The characterizing elements are:

- The pursuit of organizational change through the dismemberment of large bureaucratic entities in lower dimensional units, with greater decentralization of power and greater managerial autonomy.
- The search for new forms of management characterized by more competitiveness, with the introduction of market logic.
- The adoption of management styles and tools typical of private companies
- Particular attention to issues related to the efficient use of resources.
- The identification of measurable and quantifiable standards, to facilitate the evaluation and comparison of performances.
- The possibility of realizing the constant control forms over time, in order to allow the reorganization of the programmatic choices according to a circular logic of the programming and control activities that in the literature we also identify as rational administration (Puddu, 2001; Rainero & Brescia, 2016).
- The development of accountability tools more focused on produced outputs.

The aim of promoting this type of culture oriented towards the performance of a less centralized public sector is characterized by greater attention in terms of efficiency, effectiveness and quality of service. It also aims at the replacement of highly centralized hierarchical structures with management environments in which the decisions of the administration on the services provided allow feedback from citizens and all stakeholders. The NPM has a different approach. Public officials should help citizens to articulate and meet their common interests, rather than trying to control or steer society in new directions. Public officials should help citizens to articulate and meet their common interests, rather than trying to control or steer society in new directions. Public administrators should help build a collective and shared notion of public interest that leads to the creation of shared interests and shared responsibilities. Policies and programs could meet public needs to implement more effectively and responsibly through collective efforts and collaborative processes. Public officials should not just respond to requests as if they came from "clients" but focus on building trust and collaboration with and among citizens. Public servants must be attentive not only to the market, but also to legal and constitutional law, community values, political standards, professional standards and citizens' interests. Public organizations and the networks in which they participate are more likely to succeed in the long run if they are managed through collaborative processes and shared leadership. Public interest is best defended by public officials and citizens committed to make a significant contribution to society rather than from "business leaders" who act as if public money were theirs.

The above characteristics are applied all over the world to remodel the role of the state and its relations with citizens. Kettl (2000) has summarized the process in six characteristics (productivity, marketization, service orientation, decentralization, politics, responsibility for results), and for each point there are some important questions:

1) How can governments produce more services with less taxes?
2) How can governments use market-type incentives to eradicate the pathologies of government burocracy?
3) How can governments make more effective programs by shifting programs to more external levels of government?
4) How can governments better connect with citizens to make programs, which are more responsive to their needs?
5) How can governments improve their ability to process and monitor policies?
6) How can governments improve their ability to maintain what they promise?

The different contexts can generate different discussions, concerning different diagnoses of the problems that the government tries to solve. Some authors have argued that different decisions or solutions to the problems of public sector management are possible. These trying to react to various problems. At the highest level of generality, all governments are similar: interested in the efficiency with which public employees work, the standards of state services and the harmful effects of corruption on economic development. But on a more detailed level, differences emerge.

At the macro level, we focused on activities that were taken out of public competencies and allocated to the private sector such as transport, telecommunications and railways. This situation has occurred both in Europe and in Japan, and in a lesser extent also in the North American states.

At the micro level, we have dedicated ourselves to the way in which the remaining activities of the public sector are managed, considered and restructured to create a more responsible and organized entity.

A clarification concerns the institutional context, which includes issues such as:

- The managerial climate changes according to the geographical location.
- Time and sectors: consistent with what companies and other organizations are committed to.
- What the academies teach and advise.
- How the media describe the figure of the manager.

It is possible to identify two different systems of New Public Management, one of Anglo-Saxon matrix, which gave a significant boost following the reform actions promoted by the governments of the countries of this cultural area capable of offering better services with savings of expenditure (Osborne & Gaebler, 1992). The most powerful applications were in Australia and in New Zealand (Boston et al., 1996). These systems think that NPM mainly resides in a neo-liberal system of political and economic systems linked to important Anglo-Saxon economic strands such as public choice, principal agent theory, contracting and competition studies and business theory (O'Flynn, 2007). Therefore, the Anglo-Saxon strand focuses its attention on the fact that every public administration must be able to ensure the best possible level of service to the citizen, criticizing the conditions of monopoly in which the public sector is located. On the contrary in the continental European countries the New Public Management is mitigated by a tradition concerning State and Public Administration (Kickert, 2008). We can find these three basic conditions related to the development in these countries, the first concerns the existence of a formal legal approach, typical of the civil law countries (Caperchione, 2000; Capano, 2003), the second one is the lack of a real managerial culture in the public sphere with a first attempt at managerialism (Mussuri, 1997), and the third one an unresolved relationship of conflict between politics and administration that the provisions introduced did not help to recompose (Sancino, 2012). For several years there have been many criticisms related to NPM including the impossibility to apply the same logic and market mechanisms between public and private (Kickert, 1997a), and, moreover, the excessive costs for the creation of markets not sufficiently competitive also linked to the mechanism of contracting (Entwister & Martin, 2005), the negative effects of the market on the accountability process (Minogue, 2000), the risks linked to the conflict between private interests and public interest (Lawton, 1998), and finally the erosion of the traditional social values that public administrations should promote (Terry, 1998). The need to overcome the limitations and the highlighted problems led to the search for new accountability tools aimed at improving and overcoming the distance between public and private bodies, where the public body is seen individually. This goal can be achieved through the implementation of a communication path addressed to all stakeholders and to citizens. Comparing the various experiences of reforms, we note that modernisation is implemented through a series of "drivers" of action. Specifically, we can differentiate between "old" drivers and "new" drivers, depending if we are talking about the very early stages of NPM or a later more mature stage in which, in addition to the initial critical points, the Public Governance approach gradually emerged (Klijn, 2008). The "new" drivers, on the other hand, are seen in: greater focus on ethics, where the intrinsic ethics of efficiency is found; performance and results-based contracts and agreements based on performance, territorial pacts, planning agreements; improving regulations (Van

Dooren et al., 2015). At this stage, the role of public sector companies is to manage change whose aim is to implement the reform, new information technologies and efficiency and effectiveness and the transition from "information" technologies to technologies "information and communication". Key aspects of change highlight the need for a closer relationship between public administrations and citizens, and it is also necessary to improve accessibility and participation, establish quality standards and avoid political cronyism. Accountability emerges as an instrument of governance. One of the instruments of New Public Management is accountability of the public-sector company, which features five principles:

- Responsibility is public and not only internal.
- It involves explaining and justifying, rather than propaganda.
- It is specifically directed at a target audience, it is not a random explanation.
- It involves an obligation for the players to come forward and take responsibility.
- As a consequence, it involves discussion and assessment which do not lead to a monologue without the commitment of policy implementers (Ferli et al. 2005).

The focus of governance has thus shifted to performance assessment, with a system of benchmarks that are internal to the same group (Bovens, 2007). In the public sector, accountability has three components: compliance, transparency and responsibility (Mulgan, 2002). Compliance in New Public Management is defined as the tendency of public-sector companies to bureaucratise business systems (Pollitt et al., 1999), even though bureaucratisation does not necessarily lead to assessments of the results (Hood & Peters, 2004). Transparency is the sharing of information about the decisions and activities of governance, proper document management and access to information for all sectors of society: investors, the research and development community, the media and the public (Salvioni & Bosetti, 2006; Relly & Sabharwal, 2009). Responsibility is one of the cornerstones of public administration and management. It is based on the principle that according to which it is necessary to guarantee the information linked to the processes in order to inform and involve people who exercise public authority in the choices. Although the regimes of responsibility vary in important aspects between different political systems, they all contain processes whereby citizens hold their governors to account regarding their conduct and performance directly through elections. Representatives of citizens in legislative bodies hold political managers and public servants accountable through mechanisms of public control and auditing. Political managers hold the civil servants that report to them to account through hierarchical structures of authority and responsibility. Moreover, courts and the administrative courts hold legislators, managers and administrators accountable for the law (Aucoin & Heintzman, 2000; Stone, 1995; Mulgan, 1997).

Transparency without accountability becomes meaningless and makes a mockery of a healthy public administration. Accountability depends on the transparency or having the necessary information, and transparency and accountability without integrity may not end up serving the public interest (Armstrong, 2005). The accountability system, therefore, is not based on individual objectives of the public-sector company through financial reporting, but on a system of governance based on consolidated reporting (Levi-Faur, 2012; Stoker, 2016). This shift is due to the gradual inability of public-sector companies to respond autonomously to the needs of citizens and to the stakeholders to whom, according to the principle of subsidiarity, public-sector companies answer (Barnes & Sullivan, 2007). Governance and the capacity of local public bodies to manage the external aspects of public services is one of the most important aspects for guaranteeing the efficiency and effectiveness of services (Bouckaert et al., 2016; Hodge & Greve, 2017). In order to achieve this, useful information needs to be exchanged and a performance monitoring system needs to be in place, not only internally, but also with the external support of new IT systems (Kouzmin et al., 1999; Korac-Kakabadse, 2001). The focus has shifted to the quality of the information made available and on good reporting practices using the governance instruments that are available to the private group and their implementation in the public group (Shaoul & Stapleton, 2012).

At the beginning of the twentieth century, the interest in efficiency promoted by the "Progressive Era" led to a series of developments that will be known as "classical management" techniques. One of the elements that was used to control the work is accounting, and this can be associated with classical management techniques that have developed in a context of attention to the control of craftsmen, but that today is exploited in the control of professionals. The change that has taken hold in the last twenty years, known as NPM, which has fuelled market approaches to increase efficiency, has been more complex and does not always agree with the market's laissez-faire philosophy. The framework of rules developed by Ouchi (1979,1980), provides the opportunity to reflect on the changes of the NPM, in fact the directives provide three ideal types of market, hierarchy and clan, which characterize the different approaches of control (Table 1). Ouchi, in the exploration of the problem with the aim of achieving cooperation between individuals who may not have the same goal, extended the categorization distinguishing between markets, hierarchies and clans. Two elements define the most appropriate form of control: the extension of the knowledge of the transformation process and the ability to measure the results.

Changes in public services include bureaucracy, transparency, markets and rules control. As argued by Ouchi, all organizations tend to have elements of all types of control, albeit with different emphasis. Public services, probably before the advent of the NPM, tended to adopt hierarchical bureaucratic structures. To date, things have changed, but this change has not necessarily been accompanied by the strict control

Table 1. Ouchi revision

Hierarchy	Within this category, which may be associated with bureaucracy, there is likely to be a focus on the process.
Market	The focus must be the output, the subject of exchange. On the market the information must be on prices and a multiplicity of buyers and sellers.
Clan	Where there is neither the ability to measure outputs nor to specify behaviour through knowledge of the transaction process, Ouchi suggests that the clan becomes a means of focusing on the organization. The clan can be used to coordinate behaviour through norms and values, rituals and shared.

Source: own re-elaboration – Ouchi (1979). A conceptual framework for the design of organizational control mechanisms. In Readings in accounting for management control (pp. 63-82). Springer, Boston, MA. Ouchi (1980). Markets, bureaucracies, and clans. Administrative science quarterly, 129-141.

of activities that is required by standardization and by the costing of outputs. It has often been preferred to make force on a process-based control for workers, but not for all, in fact the management control of professionals has not been appropriate. The justification for the adoption of the NPM often responds to the fact that the bureaucracy has often been inefficient and useful only to itself. Thus, the market has been promoted as an approach that wants to eliminate these elements through the competitive logics that these incorporate. In a market there is a need to determine and evaluate a return that can be traded, the accounting mechanism provides a way to calculate prices. Accounting allows to show the efficiency of organizations, providing the calculation of financial profits. New public governance has led to the need to seek specific skills related to the consolidated financial statements and the management of corporate groups. Accounting systems and management control systems have been adapted to the needs of the public group's vision. In many cases the need arose for offices dedicated to new needs and the search for better programs that allow data transmission to national and European levels. In many European countries, public managers do not have specific competences and often the need to collect non-financial information through big data finds objective obstacles to understanding and adopting information and data processing processes, even if Europe invests by time in public services The search for new levers of governance and information useful to give real transparency to stakeholders is increasingly hampered by the difficulty of local administrations to provide specific training to staff and to build and have available to employees ready to face new challenges. The reduction in spending linked to European policies does not allow the recruitment of new qualified figures and limits the possibility of a complete development of the support of new public governance, increasingly replaced by the passage and creation of networks with public participation in the search for systems informal management and identification of professionalism within the network. Universities and supranational public bodies can intervene concretely in the process of accessibility and transparency of information.

The city management was asked to run the public-sector company according to governance criteria (Bovaird & Löffler, 2009; Lægreid & Verhoest, 2010). In order to create value for its stakeholders, while maintaining economy-efficiency-effectiveness conditions, the local public-sector company has always relied on planning and on internal control instruments, as well as the supporting information system, in other words, internal governance. Nevertheless, as a result of the rapid shift in the legislative and socio-economic landscape, whereby its role and competences have changed, and with the arrival of the "Public Governance" and "Network Management" models, the local public-sector company has to use instruments that integrate with earlier ones to be able to verify implementation of its guidelines and strategies. Moreover, this takes place in a context in which it has to deal with a growing number of external actors entrusted with public services for the benefit of the community. Specifically, the need to define a model for the overall control of the participating organizations is satisfied in the process of liberalization and privatization of public services. This element is the key to the internal reorganization based on the new information needs and on the new professional and instrumental skills required to ensure that the conduct of the participating organizations is oriented towards the protection of local authorities and, indirectly, of the citizens-users-stakeholders. This process has uncovered a need for greater use of management tools, not only within the public-sector company but also in the wider context in which it operates (Grossi et al., 2010). One of the identified instruments identified is the consolidated financial statements which provide a mosaic view of the local context, presenting the performances and results achieved at an aggregate level (Robinson, 1998; Buiter, 1983; Walker, 2011; Schick, 2007) and observing the two principles of utility and accountability (Grossi & Steccolini, 2008). Starting with the premise that there are both national and international accounting standards for the financial statements of public-sector companies, it is necessary to investigate which standards are best suited to represent transparently and accurately the consolidated financial statements of the local public group, in a way that can be read by the stakeholders. IAS/IFRS (International Accounting Standards) for the private sector: IAS 27, IAS 28, IAS 31, replaced since 2011 by IFRS 10, 11 and 12 for Groups, IPSAS (International Public Sector Accounting Standards) and specifically international public sector accounting standards IPSAS 6, IPSAS 7, IPSAS 8, for Local Public Groups, FRAB (Financial Reporting Advisory Board) and GASB (Governmental Accounting Standards) should be considered for consolidation purposes (Shaoul & Stafford, 2012; Biancone et al., 2014, 2016; Campra, Passarani, & Anna, 2010). Therefore, it is necessary to consider the need for uniform accounting systems within the different sectors of public administration. The use of different principles and competence criteria inevitably leads to a heterogeneous system that is heterogeneous and introduces strong limitations to a process of proper consolidation of the accounts (Quagli, 2017). Thus, pro forma and actual financial statements should be as uniform as possible, and with a standard, mandatory structure, which cannot be modified, at least in terms of aggregated items (Borgonovi et al., 2016). The need for an accounting harmonization of the systems between cities and between states, which considers the subsidiaries is necessary to allow real governance tools according to a set of internal indicators (within the same public institution from one year to the next) and external indicators (between entities with similar dimension and or expense characteristics).

If different accounting principles and recalls invite to reduce the information provided in the explanatory notes in order to avoid the risk of losing attention to the most important information, the obligation to draw up a document containing non-financial information has been introduced by the Directive 2014/95/EU of the European Parliament and of the Council of 22 October 2014. This Directive defines the criteria for the disclosure of non-financial information and of information about diversity by certain companies and certain large groups. In fact, the directive that introduced the obligation to draw up the Consolidated Declaration of a non-financial nature concerns only "large" public entities of interest, i.e. those that during the financial year have had, on a consolidated basis, a number of employees higher than 500 and, on the closing date of the financial year, they had a balance sheet of more than 20 million or net revenues from sales and services exceeding 40 million euros. According to the law, the public-interest group should include, among its management activities, a non-financial statement report containing information useful to understand the undertaking's development, performance, position and impact of its activity. This information should be related, as a minimum, to the environmental, social and human rights, anti-corruption and bribery matters. The obligation does not forbid all the other groups, even those who are not of public interest, to draw up this declaration. The introduction of the consolidated statement of a non-financial nature is part of the discussions about sustainability launched in the last decade, due to a progressive reduction of resources and to a greater need to identify results and company priorities with the introduction of Key Performance Indicator (KPI). On 25th September 2015, the United Nations General Assembly adopted the 2030 Agenda for Sustainable Development in which the guidelines of the activities for the following 15 years are outlined at global level. The 17 Sustainable Development Goals included in the 2030 Agenda represent the United Nations global action plan to eradicate poverty, to protect the planet and to ensure prosperity for all. In order to identify a shared statistical information framework as a tool for monitoring and evaluating progress towards the Agenda objectives, the

United Nations Statistical Commission set up the Inter Agency Expert Group on SDG which defined a set of more than 200 indicators, which can be useful to have a frame of reference. The identification of indicators in relation to the location of each public service company helps to give a scale of values and identify the objectives achieved. The context and the evaluation awarded is an essential starting point for evaluating the tendency of each company. A report by KPMG that analyses the models implemented in the last 20 years of reporting in the 41 considered countries, showed as, on average, a Sustainability Report has been achieved in 71% of the top 100 companies (Gasperini & Zambon, 2017). The most used guidelines in sustainability reports are those of the GRI, GASB and GBS. These guidelines define the principles of material information and the indicators that organizations can use to communicate performance, environmental, social and economic impacts. This is possible through a sustainability report. integrated in addition to the analysis of the ability of financial capital to create value over time (Rainero & Brescia, 2016). In order to assess the sustainability, the social aspect, despite cannot be perceived in terms of value among the fixed assets in the Consolidated Financial Statements, is more relevant. In the last 20 years, indeed, has led to an increase in investments, identifying it as the main factor for companies' success. (Corrado, Hulten, & Sichel, 2009; Edvinsson, 2000). To date, the national and international accounting standards, as well as the guidelines about financial statements and integrated reporting, have not fully implemented the legislation introduced on the consolidated non-financial statement and on the expressed need for representation of human capital. Furthermore, the European decree on the subject of a non-financial report leaves the discretion of the instrument and the guidelines to be adopted.

2.2 The Popular Financial Reporting

A relationship between socio-economic characterizations of the Municipality and the declination of Popular Financial Reporting adopted in the Anglo-Saxon countries has been highlighted (Table 2): in the analysis, it emerged that the municipalities with the prevalence of the tertiary sector in the territory of affiliation are oriented to present the efforts and accomplishment of the Report; vice versa, the municipalities with territory developed in the industrial or agricultural production sector present Popular Annual financial report. Cities with tourism sector and developed culture present a Citizen-centric financial report (Biancone & Secinaro, 2016).

Table 2. The declinations of the PFR according to the characterizations

	Prevailing Socio-economic profile	Popular Financial Type Reporting
Municipality	Tourist vocation Service vocation Industrial vocation Artisan vocation Hybrid	Citizen-centric financial report Effort and accomplishment report Popular annual financial report Citizen-centric financial report Popular annual financial report

Source: Biancone P. P., Secinaro S., (2015). Popular financial reporting, G. Giappichelli Editore, ISBN/EAN 978-88-921-5010-2

It is also imaginable and desirable that, in choosing the type, there is a relationship between the education level of the citizens of the territory and the adopted Popular Financial Reporting: this relationship is essential for orientation's information and the related methods of communication.

The Popular Financial Reporting can be compared with the most common social reporting tools to date, including the environmental balance, the gender report, the sustainability report and the integrated report.

The environmental balance is an instrument of social accountability through which the company, usually on an annual basis, reports on the actions carried out in the field of environmental sustainability through physical indicators and data concerning the destination of the expenditure sustained for environmental purposes. According to the indications provided by the European Union with the document called Agenda 21 (Cicerchia, 2006), companies must engage in the management, control and evaluation of input and output of this kind. The environmental question is a very concrete problem: it is the control of pollution, the quality of the territory, the protection policies, the availability of resources and their social distribution. Furthermore, the traditional economic-financial and budgetary planning documents are insufficient and unstructured to take account of environmental costs (Cordazzo, 2002). Their implementation is more linked to local and regional administrations that have specific expertise in the field of environmental protection. They have sanctioning power in case of crime and can link results with political planning and stipulated protocols. In the field of private and mixed companies, little is suitable, if not with a view to integration, merging for some aspects into the social budget or the integrated budget. Popular Financial Reporting takes into account the main corporate inputs and outputs, which, in public companies, are well suited to the representation, activities and results of the Department for the protection of the environment. In companies of different types, representation is strictly linked to the production process and to the resources used and represented by KPI, but it still intersects with the response to the information needs expressed by both public and private stakeholders.

The assumption of the use of social reporting tools aimed at the analysis of budgets by gender, such as gender budgeting and gender auditing, commits the company to implement neutral policies and focusing attention based on the different need. The formulation of public budgets from a gender perspective requires a new budget idea and a reclassification of expenditure that describes and evaluates the different relationship between economic facts and social dimensions, according to the so-called human development approach. A emphasis on the techniques and methods of participation of civil society in the goal-setting process. The creation of a process of defining objectives, indicators and control parameters that not only describe the actions, but also explain the outcomes of a direct or indirect policy commitment by the body (Vijayalakshmi, 2002). The gender balance is normally aimed at defining what are public programs. It normally does not consider an entire group of companies and is closely linked to the sensitivity of the private company. It adapts a lot to what are the needs and needs of a mixed company, but this aspect is often integrated into the sustainability report. Social cooperatives are closely linked to the aspect of mutuality (Congiu, 2010) and therefore also the reporting will tend to bring out these aspects. In both public companies and private companies, Popular Financial Reporting, by orienting the order and the manner of representation based on the need expressed by gender, ensures greater transparency and responds to the needs expressed. A representation of this type is complete and considers more and more of all the needs of users of the report by managing at best the resources available (Biancone et al., 2017c).

Compared to the environmental budget, the sustainability report is a “more complete” reporting tool, as it includes all the dimensions of the concept itself: environmental sustainability as a capacity to maintain the quality and reproducibility of natural resources; social sustainability as a capacity to guarantee conditions of wellbeing and growth opportunities in respect of human and labour rights; economic sustainability as a capacity to generate income, profits and work. It is possible to define the full appreciation of the environmental dimension, as well as of the economic and social ones, as distinguishing features of this reporting tool with respect to the social report; the attention to the well-being of future generations as stakeholders to whom it is necessary to “give voice”; the ability to combine global dimension and local dimension of development; the ability to be the result of an overall process of interaction in the management policies of socio-environmental variables within the organization (Gazzola, 2012). The sustainability report is the one that perhaps comes closest to what may be the needs of mixed companies and which can also pay attention to aspects related to the intangible values present in the company (Pedrini, 2012). If it is very suited to the request for identification of the added value of the company aimed at all stakeholders, it is little adapted to the need to represent the entire group and to provide consolidated information with simple language aimed at considering more those who they can be the main stakeholders of a social cooperative (users and workers). The sustainability report does not often start with a group vision, even if the instrument can be adapted to the request. The Popular Financial Reporting, on the other hand, starts from a group vision in a new public management perspective and is well suited to those that are representative of this type, including private and mixed companies.

The "International Integrated Reporting Council" (IIRC) defines the Integrated Report as "a brief communication that illustrates how an organization's strategy, governance, performance and prospects enable the creation of value in the short, medium and long term in the context in which it operates ". In other words, the integrated budget is intended to provide detailed information on the resources used and on the reports on which an organization generates influences. This tool is suitable to illustrate the factors that affect the logistical capacity to create value over time and to define the connection between information of a different nature (financial, governance, social and environmental). A structured reporting model should be able to support greater understanding because it systematically considers environmental and social factors in decision-making and communication processes, as well as helping to create a more sustainable economy. The adoption of the integrated reporting requires the identification and the overcoming of the critical elements that arise from the complex coexistence of financial and non-financial information, characterized by different characteristics (Incollingo, 2015). Normally, it does not start from the group vision.

The creation of Popular Financial Reporting in Europe starts from the vision of a consolidated public group. The Consolidated Financial Statements for companies provide the information necessary to verify the degree of achievement of the objectives relating to the entire aggregate, especially with reference to the composition of the sources and the composition of the loans (Fornaciari, 2017; Pisoni, Biancone, Busso, & Cisi, 2007). This context allows to know the financial structure of the group, the degree of financial autonomy and the level of the debt, the shareholding or the composition of the group, the total cost of the same, the structural composition of the costs, especially those that are the elements most significant part of the production. The Consolidated provides information and knowledge of the different composition of income. Furthermore, it is possible to derive from this document the analysis of the ratio between the income to be taxed as well as the capacity of the parent company. The income generated by the exchange with the subsidiaries with the possibility of forecasting for consolidated business units. This information allows the possibility of formulating programs for greater optimization in order to identify the use of resources. Both national and international accounting standards converge with the intention of providing information from the consolidated group: accessible, comprehensible and transparent (Ecchia & Zarri, 2005). Especially in the context of a corporate group, where different companies can be merged by nature and destination (profit and non-profit companies), the Popular Financial Reporting, a consolidated financial-financial reporting tool, which integrates financial information, may intervene to support it., economic, capital, quantitative and qualitative aspects of the Consolidated Group with a simple language, also understandable to non-professionals, and therefore aimed at all citizens and stakeholders (Biancone et al., 2016, 2017c). The most widespread instrument in the municipalities and in the Anglo-American States was applied for the first time in Italy with the realization of the Popular Financial Reporting of the Municipal Group of the City of Turin. The instrument in its first definition represented all aspects of the public group. Subsequent realizations are focusing on the prevailing needs of the main stakeholder, the citizen, also differentiating the group's attention to gender needs (Biancone, Secinaro, & Brescia, 2017a). In the same document are compared to the quantitative and qualitative results, representative results related to the perception of the group or some specific services by means of social indicators that many statistical bodies at international level through new social welfare reporting tools are realizing through welfare relationships some years (Biancone et al., 2017a; Biancone, Secinaro, & Brescia, 2017b). However, the tool is well suited to the needs of the group through representation: gender, environmental, quantitative and qualitative, representing both financial and non-financial aspects. Since the accessibility of information by stakeholders is the fundamental point of Popular Financial Reporting, with them the company collaborates year after year for the redefinition of content to adapt to what are requests and information priorities. Moreover, given the difficulty in reading the results compared to the financial and non-financial contents linked to the level of education, the tool is able to respond to the needs of the workers but also to the needs of investors considering the possible gap and range linked to the education (Biancone et al., 2017c). The connotation and vision of the whole group allows a truthful representation of what is the real situation and trend, giving the possibility to direct the programming aligning the needs of the workers, and the objectives of the service contracts that the social cooperatives often stipulate for the achievement of common public interests with local or regional authorities aimed at the satisfaction of the community. The definition of guidelines and suggestions to ensure transparency and ease of reading data (Hermann, 2011) well meet the needs of the declaration of non-financial information, without the need to further adapt those accounting principles and guidelines in the context of financial representation. The differences are expressed in table 3.

Table 3. Scheme for comparison between types of financial statements

Report	*Economic-Financial*	*Social*	*Sustainability*	*Integrated*	*Popular Financial Reporting*
Focus	• Economic • Financial • Patrimonial	• Economic • Financial • Patrimonial	• Economic • Financial • Patrimonial	• Economic • Financial • Patrimonial	• Economic • Financial • Patrimonial
Temporal focus	Past (final balance) Future (budget or programmatic budget)	Past with orientation to the future	• Past • Present • Future	• Past • Present • Future	• Past • Present • Future
Main recipients	- Employees (politicians, professionals, auditing firms, researchers) -Finanziatori - Central administration -Mass specialized media	-Citizens - Companies of the territory -Mass Media -Human resources - Non-profit organizations	- Interested public	- All stakeholders	- All stakeholders with content focus based on the needs of key stakeholders
Commitment level	mandatory drafting	Voluntary implementation	Voluntary implementation	Voluntary implementation	Voluntary implementation
Approach	Compliance	Based on principles	Based on principles	Based on principles	Based on principles
Function	communicative	• communicative • Strategic	• Communicative • Strategic • Internal	• Communicative • Strategic • Internal	• Communicative • Strategic • Internal • External strategy
Report with the economic-financial balance sheet	Report with the economic-financial balance sheet	complementary	complementary	Incorporation of: • Economic-Financial Report • Sustainability Report • Information on corporate governance • Possible focus on intangible capital	Incorporation of: • Consolidated Economic-Financial Report • Sustainability Report • Information on corporate governance with a gender-oriented approach • Group non-financial information • Focus on intangible capital

3. METHODOLOGY

Integration of the theory developed through reality together with different currents of thought in conjugation with practical evidence in order to better define knowledge (Klein, 1989). Theory integration is an attempt to construct and reconstruct in order to explain the social and organizational world (Di Maggio, 1995; Weick, 1995). The efficiency of the tool is linked to the type of information required by the citizen, format and means of dissemination, therefore the study deepens and analyses the aspects trying to highlight the particularities and characteristics useful to increase the transparency of the public sector and municipalities (Yusuf et al., 2013). The studies on the City of Turin, the first and only one in Europe to date, Popular

Financial Reporting is useful in defining the elements and characteristics of the instrument. As reported by Moody's Public Sector Europe: "We expect this is to raise Turin's transparency standards, which should go hand in hand with a more efficient and responsible use of resources, a credit positive" (Zambon & Beltrachi, 2016). Preliminary studies already conducted by Biancone et al. (2016) on the City of Turin are further analysed and expanded.

A fundamental characteristic is that Popular financial reporting is not just a reporting document, but a sort of re-engineering of the information and decision-making system, that is the key to managing the public manager. The reporting path according to the "POP method" requires several implementation steps. From the analysis of the characteristics highlighted it is possible to reconstruct the model necessary to define their presence. First, the recognition phase: the size of the Municipality of Turin has been mapped under different socio-economic-structural levels:

- Population.
- Reference territory (geo-political characteristics).
- Number of companies present.
- Political context.
- Technological advancement.
- Organizational structure of the Municipality.
- Offered services.
- Method of providing services.
- Mapping of companies with municipal participation.
- Mapping of non-profit companies to municipal "participation".

In the second phase the sectors to be represented were identified, the graphic form and the type of language to be applied considering the qualifications of the various potential readers (Biancone et al., 2016). The document considers preferences and language by integrating and representing information in a preference of gender and structure in line with the guidelines (Biancone et al., 2017b). In particular a reviews of gender budgeting worldwide (Budlender, 2002) indicate that the practical organisation of a gender budgeting initiative can take several forms like Political location:

- At national, regional, or local levels of government.
- Inside government departments, organised by officials and ministers.

- In elected assemblies, organised by elected representatives.
- Outside government, organised by researchers and civil society organisations.

An interactive, consultative, process involving all of the above has been found to be particularly effective. To be sustainable, gender budgeting is best organised in ways that democratise the procedures through which budgets are made and implemented, and give more voice to women's concerns (Elson, 2003). For an organic reading of programming and planning, it will be appropriate to maintain a constant gender mainstreaming approach in order to identify the possible presence of attention to gender in any intervention. In a broader view, as suggested, the reading of the documents will be supported by a grid of dynamic analysis, ie adapted to the nature of the document, as to apply to an all "gender bias" that allows to grasp general references to equal opportunities. The elements of the gender accountability can be distinguished into quantitative and qualitative and should be taken into account in order to define all the characteristics to be taken into consideration. The quantitative elements are sensitivity to gender and equal opportunities in the description of program, possible presence of an explicit goal of equal opportunities, possible provision of targeted initiatives to equality and / or positive action for women, any explanation of monitoring and evaluating indicators of gender impact. The qualitative elements are elements of particular interest or relevance from a gender perspective, involvement in the preparation phase of the program, the institution and equal subjects, critical elements and potential improvement (from a gender perspective) (Biancone et al., 2017b). This will make it possible to inaugurate a gender administration governance, expanding the synergistic capabilities of the different government levels and instruments, meaning in particular the programming phase as the site for clarification of an administration's ability to make its principles of equal opportunities and equality. Criteria Reference for the Analysis of Gender Budgeting oriented is the Purpose That, in the basis of the final application practices From the Anglo-Saxon literature (Sharp & Connolly, 2003). These are summarized in equity, awareness, efficiency and transparency. Fairness requires attention to the budget that protects the women's rights, which ensures that equality represents not only a political and strategic objective, but also an indicator of economic policy. Awareness is the gender reading of the budget, which increases in government the awareness of the impacts of their actions and ascribes to citizenship an assessment tool of the institution. With regard to efficiency, the gender differences, if not treated, lead to increasingly relevant losses in economic efficiency and human development, especially in tax policy decisions referred both to revenue and expenditure. Transparency within the framework of a budget and political action that this reflects in the gender reading, helps make formally explicit the most affected areas of focus by disparities and their discretion. The budget items must be reclassified starting from the expenditure items to the analytical level more widely available in the entity, according to aggregate categories that facilitate the reading of the revenue and expenditure, highlighting the impact of the allocation of economic resources on women and men. The gender balance is different from the preparation of financial statements in its mandatory form dictated by the regulations because, starting from the data contained in cost centres of cost accounting, proposes a regrouping according to thematic areas and major categories of genre. The reclassification does not concern only the expenditure, but the whole budget therefore including the analysis of revenue: particularly useful analysis of the combination of revenue/funded services, which produces, in short, a picture of what the budgetary levers giving greater certainty, even over time, to the actual implementation of gender policies. An essential methodological differentiation comes from the availability of analytical information of income and expenditure to enable the reclassification of the budget: the activation of procedures of management control and cost accounting within the entity are the prerequisite information necessary for the preparation of the gender balance. This is evident in municipalities that do not have in particular cost accounting, and, in smaller size municipalities, you cannot expect to activate the analytical accounts only aimed at gender balance and, therefore, it is expected a less articulated reclassification. The continuous improvement in a process has three phases and it is divided into programming, planning and control. Each phase of the economic and financial management currency in that system with other off-book items helps the definition of the activities' process, which is defined as rational administration in the definition of the activities process, this is defined as rational administration (Puddu, 2010). The unique approach of integrated improvement from the perspective of Popular Financial Reporting should involve the quantitative and qualitative elements previously described. It is possible to have a vision of gender accountability also through an approach and proposed system for the Popular Financial Reporting of public groups. Based on the continuous improvement and consolidation approach you can get an overview that meets all stakeholders' needs (Biancone et al., 2016). In particular, it is possible to insert in the system all the foregoing matters. The role of person-to-person congruence in demographic characteristics has attracted increasing attention in the field of public administration from a representative bureaucracy perspective (Dolan & Rosenbloom, 2003; Meier, 1993; Selden, 1997; Rumens, 2016).

Still in the second phase based on the statistical analysis of social welfare indicators, taking as reference those relating to the Region in absolute value (in the absence of municipal indicators) and percentage variation of the indicator with respect to the value of each index and deviation from the average value for Northern Italy identified three sectors that require greater attention and which are therefore analysed in the document, because they are considered critical. These are transport, waste and education.

In the third phase, the composition of the public group was analysed, starting from the identification of composition, roles and responsibilities of the Council and the City Council. Alongside this, an analysis was carried out on governance, organizational structure, operating mechanisms of investee companies (profit and non-profit), also identifying the various managers appointed for the management and internal audit of subsidiaries, associated companies and investee.

The fourth phase was to orientate and identify, with the governing bodies of the local public Group, what the group's stakeholders are and what information they need. The identification of stakeholders has led to a delicate process of analysis, which is always in progress, to identify increasingly complex stakeholders.

The fourth phase, more operative, has been declined on several fronts of engagement, focusing the attention where possible to the granularity of the data:

1. Collection and analysis of the reference context: statistical, social/demographic, cultural, structural and economic data on the territory.
2. Analysis and presentation of the districts in which the City of Turin is subdivided, giving evidence in participatory terms of the patrimony and characteristics of each.
3. Collection and analysis of the composition of the personnel belonging to the Consolidated Group of the Municipality of Turin. Gender analysis and where possible analysis of age groups and level of study. Preparation and analysis of the Consolidated Financial Statements: the latest consolidated financial statements approved by the City.
4. Redefinition and analysis of the City's Financial Report, restating the number of expenses per service/activity. Search for a possible equalization between income/transfers and expenses. Graphical analysis and evaluations based on the relevance of the expenditure by sectors/services.
5. Study of the Executive Management Plan and of the City Performance Report and analysis of the Executive Management Plan for the following year to identify the possible significant sectors and elements that can be represented in clear terms for each sector.
6. Elaboration of quantitative and qualitative analysis grids for each sector/activity of the City aimed at data collection.
7. Study, analysis and graphic representation of the most significant results achieved by each sector, both quantitatively and qualitatively. The representation focused

on specific elements for each sector/activity, according to the prevalence of expenditure, while ensuring transparency of the main results. Comparison and definition of in-depth analysis by sectors with the help of statistical data or from European aggregates (social or sector indicators).

8. Collection of service contracts, where present with subsidiaries and associates, and analysis of the possible evaluation criteria binding to the contract.
9. Request through open questioning of the results in quantitative and qualitative terms for the reference year and first semester, and analysis and representation where possible of the results in qualitative terms (through free management report) or quantitative (evaluation number of services and quality of service). Comparison of the results achieved where possible with respect to the budget and the initial program. This is possible in cases where there is an internal control system and an internal quality system.
10. Collection, analysis and graphic representations of quantitative and qualitative information of service present on the institutional sites of subsidiaries, associated companies and investee companies.

The sixth phase was developed in the preparation of the Pop statement, combining consolidated economic/financial/capital aspects with non-monetary reporting aspects, linked to the effects of the municipal group's policies on the territory. The challenge is to make the POP statement information simple, accessible, understandable and assessable. In this phase the graphic aspects, the diffusion, the use of the site and the social channels were also studied: the goal is that the Pop is widely distributed and understood by everyone, in such a way as to generate a virtuous cycle of comparison with the community.

4. DISCUSSION

The capacity to increase the decision-making processes of public bodies, citizens and stakeholders requires the application of instruments that can collate and summarise the various information flows, thereby ensuring a real process of accountability. Performance assessment is one of the essential requisites for transparency and accountability in public service organisations (Reichard, 1998, Pollitt & Summa, 1997). However, transparency is a weak form of accountability. The concept of accountability changes over time and provides a framework for many other aspects of the relationship between public administrations and citizens (Steccolini, 2004). The definition of accountability is given by the need of someone to provide someone else with the reasons why choices or actions have been conducted, thus empowering decisions (Robert & Scapens, 1985, page 447). How and why they become the key reasons (Mulgan, 2000, Bovens, 2005). Often, when there is only access to information, an institution is transparent but not accountable. Accountability includes the ability to impose penalties or to compensate. The intermediate category refers to the ability to ask for explanations, which here is an area of overlap between transparency and accountability (Fox, 2007). As citizens are often the providers of services in public bodies, thus unconsciously defining the quality and quantity required (Brusca & Montesinos, 2006), providing transparent information to guarantee a choice is a non-negotiable element when defining public spending and, as a result, even the taxes and duties that the public body will levy (Fox, 2007; Pina, Torres, & Acerete, 2007; Pina, Torres & Royo, 2010; Piotrowski & Van Ryzin, 2007). The ability to ask for information and the type of data that can be consulted are therefore areas for analysis. Furthermore, the literature has always highlighted the fact that companies are part of a dynamic environment, which requires them to evolve, anticipating environmental changes and, to a certain extent, trying to influence them (Joskow, 1974; Roome, 1992; Oliver & Holzinger, 2008). The above has contributed to a new approach to decision-making and reporting, rooted in the active involvement of civil society and with a multi-stakeholder perspective (Moon, 2004; Chen & Delmas, 2011). In concrete terms, it is corroborated by the considerable spread of inclusive decision-making processes and social reporting (Adams, 2002; Deegan, 2002). This is because only a proper understanding of the information received can enable those receiving it to contextualise it, to relate it, at least potentially, to actual dynamics of participation and therefore to interpret it responsibly, uninfluenced by the prejudices of a culture of suspicion and mistrust in everything that is done in the exercise of public duty or, at least, using public resources. Several studies state that the revitalisation or the renewal of local democracy has four characteristics: improving participation in local elections; improving community leadership; reforming the internal management of local authorities, mostly following private sector guidelines and providing the public with opportunities to get involved in the decision-making processes of local authorities (Boston & Pallot, 1997; Burns et al., 1994). The relationship between choice and the response of the same players leads to new forms of market of democracy in local administrations. New mechanisms have been introduced to improve the participation of the public and the local affairs that concern them, to make local authorities more aware of the concerns of citizens and to increase the choices available (Boston & Pallot, 1997, Wallis & Dollery, 2001; Northcott et al., 2012). The involvement of the public and of public employees in choices thus becomes one of the key elements that can lead to a renewal of democracy where decision-makers and the main stakeholders are involved in the assessment system, in terms of its efficiency and effectiveness (Kelly & Swindell, 2002) but also in terms of social welfare (Biancone et al., 2017). In the mechanisms introduced to guarantee the new forms of democracy, it is essential to look at the issue of transparency and the use of information. Transparency is the ability to provide credible policies free from conflicts of interest, open information and the sharing of financial reports, freedom of information and the participation of citizens in the formulation and implementation of public policies, so that state-run enterprises become accountable (Turnpenny et al., 2009). Transparency, therefore, concerns facility of access and use of government and non-profit information. The easier and more open it is for the public to obtain information, the greater the level of transparency. The situation in the reality is however very complex. If citizens have difficulty in analysing the economic and financial results provided by the financial statements or the annual reports (Jones et al., 1985; Daniels & Daniels, 1991; Steccolini, 2004), then it is necessary to identify alternative means of disclosure to be provided to the stakeholders in the municipality (Olson et al., 1998; Martin & Kloot, 2001; Burby, 2003; Steccolini, 2004; Biancone et al., 2016). Moreover, the need to consider the municipality as well as other public companies not common only body but as a hybrid organization composed of private sectors, public sectors, third sectors with complicated intertwining of properties, agreements and components aimed at realizing the services. Hybrid organizations are strictly influenced by demand. Bovens (2005) defines 5 important elements to guarantee accountability: public accountability is not internal; it is necessary the development of explanations and justifications not of propaganda, the explanations are directed to a specific audience and not to a random set of spectators, it is necessary to oblige the actors to become more accountable; the results and the judgments are not a monologue without actors. Better accountability is only possible if the citizen's democratic control can judge the government's performance and the sanctions of elected politicians (Bovens, 2005). According to Mulgan (2000) the key to accountability is provided in the relationship between public offices and citizens and not in the assessment of offices by politicians and bureaucrats. The introduction of information and communication technologies (ICT) systems has further contributed to change the methods of communication between citizens and public administrations, while offering the possibility of activating new tools for democratic participation (Montanari et al., 2013; Pina et al., 2007; Bonson et al., 2012; Ebdon & Franlin, 2004; Babeiya & Masabo, 2017; Rainero & Brescia, 2018; Biancone et al; 2018). However, the adoption of new accountability tools does not guarantee the effective participation of the population in political life, although it represents an important step to rethink and reinvent the relationship between administration and citizens (King et al., 1998). Among the tools used by local authorities for dialogue with the citizen, communicating the results of the management in a clear and accessible way also to those who do not have specific accounting training, to involve them directly in the decision-making processes, the Popular Report (Clay, 2008; Sharp et al., 1998; De Matteis et al., 2009; De Matteis, 2011; Biancone and Secinaro, 2015; Groff and Pitman, 2004). At the same time, the Popular Financial Report can play an important role in disseminating public information by making it available and educating the population about budgets and their ability to actually define a participatory budget (Franklin & Ebdon, 2007, 95).

The analysis of the European case permits to define the main characteristics in response to the need for transparency and accountability that the document should detect. Popular Financial Reporting of City of Turin is divided into chapters for easy of exposition. The introductory part defines in detail what is the Popular Financial Reporting, renamed according to the needs of the stakeholders, "the People's Budget and Transparency", which needs have been considered and the subjects involved in its implementation. Normally the working group of methodological and application is composed of internal and external components to guarantee the representative veracity and the correct methodological execution requested by the scientific committee. A chapter is dedicated to describing the composition and the main stakeholders of the group, followed by a characterization of the main activities and the mission in response to the company's external and internal needs. To better convey the communication, the consolidation of the group is graphically represented. Popular Financial Reporting always starts from a financial, economic and financial representation of the consolidated group to highlight the main items related to the Group's activity, the absorption of resources but above all the added value and sustainability linked to the value generated. The group's services are then described in quantitative and qualitative terms, with a focus on financial resources used, linking them to non-financial information that often cannot be presented in the financial statements or cannot be valued compared to the context in the explanatory notes. Where possible, social indicators are used to represent the reference context (Biancone et al., 2017a, 2017b). In all representations, simple and intuitive languages are used, also using graphics and images that recall key concepts expressed in a discursive manner (Biancone et al., 2016). The final methodological note defines the criteria of realization, the applied guidelines, the scientific evidence useful to construct the document and to represent the results in a transparent way, defining the different phases of the project. The dissemination plan is an integral part of the document and is a key element for increasing the accountability of stakeholders. It also grants the possibility to collect requests, preferences and comments from stakeholders to better represent the elements of the document. The City of Turin, which is at the second edition of the document, can give useful indications on the construction and content of a report that can be further improved but that presents some important aspects to be taken into consideration in the European context.

The first chapter starts by offering information about the context of reference. The main stakeholder of the documentary is immediately highlighted, ie the number of residents, analysing the most relevant aspects (average age, division between men and women by circumscriptions or areas of the city, prevalence of resident foreigners, trend over time in the number of residents, population density, life expectancy). The Foundation of the Entity (City of Turin) is described at the historical level and the main connotations of the territory including surface, altitude, medium temperature are reported. Subsequently, the infographics provides an immediate representation of the context, putting together elements related to the characteristics and vocations of the City with elements useful to define the system inputs (as required for non-financial documents from the European Union). The representation summarizes aspects such as energy consumed, and type of energy consumed, means of communication used in the territory, health services and social health in the area, housing, labor market broken down by sector, means of transport, educational services and related activities, tourism and related activities.

About the non-financial information, details about the employees of the public group are identified since they can be considered as a second stakeholder. The division of the personnel in the group is made based on the participation fees of the City in each institution and company. In order to give a more transparent representation, the quantity of people and the incidence that the public group has on the percentage of people employed at a city level is always defined in percentage terms. In order to give an immediate representation of the type of investee or controlled companies, information is given in tabular form of the percentage of participation, and of the type of service that is carried out. The cornerstone of representation from the point of view of the distribution of workers, participations or financial items must always be related to the need to which the group responds. The need is normally identified with the list of connected services to which the city must respond, it is rarely possible to identify holdings aimed at obtaining a financial return useful for financing other services or strategic participations for the success of regional or national actions.

The activities carried out by the main associations, foundations and consortiums in which the city is a partner is also represented. It is important to highlight that due to the accounting harmonization and national accounting standards as well as international ones, many items of expenditure and capital of associations and foundations do not enter the consolidated sector as they do not reach the percentage of participation or expenditure threshold.

For this reason, non-financial representation is important and plays a crucial role in the real understanding of the group. Moreover, in the section referring to the consolidated aspects, the type of information essential to the governance that the City has in its relations with its subsidiaries is essential. Citizens and other stakeholders must understand the type of control the City can exercise towards their investee companies. It is sometimes an indirect but significant control as the sole

Table 4. Consolidated financial statements of the city of Turin

Active Consolidated Balance Sheet (Data in Thousands of Euros)	Year 2016
A) Credits to the State and other public administrations for participation in the endowment fund	22
B) Fixed assets Intangible assets Tangible fixed assets Financial fixed assets	8,716,453 654,970 7,235,183 826,299
C) Active assets Inventories Credits Liquidity	1,258,853 13,923 1,145,530 99,400
Total active	9,990,605

lender of the service or the only body able to define service delivery criteria, while sometimes the city has a direct ability to intervene in management.

The purpose of participation in each company, the role of the members of the board of directors appointed by the city in the investee companies or subsidiaries and the duration and period of the appointment are explained to the citizen. This aspect disregards the political evaluations and allows to understand to what extent the City can use the control levers and define the characteristics of the different services. However, the public group is always a single body that must respond to many needs with limited resources. For this purpose, the economic and financial representation represents one of the main and starting aspects of understanding the quantitative and qualitative information provided subsequently. Balance sheet assets and liabilities of the consolidated group give a first information that is better explained (for the profane of accounting) through a quick representation of the main balance sheet items. The information relating to the group's receivables and payables is disaggregated and extended by dividing them for company and services provided in order to identify how much resources still need to be absorbed or the expenses to achieve the service objectives. Another important data is provided by the income statement that, through the distribution of revenues, provides a rapid representation and distribution, also in graphic terms, of revenue from the members of the public group. The result of management together with this simple information allows a first analysis by the citizen and the stakeholders of the trend without having to understand all the budget items. Obviously, over time it will be necessary to simplify this section more and more, leading to a complete understanding even for those who have never seen a budget. Surely, all public and private administrations are still far from this goal. The consistency of debts, credits and income within

Passive Consolidated Balance Sheet (Data in Thousands of Euros)	Year 2016
A) Net assets Endowment Fund Reserves Economic result of the year Shareholders' equity including the quality of minority interests Endowment fund and reserves pertaining to third parties Economic result for the year pertaining to third parties Equity attributable to non-controlling interests	3,874,593 3,288,794 613,203 (27,403) 3,874,593 158,539 16,692 175,231
B) Provision for risks and charges	72,307
C) End-of-service treatment	23,093
D) Debts Loans from financing Payables to suppliers Advances Payables for transfers and contributions Other debts	5,406,710 4,548,303 490,385 638 85,130 282,254
E) Accrued income and prepayments and investment grants	613,902
Total liabilities	9,990,605
Total order accounts	315,366

the group certainly provides a useful tool for reading the political choices of the administration and technicians as the alienation or closure of some group companies in an objective manner (Table 4).

The analysis of the City, as the main decision-maker and body identified to respond to the needs of the stakeholders in the pertinent section, includes the elements that are identifiable as important in the evaluation process, of accountability and transparency. A description of the governance, formed by councillors divided between political parties, provides a quick identification of the political decision makers in charge. The tools used, represented graphically and numerically, allow the understanding of the municipal machine and of the decisional processes. These tools are represented by the question time, the approved motions, the number of sessions, the interpellations presented, the motions presented, the approved resolutions and the percentage of attendance to the board. The citizen, as the main lender and user of the services offered by the municipality, is also interested in information closer to him. The analysis therefore starts from the general identification of the types and the amount of revenues and then move on to detail defining the type of tax paid to the municipality by citizens and companies, their amount and their definition, highlighting also the purpose of collection and the response to the service. Graphic representation and a descriptive text with a simple language guarantee transparency on the most critical aspect that can be immediately perceived by the stakeholder. The identification of outputs in response to needs immediately after the identification of revenues and sums

Consolidated Income Statement (Data in Thousands of Euros)	Year 2016
A) Positive components of management	1,926,472
1 Income from taxes	638,517
2 Income from per equative sources	181,489
3 Income from transfers and contributions	282,937
4 Revenues from sales and services and income from public services	583,066
5 Change in inventories of products in progress	(65)
6 Change of work in progress to order	(173)
7 Increases in fixed assets for internal works	65,412
8 Other revenues and income	175,290
B) Negative components of management	(1,785,304)
9 Purchasing raw materials and consumer goods	(61,224)
10 Services services	(700,704)
11 Use of third-party assets	(16,907)
12 Transfers and contributions	(73,587)
13 Personnel	(474,864)
14 Depreciation and write-downs	(354,806)
15 Change in inventories of raw materials and / or consumer goods	(12)
16 Provisions for risks	(5,429)
17 Other provisions	(3,719)
18 Different management fees	(94,052)
Difference between positive and negative components	141,168
C) Financial income and expenses	(107,697)
19 Income from participation	12,419
20 Other financial income	13,870
21 Financial charges	(133,986)
D) Value adjustments and financial assets	(43,313)
22 Revaluations	1,734
23 Write-downs	(45,047)
E) Extraordinary income and expenses	
24 Extraordinary income	71,656
25 Extraordinary expenses	(37,729)
Result before the taxes	24,085
26 Taxes	(51,488)
27 Operating Result	(24,403)
28 Operating result for third parties	16,692

collected, increases the understanding of the financial commitment undertaken and the allocation of resources in the group. Very often the regulatory and accounting changes linked to the aggregation of the items of expenditure or consolidation, limits the possibility of comparing the previous years without guaranteeing a complete response to the requirements of transparency and contextualization.

Quantitative and qualitative information is widely discussed in Popular Financial Reporting. The analysis starts from the need to which the public group must respond. Starting from this assumption, a clear information is given about the actors involved (companies, cities, foundations and associations), the main activities, the absorption of detailed resources (where possible for each specific need) and the number of users who have received the service. Graphic representations and explanatory tables accompany the descriptive textual information. It was the American journalist Frederick R. Barnard who popularized the expression "a picture is worth a thousand words" using it for the first time in an article in which he promoted the advertising applied on the sides of public transport, citing, according to an ancient Chinese proverb. It has probably become a cliché over time but is has really been demonstrated in a variety of cognitive psychology research. Information design is the discipline that aims to reprocess information in a diagrammatic form to facilitate understanding (Trotti, 2011). In the depths of our mind, understanding and seeing are two concatenated processes. We understand why we see. This relation of cause is also true in the opposite sense. Let's see why we first understood certain things. The infographics presents information through graphs, maps and statistical diagrams, while visualization offers visual tools that the public can use to explore and analyse data. While the infographic tells stories outlined by communicators, visualization helps readers discover them on their own (Cairo, 2013). In the case study of the Group we represent some significant elements as expressed in the Popular Financial Reporting and that immediately allow an overview and that can also represent the environmental elements in reference also to previous exercises. Qualitative information is accompanied by quantitative data related to the service. The activities aimed at improving the service are included in the explanations provided and support the established evaluation criteria related to the planning budget. In the management process, where possible, the management results are then added to the programmed levels to give a truthful reading of the data. The context is often highlighted with statistical data offered by national or supranational collection agencies. To date, there is still a difficulty in identifying local welfare indicators that have already been developed at regional and national levels. To give a clear message, Bertin (1983) outlined five aspects of a graphical language: definition, construction, reading, questions and limits of the image. Understanding of these basic perceptual issues of this visual communication medium provides a foundation to strategic graphing choice (Kosslyn, 1994). The principles of perceptual organization must present different concept to be clear and guarantee transparency: proximity (elements close together will tend to be grouped together), good continuation (dasher or dotter tends to be grouped/linked up), similarity (similar marks will be grouped together), common fate (lines or marks that seem to be headed in the same direction will be grouped together), good form (regular enclosed shapes are seen as single units), compatibility principle (continuous data for line graph). As well as having purpose and intent, graphical displays are designed to communicate clear messages to particular audiences. The needs of demands and the knowledge base of the intended audience should be acknowledged when information is presented graphically. Sophisticated (technically competent) users and ordinary lay users require separate considerations. The experts of communication who prepare the report may benefit from an understanding of the audience and of the perceptual/ controlling issues with different graphical choices. Often, a huge amount of data may have to be dealt with including: financial, quantitative, qualitative, ranking, opinion scaling, etc., and some could be time series or cross-sectional data. The tendency is to routinely generate common types of graphs. However, it is important to be focused to understand the nature of the phenomenon that is being measured and to note the measurement scale used. Some charts are appropriate for parametric measures only–where the assumptions of numeric additivity and a ratio scale are justified. Quality graphical presentation means more than the basic architecture, but it encompasses the purposes of the graphical presentation, such as comparative analysis and magnitude estimation. Relevance is an essential requirement for successful communication (Wainer, 1996). The displays should not give more information than the needed one. The information to be presented should be helpful for answering questions (Kosslyn, 1994). Considering the wider educational impact, first, the paper favours a paradigm shift towards an interactive mode of learning encompassing both practical and critical data analysis but with a strong emphasis on the need for communication skills.

5. CONCLUSION AND FUTURE PROSPECTS

The study conducted shows that some social reporting tools (Integrated Reporting and Popular Financial Reporting) can give a correct perception and analysis of the service of public interest. Through a study, it was observed one that the effective use of Intellectual Capital (IC) by managers and the introduction of Integrated Reporting is able to encourage the introduction of changes to management and measurement processes of IC from the perspective of value creation (Badia, Dicuonzo, Petruzzelli, & Dell'Atti, 2018). Specifically, it was shown that Popular Financial Reporting can be adopted with a view to greater transparency, accountability and sharing of results with stakeholders, responding to requests for information. The consolidated statement of a non-financial nature represents a useful tool for the representation of some elements that are important for the evaluation of investments and the absorption of resources that often are not valued in the financial statements. The representation of the intangibles needs a greater sensitivity to which the accounting principles and guidelines have not yet been able to respond. In the case study, we highlight how the values linked to the employment of disadvantaged human resources not present in the group's consolidated financial statements do not find economic expression, but, they present a real added value with consequent costs ceased (which would have been not to use the subjects involved). Business models and value disclosures are the starting points for defining non-financial elements based on group values. A total representation can be given through the adoption of the Popular Financial Reporting, which thanks to the intrinsic characteristics of the instrument, already responds to the needs of group representation in an integrated sustainability perspective, considering many aspects including the representation through the infographics and a scale of priorities linked to gender, the environment and the various priority stakeholders. The KPI elements allow easy reading and comparison. In the first version of the document, there are still several evaluative approaches that will be integrated with time. The simple language to reach everyone without distinction represents a key element of the elements that must be present especially in those companies where investors are often the same disadvantaged members. Popular Financial Reporting is a voluntary tool but can respond in a single document to information needs. The need for transparency and accountability in a period of reduction of available resources is answered in the Popular Financial Reporting now justified also in purely legislative terms by the need to have an easy reading of non-financial results to attract new investors and explain to the strategic structure and the intrinsic value of the company. The governance tools proposed in this document may favour public sector investment by assessing both the perception of the population and the performance of the committed resources. Popular Financial Reporting also ensures easy reading of the allocation. Greater governance can also facilitate the growth of BRIC states (World Bank, 2017). Recognizing the right level of spending resources, consumption and perception of well-being related to public services is also a valuable tool to reduce environmental pollution. In a long-term perspective, enhancing the various values empowerment of citizenship and public decision-makers in the direction of sustainable development (Stern, 2006), the rationalization of resources and the need for a correct allocation based on real needs reflects the requirements of Agenda 21 and requires instruments of maximum transparency and accountability of all the stakeholders. Precisely the rationalization of resources and the reduction of availability will lead to the need to identify more and more tools that can guarantee transparency and the ability to understand the resources to be committed, at the same time a process of greater understanding of wellbeing will be necessary through social indicators. Social equity can only be guaranteed through a real involvement of the greatest users, citizens. Tools such as big data (Biancone et al., 2018 a), participatory budgeting (Rainero & Brescia, 2018) and integrated information systems will be the new challenge that municipalities will face in the coming years, not as a spot project but as a redefinition of a system already addressed to accountability. It will be necessary an effort by all the actors to have the right professionalism in support, these will necessarily have to be integrated into the workforce over time. At the first time the training will play an important role if not in the realization at least in the collaboration aimed at increasing the new tools. Political change and often the rotation between public leaders has not really facilitated change. For the time being, the various proclamations and attempts to move towards models of NPM and NPG due to a difficulty of global change of the system have been limited to today despite the political proclamations. Future research could focus on the actual change and impact of popular financial reporting in the decision making of the population and politicians. It will be interesting to study also the fallout of the new active participation tools and big data useful for the realization of the document and its greater diffusion with continuous updating.

REFERENCES

Adams, C. A. (2002). Internal organisational factors influencing corporate social and ethical reporting: Beyond current theorising. *Accounting, Auditing & Accountability Journal, 15*(2), 223–250. doi:10.1108/09513570210418905

AGA. (2010). *Public Attitudes Toward Government Accountability and Trasparency*. Available at: www.agacgfm.org/AGA/ToolsResources/CCR/Survey-WhitePaper10.pdf

Armstrong, E. (2005). Integrity, transparency and accountability in public administration: Recent trends, regional and international developments and emerging issues. United Nations, Department of Economic and Social Affairs.

Aucoin, P., & Heintzman, R. (2000). The dialectics of accountability for performance in public management reform. *International Review of Administrative Sciences, 66*(1), 45–55. doi:10.1177/0020852300661005

Babeiya, E. E., & Masabo, C. J. (2017). The role of ICTs in enhancing citizens' involvement in decision-making in local governments in Tanzania. *International Journal of Technology Management, 2*(2), 1–13.

Bäckstrand, K. (2003). Civic science for sustainability: Reframing the role of experts, policy-makers and citizens in environmental governance. *Global Environmental Politics, 3*(4), 24–41. doi:10.1162/152638003322757916

Badia, F., Dicuonzo, G., Petruzzelli, S., & Dell'Atti, V. (2018). *Integrated reporting in action: mobilizing intellectual capital to improve management and governance practices*. Academic Press.

Barnes, M., Newman, J., & Sullivan, H. C. (2007). *Power, participation and political renewal: Case studies in public participation*. Policy Press. doi:10.2307/j.ctt9qgrqs

Belal, A. R. (2002). Stakeholder accountability or stakeholder management: A review of UK firms' social and ethical accounting, auditing and reporting (SEAAR) practices. *Corporate Social Responsibility and Environmental Management, 9*(1), 8–25. doi:10.1002/csr.5

Biancone, P., & Secinaro, S. (2015). *Popular Financial Reporting. Un nuovo strumento di rendicontazione per le municipalità*. Giappichelli Editore.

Biancone, P. P., Secinaro, S., & Brescia, V. (2016). The Popular Financial Reporting: Focus on Stakeholders—The first European Experience. *International Journal of Business and Management, 11*(11), 115. doi:10.5539/ijbm.v11n11p115

Biancone, P. P., Secinaro, S., & Brescia, V. (2017a). L'informazione consolidata e gli indicatori Bes: strumenti per una rendicontazione più accessibile ai cittadini. *L'esperienza Italiana del Popular Financial. Rivista Italiana Di Ragioneria E Di Economia Aziendale*, 339 – 354.

Biancone, P. P., Secinaro, S., & Brescia, V. (2017b). Popular financial reporting: Results, expense and welfare markers. *African Journal of Business Management, 11*(18), 491–501. doi:10.5897/AJBM2017.8367

Biancone, P. P., Secinaro, S., & Brescia, V. (2017c). The Popular Financial Reporting and Gender Accountability, the Integrated Approach in Municipalities and Public Bodies. *American International Journal of Contemporary Research, 7*, 1–11.

Biancone, P. P., Secinaro, S., & Brescia, V. (2018). The innovation of local public-sector companies: Processing big data for transparency and accountability. *African Journal of Business Management*, *12*(15), 486–500. doi:10.5897/AJBM2018.8596

Biancone, P. P., Secinaro, S., & Brescia, V. (2018 a). A Review of Big Data Quality and an Assessment Method and features of Data Quality for Public Health Information Systems. *International Journal of Management Sciences and Business Research*, *7*(1), 19–33.

Bonsón, E., Torres, L., Royo, S., & Flores, F. (2012). Local e-government 2.0: Social media and corporate transparency in municipalities. *Government Information Quarterly*, *29*(2), 123–132. doi:10.1016/j.giq.2011.10.001

Borgonovi, E. (2005). *Principi e sistemi aziendali per le amministrazioni pubbliche*. Egea.

Borgonovi, E., De Matteis, F., & Preite, D. (2016). *La rilevanza delle spese per organi di governo nei comuni italiani medio-grandi fra possibilità di efficienza e recupero di legittimazione politica*. Management Control. doi:10.3280/MACO2016-003007

Boston, J., Martin, J., Pallot, J., & Walsh, P. (1996). *Public Management: The New Zeland Model.-Melburne*. Victoria: Oxford University Press.

Boston, J., & Pallot, J. (1997). Linking strategy and performance: Developments in the New Zealand public sector. *Journal of Policy Analysis and Management*, *16*(3), 382–404. doi:10.1002/1520-6688(199722)16:3<382::AID-PAM18>3.0.CO;2-S

Bouckaert, G., Peters, B. G., & Verhoest, K. (2016). *Coordination of Public Sector Organizations*. Palgrave Macmillan.

Bovaird, T. (2006). Developing new forms of partnership with the 'market'in the procurement of public services. *Public Administration*, *84*(1), 81–102. doi:10.1111/j.0033-3298.2006.00494.x

Bovaird, T., & Löffler, E. (Eds.). (2009). *Public management and governance*. Taylor & Francis.

Bovens, M. (2005). Public Accountability. In E. Ferlie, L. E. Lynn, & C. Pollitt (Eds.), *The Oxford Handbook of Public Management* (pp. 182–208). Oxford, UK: Oxford University Press.

Bovens, M. (2007). Analysing and assessing accountability: A conceptual framework. *European Law Journal*, *13*(4), 447–468. doi:10.1111/j.1468-0386.2007.00378.x

Buiter, W. H. (1983). Measurement of the public sector deficit and its implications for policy evaluation and design. *Staff Papers, 30*(2), 306–349. doi:10.2307/3867002

Burby, R. J. (2003). Making plans that matter: Citizen involvement and government action. *Journal of the American Planning Association, 69*(1), 33–49. doi:10.1080/01944360308976292

Burns, D., Hambleton, R., & Hoggett, P. (1994). *The politics of decentralisation: revitalising local democracy* (Vol. 4). London: Macmillan. doi:10.1007/978-1-349-23397-7

Cairo, A. (2013). *L'arte funzionale: Infografica e visualizzazione delle informazioni*. Pearson Italia.

Capano, G. (2003). Administrative traditions and policy change: When policy paradigms matter. The case of Italian administrative reform during the 1990s. *Public Administration, 81*(4), 781–801. doi:10.1111/j.0033-3298.2003.00371.x

Caperchione, E. (2000). *Sistemi informativo-contabili nella pubblica amministrazione. Profili comparati, evoluzione e criteri per la progettazione*. Egea.

Caperchione, E. (2003). Local government accounting system reform in Italy: A critical analysis. Journal of Public Budgeting, Accounting &. *Financial Management, 15*(1), 110.

Carroll, A. B. (1996). *Ethics and Stakeholder Management* (3rd ed.). Cincinnati, OH: South-Western College Publishing.

Chen, C. M., & Delmas, M. (2011). Measuring corporate social performance: An efficiency perspective. *Production and Operations Management, 20*(6), 789–804. doi:10.1111/j.1937-5956.2010.01202.x

Chess, C., & Purcell, K. (1999). Public participation and the environment: Do we know what works? *Environmental Science & Technology, 33*(16), 2685–2692. doi:10.1021/es980500g

Christiaens, J., Reyniers, B., & Rollé, C. (2010). Impact of IPSAS on reforming governmental financial information systems: A comparative study. *International Review of Administrative Sciences, 76*(3), 537–554. doi:10.1177/0020852310372449

Cicerchia, A. (2006). *Strumenti per le politiche di sviluppo sostenibile: contabilità, indicatori e acquisti pubblici verdi* (417th ed.). FrancoAngeli.

City of Turin, Department of Management University of Turin. (2018). *Bilancio Pop della Città di Torino - Popular Financial Reporting City of Turin 2016/2017.* DOI: doi:10.13140/RG.2.2.18927.53920

Clarkson, M. E. (1995). A stakeholder framework for analyzing and evaluating corporate social performance. *Academy of Management Review, 20*(1), 92–117. doi:10.5465/amr.1995.9503271994

Clay, J. A. (2008). Popular Reporting. In E. M. Berman (Ed.), *Encyclopedia of Public Administration and Public Policy* (2nd ed.). New York: Taylor & Francis.

Collier, P. M. (2008). Stakeholder accountability: A field study of the implementation of a governance improvement plan. *Accounting, Auditing & Accountability Journal, 21*(7), 933–954. doi:10.1108/09513570810907429

Congiu, P. (2010). *Il bilancio sociale delle imprese cooperative. La rendicontazione della mutualità*. Giuffrè.

Cordazzo, M. (2002). *I bilanci ambientali e sociali in Italia: un'analisi empirica dei contenuti e delle metodologie*. Rirea.

Corrado, C., Hulten, C., & Sichel, D. (2009). Intangible capital and U.S. economic growth. *Review of Income and Wealth, 55*(3), 661–685. doi:10.1111/j.1475-4991.2009.00343.x

Daniels, J. D., & Daniels, C. E. (1991). Municipal financial reports: What users want. *Journal of Accounting and Public Policy, 10*(1), 15–38. doi:10.1016/0278-4254(91)90018-F

De Matteis, F. (2011). I contributi della letteratura internazionale e nazionale in tema di social accounting: quali criticità e quali spazi per un Bilancio per il cittadino negli enti locali? *Rivista Italiana di Ragioneria e di Economia Aziendale*, (2).

De Matteis, F., Preite, D., & Steccolini, I. (2009). Quali strumenti di rendicontazione per il cittadino? Milano e Memphis a confronto. Rivista Italiana di Ragioneria e di Economia Aziendale, 1-15.

Deegan, C. (2002). Introduction: The legitimising effect of social and environmental disclosures–a theoretical foundation. *Accounting, Auditing & Accountability Journal, 15*(3), 282–311. doi:10.1108/09513570210435852

Denhardt, J. V., & Denhardt, R. B. (2015). *The new public service: Serving, not steering*. Routledge.

Denhardt, R. B., & Denhardt, J. V. (2000). The new public service: Serving rather than steering. *Public Administration Review*, *60*(6), 549–559. doi:10.1111/0033-3352.00117

DiMaggio, P. J. (1995). Comments on What theory is not. *Administrative Science Quarterly*, *40*(3), 391–397. doi:10.2307/2393790

Doh, J. P., & Guay, T. R. (2006). Corporate social responsibility, public policy, and NGO activism in Europe and the United States: An Institutional-Stakeholder perspective. *Journal of Management Studies*, *43*(1), 47–73. doi:10.1111/j.1467-6486.2006.00582.x

Donaldson, T., & Preston, L. E. (1995). The stakeholder theory of the corporation: Concepts, evidence, and implications. *Academy of Management Review*, *20*(1), 65–91. doi:10.5465/amr.1995.9503271992

Ebdon, C., & Franklin, A. (2004). Searching for a role for citizens in the budget process. *Public Budgeting & Finance*, *24*(1), 32–49. doi:10.1111/j.0275-1100.2004.02401002.x

Edvinsson, L. (2000). Some perspectives on intangibles and intellectual capital 2000. *Journal of Intellectual Capital*, *1*(1), 12–16. doi:10.1108/14691930010371618

Entwistle, T., & Martin, S. (2005). From competition to collaboration in public service delivery: A new agenda for research. *Public Administration*, *83*(1), 233–242. doi:10.1111/j.0033-3298.2005.00446.x

Farneti, G., & Pozzoli, S. (Eds.). (2005). *Principi e sistemi contabili negli enti locali: il panorama internazionale, le prospettive in Italia* (Vol. 365). FrancoAngeli.

Ferlie, E., Lynn, L. E., & Pollitt, C. (Eds.). (2005). *The Oxford handbook of public management*. Oxford University Press.

Fornaciari, L. (2017). *Gruppi aziendali e bilancio consolidato in Italia*. Torino: G Giappichelli Editore.

Fox, J. (2007). The uncertain relationship between transparency and accountability. *Development in Practice*, *17*(4-5), 663–671. doi:10.1080/09614520701469955

Franklin, A. L., & Ebdon, C. (2007). Democracy, Public Participation, and Budgeting: Mutually Exclusive or Just Exhausting. In R. C. Box (Ed.), *Democracy and Public Administration* (pp. 84–106). New York: M.E. Sharpe.

Gasperini, A., & Zambon, S. (2017). Impresa progetto. *DITEA*. Retrieved from https://www.impresaprogetto.it/contributi/2017-1/gasperini-zambon

Gazzola, P. (2012). CSR e reputazione nella creazione di valore sostenibile. *Economia Aziendale Online*, *2*, 27–45.

Groff, J. E., & Pitman, M. K. (2004). Municipal financial reporting on the world wide web: A survey of financial data displayed on the official websites of the 100 largest US municipalities. *Journal of Government Financial Management*, *53*(2), 20.

Grossi, G., Marcou, G., & Reichard, C. (2010). *Comparative aspects of institutional variants for local public service provision. The provision of public services in Europe: Between state, local government and market*. Academic Press.

Grossi, G., & Steccolini, I. (2008). Il bilancio consolidato negli enti locali: principi contabili e condizioni operative. *Azienda pubblica, 4*, 395-411.

Harris, J., McKenzie, K., & Rentfro, R. (2008). Efforts and Accomplishments in Communicating Efforts and Accomplishments in Communicating with the Citizenry. *Journal of Government Financial Management*, *57*(3).

Hermann, K. R. (2011). Creating an Excellent Popular Financial Report. *Government Finance Review*, *27*(5), 41–44.

Hodge, G. A., & Greve, C. (2017). On public–private partnership performance: A contemporary review. *Public Works Management & Policy*, *22*(1), 55–78. doi:10.1177/1087724X16657830

Hood, C. (1991). A public management for all seasons? *Public Administration*, *69*(1), 3–19. doi:10.1111/j.1467-9299.1991.tb00779.x

Hood, C. (1995). The "New Public Management" in the 1980s: Variations on a theme. *Accounting, Organizations and Society*, *20*(2-3), 93–109. doi:10.1016/0361-3682(93)E0001-W

Hood, C., & Peters, G. (2004). The middle aging of new public management: Into the age of paradox? *Journal of Public Administration: Research and Theory*, *14*(3), 267–282. doi:10.1093/jopart/muh019

Incollingo, A. (2015). *Le prime esperienze di bilancio integrato: analisi e riflessioni*. Torino: G Giappichelli Editore.

IPSASB (International Public Sector Accounting Standards Board). (2013). *Handbook of International Public Sector Accounting Pronouncements Edition*. International Federation of Accountants.

Jones, D. B., Scott, R. B., Kimbro, L., & Ingram, R. W. (1985). *The needs of users of governmental financial reports*. Governmental Accounting Standards Board of the Financial Accounting Foundation.

Jones, R. (1992). The development of conceptual frameworks of accounting for the public sector. *Financial Accountability & Management*, *8*(4), 249–264. doi:10.1111/j.1468-0408.1992.tb00442.x

Joskow, P. L. (1974). Inflation and environmental concern: Structural change in the process of public utility price regulation. *The Journal of Law & Economics*, *17*(2), 291–327. doi:10.1086/466794

Kelly, J. M., & Swindell, D. (2002). A multiple–indicator approach to municipal service evaluation: Correlating performance measurement and citizen satisfaction across jurisdictions. *Public Administration Review*, *62*(5), 610–621. doi:10.1111/1540-6210.00241

Kettl, D. F. (2006). *The global public management revolution*. Brookings Institution Press.

Kickert, W. J. (1997). Public governance in The Netherlands: An alternative to Anglo-American 'managerialism'. *Public Administration*, *75*(4), 731–752. doi:10.1111/1467-9299.00084

Kickert, W. J. (2008). The Study of Public Management in Europe and the United States. A Comparative Analysis of National Distinctiveness. der moderne staat–dms: Zeitschrift für Public Policy. *Recht und Management*, *1*(1).

King, C. S., Feltey, K. M., & Susel, B. O. N. (1998). The question of participation: Toward authentic public participation in public administration. *Public Administration Review*, *58*(4), 317–326. doi:10.2307/977561

Klein, H. J. (1989). An integrated control theory model of work motivation. *Academy of Management Review*, *14*(2), 150–172. doi:10.5465/amr.1989.4282072

Klijn, E. H. (2008). Governance and governance networks in Europe: An assessment of ten years of research on the theme. *Public Management Review*, *10*(4), 505–525. doi:10.1080/14719030802263954

Korac-Kakabadse, N., & Kakabadse, A. (2001). IS/IT governance: Need for an integrated model. *Corporate Governance: The International Journal of Business in Society*, *1*(4), 9-11.

Kouzmin, A., Löffler, E., Klages, H., & Korac-Kakabadse, N. (1999). Benchmarking and performance measurement in public sectors: Towards learning for agency effectiveness. *International Journal of Public Sector Management*, *12*(2), 121–144. doi:10.1108/09513559910263462

Lægreid, P., & Verhoest, K. (Eds.). (2010). *Governance of public sector organizations: Proliferation, autonomy and performance*. Springer. doi:10.1057/9780230290600

Lawton, A. (1998). *Ethical management for the public services*. McGraw-Hill Education.

Levi-Faur, D. (Ed.). (2012). *The Oxford handbook of governance*. Oxford University Press. doi:10.1093/oxfordhb/9780199560530.001.0001

Martin, J., & Kloot, L. (2001). Local government accountability: Explaining differences. Accounting. *Accountability & Performance*, *7*(1), 51.

Minogue, M. (2000). *Should flawed models of public management be exported? Issues and practices*. Academic Press.

Mitchell, R. K., Agle, B. R., & Wood, D. J. (1997). Toward a theory of stakeholder identification and salience: Defining the principle of who and what really counts. *Academy of Management Review*, *22*(4), 853–886. doi:10.5465/amr.1997.9711022105

Montanari, F., Pattaro, A. F., & Scapolan, A. (2013). Comuni 2.0. Un'indagine esplorativa sull'utilizzo dei social media nei Comuni italiani di medie e grandi dimensioni. *Azienda Pubblica*, *2*, 191–220.

Moon, J. (2004). *Government as a driver of corporate social responsibility: the UK in comparative perspective*. Academic Press.

Mulgan, R. (1997). Contracting out and accountability. *Australian Journal of Public Administration*, *56*(4), 106–116. doi:10.1111/j.1467-8500.1997.tb02493.x

Mulgan, R. (2000). 'Accountability': An ever-expanding concept? *Public Administration*, *78*(3), 555–573. doi:10.1111/1467-9299.00218

Mulgan, R. (2002). Public accountability of provider agencies: The case of the Australian 'Centrelink'. *International Review of Administrative Sciences*, *68*(1), 45–59. doi:10.1177/0020852302681003

Mussari, R. (1997). Autonomy, responsibility, and new public management in Italy. *Advances in International Comparative Management*, 185-202.

Northcott, D., & Ma'amora Taulapapa, T. (2012). Using the balanced scorecard to manage performance in public sector organizations: Issues and challenges. *International Journal of Public Sector Management*, *25*(3), 166–191. doi:10.1108/09513551211224234

O'Flynn, J. (2007). From new public management to public value: Paradigmatic change and managerial implications. *Australian Journal of Public Administration*, *66*(3), 353–366. doi:10.1111/j.1467-8500.2007.00545.x

Oliver, C., & Holzinger, I. (2008). The effectiveness of strategic political management: A dynamic capabilities framework. *Academy of Management Review*, *33*(2), 496–520. doi:10.5465/amr.2008.31193538

Olson, O., Guthrie, J., & Humphrey, C. (1998). International experiences with 'new'public financial management (NPFM) reforms: New world? Small world? Better world. *Global warning: Debating international developments in new public financial management*, 17-48.

Osborne, D., & Gaebler, T. (1992). *Reinventing government: How the entrepreneurial spirit is transforming government*. Reading, MA: Adison Wesley Public Comp.

Osborne, S. (2010). Delivering public services: Time for a new theory? *Public Management Review*, *12*(1), 1–10. doi:10.1080/14719030903495232

Osborne, S. P., Radnor, Z., & Nasi, G. (2013). A new theory for public service management? Toward a (public) service-dominant approach. *American Review of Public Administration*, *43*(2), 135–158. doi:10.1177/0275074012466935

Ouchi, W. G. (1979). A conceptual framework for the design of organizational control mechanisms. In *Readings in accounting for management control* (pp. 63–82). Boston, MA: Springer. doi:10.1007/978-1-4899-7138-8_4

Ouchi, W. G. (1980). Markets, bureaucracies, and clans. *Administrative Science Quarterly*, *25*(1), 129–141. doi:10.2307/2392231

Pedrini, M. (2012). I bilanci di sostenibilità e delle risorse intangibili: il processo di integrazione nelle aziende italiane. *Economia Aziendale Online*, (1), 117–146.

Pina, V., Torres, L., & Acerete, B. (2007). Are ICTs promoting government accountability? A comparative analysis of E-Governance developments in 19 OECD countries. *Critical Perspectives on Accounting*, *18*(5), 583–602. doi:10.1016/j.cpa.2006.01.012

Pina, V., Torres, L., & Royo, S. (2010). Is e-government leading to more accountable and transparent local governments? An overall view. *Financial Accountability & Management, 26*(1), 3–20. doi:10.1111/j.1468-0408.2009.00488.x

Piotrowski, S. J., & Van Ryzin, G. G. (2007). Citizen attitudes toward transparency in local government. *American Review of Public Administration, 37*(3), 306–323. doi:10.1177/0275074006296777

Pisoni, P., Biancone, P., Busso, D., & Cisi, M. (2007). Il bilancio consolidato IAS/IFRS. Milano: A. Giuffrè Editore.

Pollitt, C. (2010). Cuts and reforms—Public services as we move into a new era. *Society and Economy, 32*(1), 17–31. doi:10.1556/SocEc.32.2010.1.3

Pollitt, C., & Bouckaert, G. (2004). *Public management reform: A comparative analysis*. Oxford University Press.

Pollitt, C., & Bouckaert, G. (2011). *Public Management Reform: A comparative analysis-new public management, governance, and the Neo-Weberian state*. Oxford University Press.

Pollitt, C., Girre, X., Lonsdale, J., Mul, R., Summa, H., & Waerness, M. (1999). *Performance or compliance? Performance audit and public management in five countries*. Oxford, UK: Oxford University Press. doi:10.1093/acprof:oso/9780198296003.001.0001

Pollitt, C., & Summa, H. (1997). Trajectories of reform: Public management change in four countries. *Public Money & Management, 17*(1), 7–18. doi:10.1111/1467-9302.00051

Puddu, L. (2001). *Ragioneria Pubblica. Il bilancio degli enti locali*. Milano: Giuffrè.

Quagli, A. (2017). *Bilancio di esercizio e principi contabili* (Vol. 5). G Giappichelli Editore.

Rainero, C., & Brescia, V. (2016). Corporate Social Responsibility and Social Reporting: The Model of Innovation Piedmont Method. *International Journal Series in Multidisciplinary Research, 2*(3), 18-40.

Rainero, C., & Brescia, V. (2018). The Participatory Budgeting Towards a New Governance and Accountability. *International Journal of Management Sciences and Business Research, 7*(2), 54–67.

Rebora, G. (1999). *Un decennio di riforme: nuovi modelli organizzativi e processi di cambiamento delle amministrazioni pubbliche*. Academic Press.

Reichard, C. (1998). The impact of performance management on transparency and accountability in the public sector. In A. Hondeghem (Ed.), Ethics and accountability in a context of governance and New Public Management (pp. 123–137). Academic Press.

Relly, J. E., & Sabharwal, M. (2009). Perceptions of transparency of government policymaking: A cross-national study. *Government Information Quarterly*, *26*(1), 148–157. doi:10.1016/j.giq.2008.04.002

Roberts, J., & Scapens, R. (1985). Accounting systems and systems of accountability—Understanding accounting practices in their organisational contexts. *Accounting, Organizations and Society*, *10*(4), 443–456. doi:10.1016/0361-3682(85)90005-4

Robinson, M. (1998). Accrual accounting and the efficiency of the core public sector. *Financial Accountability & Management*, *14*(1), 21–37. doi:10.1111/1468-0408.00048

Roome, N. (1992). Developing environmental management strategies. *Business Strategy and the Environment*, *1*(1), 11–24. doi:10.1002/bse.3280010104

Sancino, A. (2012). Il Direttore Generale dei Comuni tra (city) management, politica e governance locale. *Economia & Management*, (2), 101-119.

Schick, A. (2007). Performance budgeting and accrual budgeting: Decision rules or analytic tools? *OECD Journal on Budgeting*, *7*(2), 109–138. doi:10.1787/budget-v7-art11-en

Shaoul, J., Stafford, A., & Stapleton, P. (2012). Accountability and corporate governance of public private partnerships. *Critical Perspectives on Accounting*, *23*(3), 213–229. doi:10.1016/j.cpa.2011.12.006

Sharp, F., Carpenter, F. H., & Sharp, R. F. (1998). Popular Financial Reports for Citizens. *The CPA Journal*, *68*(3), 34–38.

Steccolini, I. (2004). Is the annual report an accountability medium? An empirical investigation into Italian local governments. *Financial Accountability & Management*, *20*(3), 327–350. doi:10.1111/j.0267-4424.2004.00389.x

Stern, N. (2006). What is the economics of climate change? *World Economics-Henley on Thames*, *7*(2), 1.

Sternberg, E. (1997). The defects of stakeholder theory. *Corporate Governance*, *5*(1), 3–10. doi:10.1111/1467-8683.00034

Stoker, G. (2006). Public value management: A new narrative for networked governance? *American Review of Public Administration*, *36*(1), 41–57. doi:10.1177/0275074005282583

Stone, N. (1995). *The management and practice of public relations*. Macmillan. doi:10.1007/978-1-349-24158-3

Taylor, F. W. (1911). Principles and methods of scientific management. *Journal of Accountancy*, *12*(2), 117–124.

Terry, L. D. (1998). Administrative leadership, neo-managerialism, and the public management movement. *Public Administration Review*, *58*(3), 194–200. doi:10.2307/976559

Trotti, S. (2011). *Infografica e/o infotainment. L'accesso ai fatti durante la crisi delle testate giornalistiche*. Retrieved from https://www.politesi.polimi.it/handle/10589/18383

Turnpenny, J., Radaelli, C. M., Jordan, A., & Jacob, K. (2009). The policy and politics of policy appraisal: Emerging trends and new directions. *Journal of European Public Policy*, *16*(4), 640–653. doi:10.1080/13501760902872783

Van Dooren, W., Bouckaert, G., & Halligan, J. (2015). *Performance management in the public sector*. Routledge.

Vijayalakshmi, V. (2002). *Gender Accountability and Political Representation in Local Government*. Working Papers.

Walker, R. G. (2011). Issues in the preparation of public sector consolidated statements. *Abacus*, *47*(4), 477–500. doi:10.1111/j.1467-6281.2011.00349.x

Wallis, J., & Dollery, B. (2001). Local government policy evolution in New Zealand: Radical reform and the ex post emergence of consensus or rival advocacy coalitions. *Public Administration*, *79*(3), 533–560. doi:10.1111/1467-9299.00268

Weber, M. (1922). Wirtschaft und Gesellschaft, Tübingen. Max Weber im Kontext. InfoS-oftWare Karsten Worm, 2.

Weick, K. E. (1995). What theory is not, theorizing is. *Administrative Science Quarterly*, *40*(3), 385–390. doi:10.2307/2393789

Wilkinson, M. J. (1995). Love is not a marketable commodity: New public management in the British National Health Service. *Journal of Advanced Nursing*, *21*(5), 980–987. doi:10.1046/j.1365-2648.1995.21050980.x PMID:7602008

Wilson, W. (1887). The study of administration. *Political Science Quarterly*, *2*(2), 197–222. doi:10.2307/2139277 PMID:4591257

Woods, P. (2013). *Researching the art of teaching: Ethnography for educational use*. Routledge. doi:10.4324/9781315004389

World Bank. (2017). *Global Economic Prospects, January 2017: Weak Investment in Uncertain Times*. Washington, DC: World Bank. Retrieved from https://openknowledge.worldbank.org/handle/10986/25823

World Bank Staff. (2004). *World Development Report 2005: Investment Climate, Growth and Poverty*. World Bank Publications.

Yusuf, J. E., Jordan, M. M., Neill, K. A., & Hackbart, M. (2013). For the people: Popular financial reporting practices of local governments. *Public Budgeting & Finance*, *33*(1), 95–113. doi:10.1111/j.1540-5850.2013.12003.x

Zambon, F., & Beltrachi, G. (2016). *City of Turin's (Italy) Popular Financial Reporting is credit positive*. Moody's Public Sector Europe.

Chapter 7
The Case of Accounting Information for Infrastructural Assets Reporting:
Local Government Borrowings and Investment Choices in the Context of Moral Hazard and Local Government Politics

Dimu Ehalaiye
https://orcid.org/0000-0002-0424-9108
Massey University, New Zealand

Nives Botica Redmayne
Massey University, New Zealand

Fawzi Laswad
Massey University, New Zealand

ABSTRACT

In a civil society, citizens require information to assist them in understanding and monitoring how public resources are managed. Accounting information produced by public managers allows such monitoring and helps citizens to participate in the political process when it comes to election or re-election of the politicians. This chapter discusses the case of investments in infrastructural assets and local government borrowing in New Zealand, with an emphasis on the role of accounting information in the context of moral hazard and fiscal accountability of local government politicians and leadership. The evidence in this chapter shows that New Zealand local governments tend to invest significantly more in visible infrastructural assets such as roads, land, and buildings. This confirms the moral hazard theory that local politicians may be prioritizing infrastructure investments that can be seen by their electorate as evidence of their performance in government, presenting a more favourable picture that leads to politicians' election or re-election on local government bodies.

DOI: 10.4018/978-1-5225-7820-8.ch007

1. INTRODUCTION

In a civil society, citizens require information to assist them in understanding and monitoring the management of public resources. Accounting information produced by public managers allows such monitoring and enables transparency and accountability in the public sector. Such information also helps citizens to participate in the political process when it comes to election or re-election of politicians or other citizen representatives. Accounting information, therefore, has both social and economic influence on the political process. At local government[1] level, the information about infrastructural assets and borrowing is of particular interest to citizens. This is because local government borrowing, and infrastructural investment priorities can be of large magnitude and can evoke issues around intergenerational equity as well as managerial accountability and moral hazard. Local government politicians often use the rhetoric around debt conservatism, and the state of infrastructural assets and investment in them, as election platforms. However, both issues can be fraught with moral hazard.

This chapter reviews and discusses the case of investments in infrastructural assets and local government borrowing in New Zealand. It emphasises the role of accounting information in the management of both issues in the context of moral hazard and fiscal accountability for local government politicians and leadership. The research evidence reviewed and discussed in this chapter shows that the supply side of credit through central government funding agencies can strongly influence and control local government borrowing and investment. It is argued that government policy can be effective in controlling moral hazard for local government, since debt, and the related investment in infrastructural assets, are based on accounting measures that must be met before local governments can access debt financing from suppliers of credit.

The evidence reviewed in this chapter also shows that there are shortcomings in the accounting information communicated by New Zealand local governments in annual reports regarding infrastructural assets. However, a case is made that some form of condensed information about the annual net investment in infrastructural assets and the sources of funding of infrastructural assets should be provided in local authorities' annual reports. It is argued that this information is more useful for assessing the level and the type of infrastructural investment for public asset management, especially in comparison to the net book values (NBVs) of the infrastructural assets that usually provide estimations in local authorities' annual reports. Users of local authorities' financial statements could then deduce the priorities of their local councils' infrastructure investment strategy, while evaluating the net investment figures; and citizens could evaluate the performance of their representatives/politicians, particularly for the purpose of electing or re-electing them.

Moreover, when it comes to the actual investment in a particular type of infrastructural asset, the evidence reviewed and discussed in this chapter shows that New Zealand local governments tend to invest significantly more in visible infrastructural assets such as roads, land and buildings. This is so, when compared to the lesser investments made for infrastructural assets that are not as visible, such as waste and storm water systems. This confirms the moral hazard theory, that local politicians may be prioritizing infrastructure investments that can be seen by their electorate as evidence of their performance in government, thus, presenting a more favourable picture that leads to their election or re-election.

The remainder of the chapter is organised as follows. In Section 2, we discuss the theoretical framework of fiscal accountability and moral hazard in relation to local politicians, local government borrowing and investment priorities. In Section 3, we provide an overview of the literature on infrastructural assets, accounting and local government borrowing. In Section 4, we discuss New Zealand local government structure, and the borrowing and infrastructural assets accounting framework. In Section 5, we review and discuss the research evidence on New Zealand local government borrowing and infrastructural assets accounting. In Section 6, we provide some conclusions, and suggest some future research directions.

2. THEORETICAL FRAMEWORK

In a representative democracy there is a significant degree of agency between politicians elected to govern the affairs of a state and the citizens (the public), over which they govern (Zimmerman, 1977, Benito et al., 2019). This relationship also makes such elected representatives accountable to the public for the exercise of government power (Stewart, 1984). Agency theory and the theory of managerial accountability, particularly fiscal accountability, are relevant in exploring the drivers for infrastructural investments and borrowing by local governments. The theory of managerial accountability suggests that those with a delegated authority are answerable for producing outputs, or the use of resources to achieve certain ends (Sinclair, 1995; Mulgan, 2000). Fiscal accountability is a subset of managerial accountability, and it assesses whether money has been spent as agreed or, if based on a projected budget, whether particular processes have been implemented and outcomes, or defined results, have been accomplished (Sinclair, 1995; Walker, 2002; Goddard, 2005). Fiscal accountability is predominantly pertinent within the local government sector, where managerial accountability by local government officials is towards both local government citizens (rate or taxpayers) and central government, which typically has a ministry of local government affairs.

The concept of moral hazard based on agency theory (Jensen & Meckling, 1976; Eisenhardt, 1989) is also relevant when it comes to how local governments manage their borrowings and invest in infrastructural assets. In this situation, moral hazard refers to the subsidization by taxpayers/ratepayers of unaffordable obligations committed by their local political representatives (Ehalaiye et al., 2017). Krugman (2009) also describes moral hazard as "… any situation in which one person makes the decision about how much risk to take, while someone else bears the cost if things go badly." Moral hazard theory is applicable within the local government context primarily because there is an information asymmetry between the governors (i.e. the politicians) and the governed (the public). Politicians have more information and less concern about the consequences of their behaviour, particularly if they are self-interested, than the public (taxpayers/ratepayers) who must pay for those consequences, ultimately (Krugman, 2009; Pitesa & Thau, 2013; Myerson, 2015). The theoretical case is that local politicians principally spend and commit future public funds through borrowing and choose to fund infrastructural investment priorities with far less care than they would have they spent their own, private funds. The argument is that, politicians tend to borrow, spend and commit current and future taxpayer (or rate payer) funds for infrastructural investment priorities that are chosen based on the desire to gain public support, rather than on the genuine infrastructural needs of the local community. Politicians tend towards this behaviour, because of a desire to gain the support of the public, especially during election times (Pereira & Bhavnani, 2008; Winters & Weitz-Shapiro, 2013). A generally ignorant or unsuspecting public facilitates such behaviour, mainly because of the information gap between politicians and the public. This information gap, therefore, needs to be bridged, in order to reduce the moral hazard conundrum. We argue that appropriate accounting information can assist in reducing this information asymmetry and, ultimately, the moral hazard challenge.

The moral hazard problem in local government is amplified, because central government can prevent defaults on local government loans (Letelier, 2011; Beck et al., 2017). This implicit central government guarantee, or unwritten bailout fund, therefore, provides conditions that can encourage local governments to take on higher levels of debt (Beck et al., 2017). Thus, considering the self-interest of politicians to achieve re-election, this implicit guarantee can increase the moral hazard problem. Indeed, Aghon and Letelier (2016) note that funding local councils through borrowing could stimulate imprudent practices by local governments, especially if local governments issue nonguaranteed bonds.

Thus, in this chapter, the theories of fiscal accountability and moral hazard serve as a base on which the discussion on local government borrowing behaviour and infrastructural investment choices are centred, given the context of information asymmetry between local politicians and the public they were elected to serve. Further, in this context, we evaluate the research evidence on the role of accounting information in managing issues concerning both accountability and moral hazard in New Zealand local government, particularly with regard to borrowing and infrastructural asset investment.

3. INFRASTRUCTURAL ASSETS ACCOUNTING AND LOCAL GOVERNMENT BORROWING- AN OVERVIEW

3.1 Infrastructural Assets Accounting in the Public Sector

Accounting for infrastructural assets in the public sector has been subject to significant debate in the last four decades. Most of the earlier discussion concerned conceptual questions about including public sector infrastructural assets as capital assets in the financial statements of public sector organisations (Anthony, 1985; Mautz, 1988; Pallot, 1992; Likierman, 1994; Lapsley & Pallot, 1997; Rowles, et al., 1998). Such discussion focused on the differences between public infrastructural assets and capital assets in for-profit firms (Mautz, 1988; Pallott, 1990), the valuation practices for infrastructural assets (Pallott, 1997; Barnes & Lord, 2017); the depreciation of such assets (Cheng & Harris, 2000; Drew, 2018), and inter-generational equity in relation to infrastructural assets (Mccrae & Aiken, 2000; Barnes and Lord, 2017) . Further studies such as Christiaens and Vahnee (2003), Walker et al. (2000a), Walker et al. (2004) and Tan-Kantor et al. (2017) have raised issues over the usefulness of accounting information on infrastructural assets.

The use of conventional, private sector reporting standards for infrastructural assets, especially when it comes to depreciation, has been criticised, particularly in terms of depreciation as a measure of actual resource consumption in the public sector (Pallot, 1992; Drew, 2018; Pilcher, 2018). Pallot (1997) also questioned the appropriateness of the use of infrastructural assets information, and whether its preparation for public assets management under conventional private sector accounting standards is relevant in the public sector environment of higher fiscal accountability. Further, it has been argued that private sector accounting standards do not support the accounting for inter-generational equity in terms of costs and benefits that is a feature of public infrastructural assets (Mccrae & Aiken, 2000; Barnes & Lord, 2017). Christiaens and Vahnee (2003) provided evidence of governmental accounting standards and practices for capital assets/infrastructural assets in Flemish governments and underscored the conflicts and implementation problems of adopting accrual accounting for infrastructural assets in the environment of budgetary accounting.

Walker et al. (1999, 2000a) analysed infrastructure reporting in Australia, particularly the competing forms of valuation based on replacement prices in the public sector. They found that local Australian councils recorded significant amounts of expenditure on proposed infrastructure upgrading. Walker et al. (2000b) also discussed infrastructural reporting options so that public sector stakeholders might be better informed about critical financial and other infrastructural characteristics in order to assess future expenditure needs. They found that private sector firms have interest in both their current and long-term future financial information on infrastructural assets, given that those assets are often funded through loan finance. They suggested that a combination of financial data and some non-financial quantitative and qualitative information about infrastructural assets is likely be more relevant to users of local governments' reports and, as such, could assist in closing the information asymmetry gap between the local politicians and the public. Walker et al. (2004) further investigated attitudes of preparers and users of infrastructure information in Australian local governments and found that the reports, as currently prepared and presented, were likely to be ineffective in communicating information about infrastructural issues, including long-term investment in assets. Tan-Kantor et al. (2017), using the case of a desalination plant in the state of Victoria in Australia, also found that implementing accounting standard requirements for valuing infrastructural assets was inconsistent with the generally accepted accounting principles based on private sector accounting standards.

3.2 Local Government Borrowing: Determinants and Limits

Several studies globally of local government borrowing, or municipal indebtedness, have focused on factors that drive or determine local government borrowing and its control or limitation, especially given the context of moral hazard inherent in local government borrowing. The determinants of local government debt are usually discussed in the literature under two broad categories: financial (such as capital expenditure and infrastructural asset investment, taxation/rates revenue), and socioeconomic/political (such as population size, government fragmentation, state regulation of debt) (Cropf & Wendel, 1998). Several Spanish studies show that the level of capital expenditure, disposable family income, population, debt servicing cost, legal borrowing limit, electoral cycles, political ideology, geographic location as well as capital and taxation income, all have significant impacts on the indebtedness levels of Spanish municipalities (Benito & Bastida, 2004; Cabasés et al., 2007; Bastida et al., 2013; Park, 2013; Balaguer-Coll et al., 2015; Navarro-Galera, et al.,

2017; Bolivar et al., 2018; Vera, 2018). A study of Switzerland municipalities also showed that a higher median tax rate and a higher proportion of own revenue to total revenue in a municipality, are associated with lower municipal borrowing (Feld et al., 2011). Liu et al. (2017) also provide evidence of a significant relationship between greater intensity of public corruption and higher aggregate levels of debt among states and local governments in the US.

Significant literature has also been devoted to the effectiveness of limits/controls on the amounts that is, or can be, borrowed by local governments. Usually, governments at the national level or their agencies impose these limits on borrowings (Lim & Hong, 2012). Debt limits are established on local governments mainly to guard against moral hazard, as discussed in section 2. The effectiveness of such limits/controls on how much local governments can borrow has been the subject of debate, but the empirical evidence favours the use of such controls.

Ter-Minassian and Craig (1997), studied the experience of a broad range of countries with controls on sub-national borrowing and found significant diversity in countries' perspectives on such controls. This depended on individual country peculiarities with respect to history, constitutional provisions, level of political and administrative control of the central over local government, overall tradition of financial discipline and level of financial market development among other things. In Spain, Cabasés et al. (2007) found evidence that supported the effectiveness of institutional borrowing restrictions on the borrowing policies adopted by Spanish local governments. Derycke and Gilbert (1985) found evidence that macroeconomic policy measures instituted by the French central government had a positive influence on the borrowing behaviour of French local governments. Similarly, Farnham (1985) found that state-imposed debt limits in the US had a significant depressing influence on local per capita gross debt levels, as such limits brought about both lower general obligation debt and decreased non-guaranteed debt. Poterba (1996, 1997) also argue that changes in fiscal rules at the U.S. state level could affect fiscal behaviour and outcomes in US states. Kennedy and Robbins (2003) in a review of studies that examine the effects of fiscal rules on fiscal performance in a number of countries found that many studies show that fiscal rules can have an impact on fiscal policy consequences, depending on the constitution of the fiscal rules. Yang (2017) investigated the relationship between tax and expenditure limits (TEL) and local government deficit financing in the 50 largest US cities following the global financial crises. She found that cities subject to a binding TEL were more likely to control expenditure growth from the pre-crisis years to years following the GFC. Kioko and Zhang (2019) also found that TELs have a negative impact on US local government use of tax-supported debt, particularly if the local government is subject to a limitation on assessed valuation or a property tax levy. Corsetti and Roubini (1996) argue that fiscal rules such as the balanced-budget rules employed in some

US states are more fitting to subnational governments than to national governments. Overall, most studies make the case that imposing debt limits on local government borrowing, can reduce the effects of moral hazard resulting from irresponsible borrowing.

4. NEW ZEALAND LOCAL GOVERNMENT DEBT, INFRASTRUCTURAL ASSETS AND ACCOUNTING

4.1 New Zealand Local Government Structure and Borrowing

New Zealand is a unitary state rather than a federation, meaning that regions and local governments are created by the authority of the central government, rather than the central government being created by the authority of the regions. Local government in New Zealand has powers conferred upon it by acts of parliament. These powers have traditionally been distinctly fewer than in some other countries. For example, central government runs police and education, while the provision of low-cost housing is optional for local councils (Ehalaiye et al., 2017).

The Local Government Act 2002 states the purpose of local government in New Zealand. According to the Act, local government enables democratic local decision-making and action by, and on behalf of, communities to meet their current and future needs for good-quality local infrastructure and public services, and to perform regulatory functions that are cost-effective for households and businesses.

In New Zealand, there are two tiers of local government. The top tier consists of 11 regional councils. The second tier consists of 67 territorial authorities (12 city councils and 53 district councils, Auckland Council and Chatham Island Council). New Zealand has 16 regions, administered by the 11 regional councils and the five unitary authorities[2]. Most territorial authorities are wholly within one region, but there are a few that cross regional boundaries. Regional council areas are based on water catchment areas. Territorial authorities (city councils and district councils) are based on communities of interest and road access. Regional councils are concerned primarily with environmental resource management, flood control, air and water quality, pest control, and, in specific cases, public transport, regional parks and bulk water supply. Territorial authorities are responsible for a wide range of local services including roads, water reticulation, sewerage and refuse collection, libraries, parks, recreation services, local regulations, community and economic development, and town planning. Each of the regions and territorial authorities is governed by a council, which is directly elected by the residents of that region, district or city. Table 1 presents some of the key financial statistics of local government in New Zealand, which indicate the significance of this sector and its debt.

Table 1. New Zealand local government key financial statistics

Share of GDP	3.8%
Share of Public Spending	11%
Total assets	$124 billion
Debt as % of Assets	8.6%
Proportion of Household Expenditure Spent on Rates	2.25%
Proportion of Council Debt Spent on Debt Servicing	6.4%
Proportion of Own-sourced Income	90%

Source: Local Government New Zealand (LGNZ). Available at: https://www.lgnz.co.nz/nzs-local-government/new-section-page/

Local council-provided services are paid for from a limited range of income sources with local councils relying mostly on a single form of tax, property tax (often referred to as rates), as a source of income. The power to levy a property tax is given to councils by the Local Government (Rating) Act 2002. The other sources of local council income include sale of goods and services (user charges for example, use of swimming pools); regulatory fees (parking fees and fines); interest earned from investments (including investments in Council Controlled Trading Organisations) and grants and subsidies (local government share of road taxes and development contributions from central government).

There are limitations to income growth for New Zealand local councils as there are rating exemptions for various categories of land, and the central government frequently regulates specific fees and user charges. This means that there are constraints placed on the income-raising abilities of local government in New Zealand. Moreover, in the period of 1996-2006, 28 out of the then 73 councils experienced population decreases, further limiting their income-raising via a rating base decline (LGRI, 2007).

Borrowing is, therefore, a critical source of New Zealand local government funding, particularly for capital expenditure. Until 1996 when Local Government Amendment Act No. 3 1996 (LGAA3) was issued, councils in New Zealand could borrow from the Local Government Loans Board only (Pallot, 2001), which restricted what local authorities could borrow, and fixed the maximum term of borrowing in relation to its estimate of the life expectancy of the assets concerned. The LGAA3 1996 allowed local councils to borrow from the market directly by issuing bonds and, more often, by borrowing from commercial banks. New Zealand local councils are unable to borrow in international currency, with the exception of Auckland Council and the Local Government Funding Agency (LGFA). The Local Government Borrowing Act 2011 established the Local Government Funding Agency (LGFA).

The LGFA can issue its own bonds and is able to lend to councils at interest rates below those charged by major commercial banks and financial institutions. The central government and participating local authorities jointly own the LGFA. Its main objective is to optimise debt funding for local authorities. In 2013, of the 78 New Zealand local authorities 42 were borrowers from the LGFA (Grant Thornton, 2014). These borrowings represented 90% of the total New Zealand local government sector debt. In 2013, the LGFA advanced loans of over three billion dollars in total. The LGFA projects that it will lend just over nine billion dollars to the New Zealand local government sector by 2020 (LGFA, 2019).

According to Section 14 (c) of the Local Government Act, 2002, to make decisions on borrowing, New Zealand local councils are required to take account of the interests of future, as well as current, communities in their decision-making process. Unlike the central government, which is free to borrow for operational expenditure, councils must use debt only to invest: not to fund operational expenditure (Grant Thornton 2014). New Zealand councils are required by The Local Government Act 2002 to provide financial strategies quantifying limits on rates and borrowing. The debt limits are set in consultation with their citizens, and councils must ensure that debt limits remain sustainable (Pallot, 2001). The Office of the Auditor General (OAG) ensures that debt limits are prudent, and if any council acts imprudently, the OAG's reports it to Parliament. The LGFA generally lends to councils only if the proportion of their income spent on interest payments is less than 20 per cent. Two measures are usually used in the local government sector to assess whether a council can deal with the amount of debt they have or want to have. These are the gearing ratio (ratio of debt to total assets) and the interest cover ratio (ratio of interest paid on debt to the income stream). These accounting-based measures affirm the role of accounting information as a tool for ensuring fiscal accountability within New Zealand local governments and limit the morally hazardous potential for local government politicians to borrow without restraint.

The OAG reported to Parliament in 2012 (OAG, 2012) that there has been a steady increase in New Zealand councils using debt. It also reported that:

- The gross debt for local authorities in New Zealand was $9.8 billion and is expected to rise to $18.7 billion by 2021/22.
- Only five out of 77 local authorities forecast no debt in their 10-year plans.
- The overall local New Zealand authorities' debt is influenced significantly by the debt of Auckland Council, which was forecast to increase from $5billion to $6.2 billion in 2017/18 and drop to $6.0 billion by 2021/22.

The New Zealand Institute of Economic research (NZIER) report in 2012, notes that the gearing ratio of New Zealand councils has trended upwards since 2000, and in 2010 reached about 6.8%, while the interest cover ratio was 6.4 in 2011. Both the NZIER (2012) report and the later study by Grant Thornton (2014) on the New Zealand local government financial position found that the level of debt undertaken by New Zealand local authorities was, nevertheless, prudent and sustainable. However, the Grant Thornton (2014) report noted that regional councils faced growing cost drivers owing to increases in environmental standards and severe weather events (that intensify pressure on flood prevention), as well as additional costs arising from new regulatory standards (such as earthquake strengthening).

4.2 Infrastructural Assets Accounting Framework in New Zealand

Infrastructural assets make up a significant amount public investment in New Zealand. According to the New Zealand Treasury (2018), there are over $200 billion of infrastructural assets owned by New Zealand central and local governments. By 2025, new infrastructure investment is forecasted to be over $110 billion. Some of the main infrastructural asset challenges that New Zealand and other countries face include ageing infrastructure networks that need renewing or replacing, an ageing population, the growth of some regions and the stagnation of others, technological changes, and climate change that puts natural resources under pressure.

In 2015, the New Zealand Treasury issued the Thirty-Year New Zealand Infrastructure Plan 2015, providing national direction on infrastructure development in New Zealand (New Zealand Treasury, 2015). Long-term plans (LTPs) were also prepared under The Local Government Act 2002 and are the key planning tool for New Zealand local councils. The LTP must include information on activities, goods or services provided by a council, and specific funding and financial management policies and information. LTPs outline all things a council does and how they fit together, including investments and costs. Rate payers can express their views on the LTPs when they are reviewed every three years. The LTPs are supplemented by the annual plan, which focuses on year-to-year budgets. Local councils prepare an annual plan in each of the two years between LTP reviews and set out in them what the council plans to do in the next 12 months to move towards achieving their goals. These plans are adopted before the start of the financial year, in July. Local councils in New Zealand are required to establish consultative processes around their policy-making activities. Finally, the LTPs and annual plans are reinforced by local councils' annual reports. The annual report tells the community whether the council has done what the LTP and/or annual plan said it intended to do and provides details on what has been spent. Annual reports are adopted by 31 October each year. In addition, when making significant decisions for funding infrastructural assets to be used from one generation to another, the New Zealand local councils are expected to consider each generation's benefits from the investment, and their contribution to the cost of that investment's service, in order to foster intergenerational equity (Premchand, 1993).

In terms of accounting for infrastructural assets, the annual reports of New Zealand local councils included (until 2015) those assets in Property, Plant and Equipment, and reported them under NZ IAS 16 (PBE) Property, Plant and Equipment, which was the IFRS-based reporting standard. This reporting was in accordance with the sector neutral reporting regime in operation until 2015, after which the New Zealand public sector adopted the IPSAS-based standards. From 2015 onwards, the applicable reporting standard for such assets became PBE IPSAS 17 Property, Plant and Equipment. NZ IAS 16 (PBE) did not define infrastructural assets separately, while PBE IPSAS 17 states in section 21 (XRB, 2017) that:

Some assets are commonly described as infrastructure assets. While there is no universally accepted definition of infrastructure assets, these assets usually display some or all of the following characteristics:

(a) They are part of a system or network.
(b) They are specialised in nature and do not usually have alternative uses.
(c) They are immovable.
(d) They may be subject to constraints on disposal.

Although ownership of infrastructure assets is not confined to entities in the public sector, significant infrastructural assets are frequently found in the public sector. Examples of infrastructural assets include road networks, sewer systems, water and power supply systems, and communication networks.

This definition is consistent with the way infrastructural assets are generally defined in the literature, by either describing their common features or by listing examples (Van Daniker & Kwiatkowski, 1986; Pallot 1997, Van Daniker & Harris, 1999; Christiaens & Vanhee, 2003; Walker et al., 2000b). Walker et al. (2000b) note that, "... infrastructure is virtually everything put to the service of the public in general – a heterogeneous collection of physical and environmental facilities, with their acquisition and maintenance funding from the public purse the only element in common".

Overall, the information required and presented by the applicable reporting standards on infrastructural assets is possibly appropriate for general property, plant and equipment reporting purposes. However, this information may not be sufficient for discussing the specific questions of the renewal of infrastructural assets and the funding of such renewals, and for addressing accountability issues around local authorities' debt for infrastructural assets financing.

In New Zealand, local government infrastructural assets can be funded through council income or debt. However, New Zealand local councils are able to use debt to invest in long-term assets only, such as infrastructural assets, and not to fund operational expenditure (Grant Thornton, 2014). Furthermore, recent reports indicate underinvestment in New Zealand infrastructure (OAG 2013, 2014, 2015; Walls, 2018). The question, therefore, remains as to whether the funding obtained via borrowing by New Zealand authorities has been invested in infrastructure, and to what extent. Additionally, the question arises as to what kind of infrastructure investments are made, and whether that information is obtainable from publicly available local authority reports. This is important to ratepayers and voters in local elections, as the investment in infrastructure has not only short- but also long-term effects on their quality of living.

5. NEW ZEALAND LOCAL GOVERNMENT BORROWING AND INFRASTRUCTURAL ASSETS ACCOUNTING- A REVIEW OF THE CURRENT RESEARCH EVIDENCE

Having discussed the structure of the local government system and the framework for local government borrowing and infrastructural asset accounting in New Zealand, we now review the research evidence on New Zealand local government borrowing, and the role of accounting information in its management, focussing on issues of moral hazard and fiscal accountability. We also review the research evidence on accounting for infrastructural assets in New Zealand with the same focus.

Pallot (2001) was the first significant study to examine borrowing management and investment policies in New Zealand local governments from an accounting and transparency perspective. The study investigated the budgeting and accounting reforms in New Zealand local government that were introduced in July 1998, following the Local Government Amendment (No. 3) Act 1996. The emphasis of these reforms was on a long-term financial planning regime for local governments. Owing to these reforms, New Zealand local governments are required to have a borrowing management policy that includes policies on (a) interest rate exposure; (b) liquidity; (c) credit exposure; (d) debt repayment; (e) any specific borrowing limits; and (f) any specific policy for security. Further, the investment policy must include the local authority's policies on management of financial assets, acquisition and disposal of assets and investments, and the mix of investments. In addition, an outline of the procedures by which investments are to be managed and reported to the council and an outline of how risks associated with investments are to be assessed and managed must be provided (Pallot, 2001). Pallot (2001) also found that the reforms insisted that New Zealand local governments make publicly available their financial intentions over an extensive period (at least ten years) and consult the public on these plans in view of the importance of planning for infrastructural assets that entail a longer time horizon and intergenerational equity concerns. These findings suggest the importance of fiscal accountability from the local government elected representatives to the public, particularly regarding borrowing and investment priorities.

Ehalaiye et al. (2017) studied all local authorities in New Zealand during the twelve-year period from 2004-2015 and investigated the financial determinants of local government debt in New Zealand. They found that council income (rates and other income) was the major financial determinant of debt, rather than infrastructural spending. Figure 1 shows the relationship between average rates income and average total liabilities of New Zealand local governments during the period 2004-2015. On average when rates increased by $NZ 103,906 the average total liabilities increased by $NZ 378,500 during this period. This provides the insight that suppliers of credit are keener to lend to New Zealand local councils who can service debts via their income and, ultimately, repay loans, thus, implying that the supply side of credit through the Local Government Funding Agency (LGFA) in New Zealand has a strong influence on local government borrowing in New Zealand. This provides indirect evidence of the use of central government policy to control moral hazard in relation to New Zealand local government borrowing.

The study also found that spending on assets other than infrastructural assets predictably leads to an overall increase in borrowings to finance infrastructural assets. Furthermore, this study found that post-global financial crisis (GFC) there was an increase in infrastructural spending and the use of debt financing, which suggests that lower interest rates brought on by the GFC, did stimulate increased borrowing activity by New Zealand local authorities. Thus, local councils in New Zealand do take advantage of debt at cheaper interest rates to fund capital expenditure, suggesting an element of fiscal accountability and prudence from their elected representatives.

On infrastructural asset reporting by New Zealand local authorities, Chatterjee et al. (2017) surveyed and interviewed a sample of the annual report recipients (users) and infrastructure information preparers, together with an assessment of the extent of infrastructure information disclosure in the annual reports of New Zealand local authorities. They found that most users considered infrastructure information important, and that most of their required infrastructure information items were not reported in annual reports. Hence, there was an information dissemination gap

Figure 1. Influence of rates on New Zealand local government debt (2004-2015)

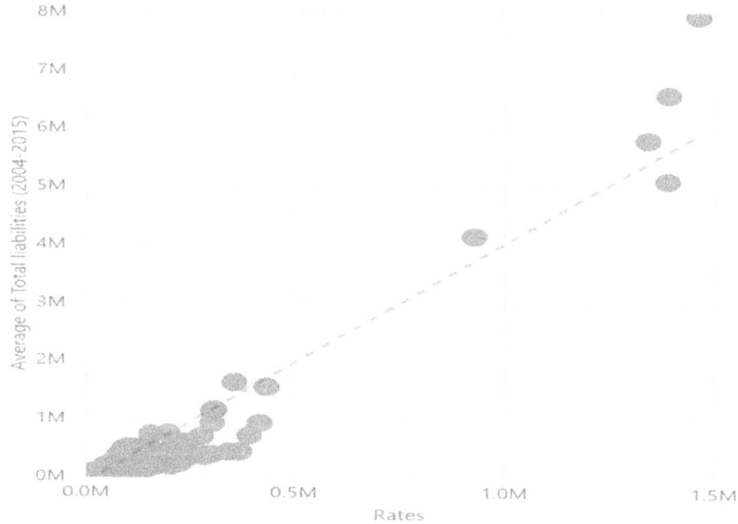

between the perceptions of the users and the preparers of annual reports regarding infrastructure information in these annual reports. They attributed this information dissemination gap to the inadequacy of private sector financial reporting standards (IFRS) in meeting the public sector reporting and accountability requirements. They recommended that additional information be provided on infrastructural assets to the users.

Ehalaiye et al. (2019) analysed the data on specific infrastructural assets in the annual reports of the 67 city and district local councils in New Zealand, from 2010-2015, focussing on the funding of these assets. They investigated precisely, whether the accounting information on infrastructural asset investment in their financial reports was useful for assessing the funding level and sources for investment infrastructural assets. This study provides evidence that the publicly available accounting information on the 'annual net investment in infrastructural assets' in local council financial statements is a useful source of information in assessing the level and the type of infrastructural asset investment. The study also indicates that infrastructural assets in New Zealand local councils are funded significantly more by borrowing than by income, thus, highlighting the need for intergenerational equity when it comes to infrastructural asset investment. The results of the study also show that councils tend to invest significantly more in visible infrastructural assets such as roads, land and buildings in comparison to their investment in less-visible infrastructural assets, such as waste and storm water systems (Ehalaiye et al., 2019). Figure 2 presents the average net investment in visible infrastructural assets (such as roads, lands and

Figure 2. Average net investment in specific infrastructural assets by New Zealand local governments (2004-2015)

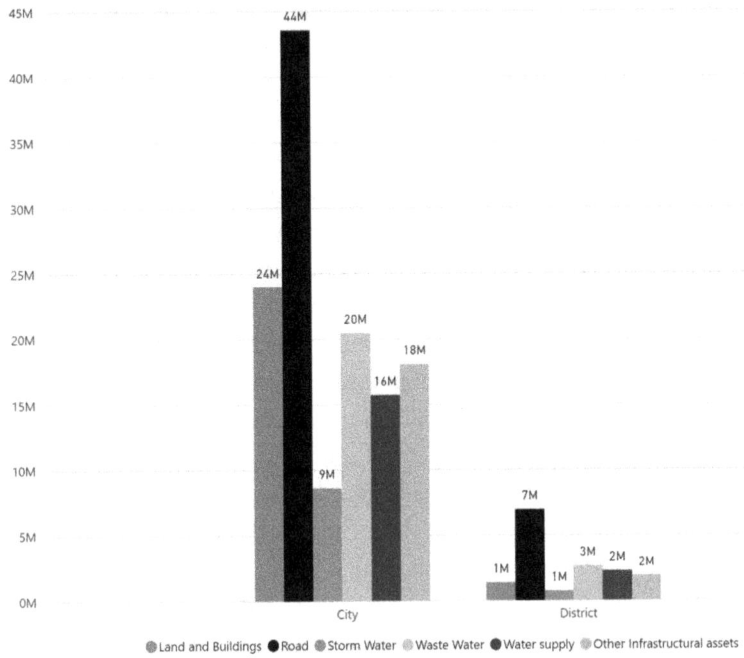

buildings) and in less-visible infrastructural assets (such as storm water, water supply and wastewater systems) during the period 2004 to 2015 in New Zealand city and district local governments. Figure 2 suggests significant investment in visible assets, particularly roads, among New Zealand local governments.

This confirms the moral hazard theory that local politicians may be prioritizing infrastructure investments that are visible to their electorate as evidence of their performance in government. An additional and complementary explanation for this finding, might be in the very long useful lives of the invisible underground infrastructural assets like waste and storm water systems, hence, there is generally less need to renew such assets regularly. The study made the case that the more useful accounting information to assess the level and the type of infrastructural investment for public asset management is the information on the 'annual net investment in infrastructural assets', and not the reported net book values (NBVs) of the infrastructural assets that provide estimations. Therefore, it was recommended that some form of condensed report, highlighting annual net investment in infrastructural assets and the sources of funding of infrastructural assets, should be provided by, say, a note in the information additional to financial information in local authority annual reports. This would enable users of council financial statements to deduce the priorities of their local councils' infrastructure investment strategy while evaluating the net investment figures. This recommendation is consistent with Walker et al.'s (2000b) suggestion that a combination of financial data, and some non-financial quantitative and qualitative information about infrastructure, is likely to be more relevant to users of local authority reports.

In summary, the research evidence on New Zealand local government borrowing and infrastructural asset accounting describes clear processes for fiscal accountability in relation to local government borrowing and infrastructure investment. In addition, the evidence shows that local politicians in New Zealand exhibit a reasonable degree of responsibility in borrowing, especially because of the indirect limits/controls by suppliers of credit who have a strong influence on local government borrowing. This serves as a limit to the moral hazard challenge to local politicians in New Zealand. On the other hand, the studies reviewed provide evidence of an information dissemination gap in perceived infrastructure information between the users and preparers of New Zealand local authorities' annual reports. Arguably, however, this information gap could be bridged if New Zealand local governments were to provide a condensed report in their financial statements, given their actual annual net investment in infrastructural assets. This accounting information would support more local politician fiscal accountability in New Zealand. Further, Ehalaiye et al. (2019) also suggest a degree of moral hazard arises, whereby local politicians' priorities in infrastructure tend to favour visible assets, like roads, land, buildings and machinery, in contrast to those that are less visible, such as waste and storm water systems.

6. CONCLUSIONS, STUDY LIMITATIONS AND FUTURE RESEARCH DIRECTIONS

In this chapter, we review and discuss the case of accounting for investments in infrastructural assets and local government borrowing in New Zealand in the context of moral hazard and fiscal accountability of local government politicians and leadership. From the research evidence reviewed, we can infer that local politicians in New Zealand exhibit fiscal accountability, particularly regarding borrowing on behalf of their local councils, especially because indirect limits/controls imposed by the suppliers of credit have a strong influence on local government borrowing. This significantly reduces their common moral hazards: excessive borrowing or failing to prioritise investment borrowing in the best interests of the local government public.

The research evidence reviewed in this chapter also indicates that infrastructural assets in New Zealand local councils are funded significantly by borrowings. While council income is used to fund infrastructural assets, New Zealand local councils tend to use more borrowings than income to fund infrastructural assets. This is expected, given the need for intergenerational equity when it comes to investment in infrastructural assets.

The review also shows that councils tend to invest significantly more in visible infrastructural assets such as roads, land and buildings in comparison to those less visible, such as waste water systems. This confirms the moral hazard theory that local politicians may prioritize infrastructural investments that give their electorate obvious evidence of their performance in government. Additionally, the review highlights a gap in the perceived accounting information disseminated on infrastructural investment decision-making, and how this decision-making balances the competing priorities of ratepayers and politicians for specific infrastructural asset investments. The reviewed research evidence provides support for the publicly available accounting information on the 'annual net investment in infrastructural assets' in local authorities' financial statements as a useful source of information in assessing the level and type of infrastructural asset investment. Thus, for public asset management, there is a strong argument that the information on the 'annual net investment in infrastructural assets' is more useful in assessing the level and type of infrastructural investment than the reported net book values (NBVs) of the infrastructural assets, which provide estimations of their value only.

Therefore, some form of condensed information about the annual net investment and the sources of funding for infrastructural assets should be provided by, say, a note in the additional information to financial information in local authorities' annual reports. This would enable users of council financial statements to deduce the priorities of their local councils' infrastructure investment strategy, while evaluating the net investment figures. Moreover, the councils could make it easier for users to find and understand the information about net investments in infrastructure through a condensed report, highlighting annual net investment in infrastructural assets. This recommendation is consistent with Walker et al.'s (2000b) proposition that a combination of financial data and some non-financial qualitative information about infrastructure would be likely to be more relevant to users of local authorities' reports, ratepayers, and the voters in local government elections. In conclusion, this chapter posits that there is a role for accounting information, albeit in an easier to understand and more condensed form, to enable ratepayers and voters' understanding of public asset management practices and for their potential evaluation of the borrowing and investment choices made by their local government representatives and politicians.

From the reviewed research evidence on local government infrastructural asset accounting and borrowing in New Zealand, some future research directions are identifiable. These include investigating the influence of political and socio-economic factors on local government borrowing. Future studies could also examine how the unique non-partisanship status of New Zealand local government politicians (New Zealand local politicians are elected as independents, without party affiliation) influences their decision-making in relation to borrowing and infrastructural investment choices. This study has two main limitations. Firstly, the study reviews existing research evidence and has not evaluated new local government data empirically. Thus, there is a possibility that new empirical research may provide novel insights on the issues covered in this chapter. Future research could examine this possibility. Secondly, the main focus of the study was on New Zealand local governments. Thus, there is a possibility that examination of the issues discussed in this chapter in jurisdictions using different accounting frameworks and governance systems may yield different results. As such, there are difficulties in generalising the inferences of this chapter.

REFERENCES

Aghón, G., & Letelier, L. (2016). Local urban governments financing a comparison between countries. *Estudos Economicos*, *23*(3), 77–97.

Anthony, R. N. (1985). Games government accountants play. *Harvard Business Review*, *63*(5), 161–170.

Balaguer-Coll, M. T., Prior, D., & Tortosa-Ausina, E. (2015). On the determinants of local government debt: Does one size fit all? *International Public Management Journal*, *19*(4), 513–542. doi:10.1080/10967494.2015.1104403

Barnes, K., & Lord, B. (2017). Intergenerational Equity: Treatment of Infrastructure in New Zealand Local Government Financial Planning. *Financial Accountability & Management*, *33*(2), 127–145. doi:10.1111/faam.12120

Bastida, F., Beyaert, A., & Benito, B. (2013). Electoral cycles and local government debt management. *Local Government Studies*, *39*(1), 107–132. doi:10.1080/03003930.2012.683861

Beck, R., Ferrucci, G., Hantzsche, A., & Rau-Goehring, M. (2017). Determinants of sub-sovereign bond yield spreads–The role of fiscal fundamentals and federal bailout expectations. *Journal of International Money and Finance*, *79*, 72–98. doi:10.1016/j.jimonfin.2017.08.003

Benito, B., & Bastida, F. (2004). The determinants of the municipal debt policy in Spain. *Journal of Public Budgeting, Accounting & Financial Management*, *16*(44), 492–525. doi:10.1108/JPBAFM-16-04-2004-B002

Benito, B., Guillamón, M. D., Ríos, A. M., & Bastida, F. (2019). Do the illegal and legal rents of politicians affect municipal election outcomes? Empirical evidence. *Local Government Studies*, 1–23.

Bolívar, M. P. R., Navarro Galera, A., López Subirés, M. D., & Alcaide Muñoz, L. (2018). Analysing the accounting measurement of financial sustainability in local governments through political factors. *Accounting, Auditing & Accountability Journal*, *31*(8), 2135–2164. doi:10.1108/AAAJ-10-2016-2754

Cabasés, F., Pascual, P., & Vallés, J. (2007). The effectiveness of institutional borrowing restrictions: Empirical evidence from Spanish municipalities. *Public Choice*, *131*(3-4), 293–313. doi:10.100711127-006-9116-y

Chatterjee, B., Mir, M. Z., Eddie, I. A., & Wise, V. (2017). Infrastructure reporting by New Zealand local authorities – perceptions and expectations. *Accounting Research Journal*, *30*(1), 36–57. doi:10.1108/ARJ-10-2013-0076

Cheng, R. H., & Harris, J. E. (2000). External reporting of capital assets: a sources and uses model. In E. Caperchione & R. Mussari (Eds.), *Comparative Issues in Local Government Accounting* (pp. 191–209). Kluwer Academic Publishers. doi:10.1007/978-1-4615-4581-1_12

Christiaens, J., & Vanhee, C. (2003). *Capital assets in governmental accounting reforms*. Working Paper, University of Gent.

Corsetti, G., & Roubini, N. (1996). European versus American perspectives on balanced-budget rules. *The American Economic Review*, *86*(2), 408–413.

Cropf, R. A., & Wendel, G. D. (1998). The determinants of municipal debt policy: A pooled time-series analysis. *Environment and Planning. C, Government & Policy*, *16*(2), 211–224. doi:10.1068/c160211

Derycke, P. H., & Gilbert, G. (1985). The public debt of French local government. *Journal of Public Policy*, *5*(3), 387–399. doi:10.1017/S0143814X00003172

Drew, J. (2018). Playing for keeps: Local government distortion of depreciation accruals in response to high-stakes public policy-making. *Public Money & Management*, *38*(1), 57–64. doi:10.1080/09540962.2017.1389542

Ehalaiye, D., Botica Redmayne, N., & Laswad, F. (2017). Financial determinants of local government debt in New Zealand. *Pacific Accounting Review*, *29*(4), 512–533.

Ehalaiye, D., Botica Redmayne, N., & Laswad, F. (2019). Does accounting information contribute to a better understanding of public assets management? The case of local government infrastructural assets. *Public Money & Management*. (forthcoming)

Eisenhardt, K. M. (1989). Agency theory: An assessment and review. *Academy of Management Review*, *14*(1), 57–74. doi:10.5465/amr.1989.4279003

Farnham, P. G. (1985). Re-examining local debt limits: A disaggregated analysis. *Southern Economic Journal*, *51*(4), 1186–1201. doi:10.2307/1058388

Feld, L. P., Kirchgässner, G., & Schaltegger, C. A. (2011). Municipal debt in Switzerland: New empirical results. *Public Choice*, *149*(1-2), 49–64. doi:10.100711127-011-9828-5

Goddard, A. (2005). Accounting and NPM in UK local government–contributions towards governance and accountability. *Financial Accountability & Management*, *21*(2), 191–218. doi:10.1111/j.1468-0408.2005.00215.x

Grant Thornton. (2014). *Local Government: A Financial Snapshot*. Grant Thornton.

IPSASB. (2015). *The IPSASB's Strategy for 2015 forward: leading through change*. Available online: https://www.ifac.org/system/files/publications/files/IPSASB-Strategy-2015-Forward-2.pdf

Jensen, M. C., & Meckling, W. H. (1976). Theory of the firm: Managerial behavior, agency costs and ownership structure. *Journal of Financial Economics*, *3*(4), 305–360. doi:10.1016/0304-405X(76)90026-X

Kennedy, S., & Robbins, J. (2003). *The Role of Fiscal Rules in Determining Fiscal Performance*. Working paper. Department of Finance Canada.

Kioko, S. N., & Zhang, P. (2019). Impact of Tax and Expenditure Limits on Local Government Use of Tax-supported Debt. *Public Finance Review*, *47*(2), 409–432. doi:10.1177/1091142117723706

Krugman, P. (2009). *The Return of Depression Economics and the Crisis of 2008*. New York, NY: W.W. Norton & Company, Inc.

Lapsley, I., & Pallott, J. (1997). *The capital accounting controversy in local government – A New Zealand – UK comparison*. Working paper, Comparative International Governmental Accounting Research.

Letelier, S. L. E. (2011). Theory and evidence of municipal borrowing in Chile. *Public Choice*, *146*(3), 395–411. doi:10.100711127-010-9596-7

LGFA. (2019). *Statement of intent 2019/20*. Available at: https://www.lgfa.co.nz/about-lgfa/lgfa-news/lgfa-statement-of-intent-2019-2020

Likierman, A. (1994). *Resource accounting and budgeting in the UK: Current developments*. Working paper, Workshop on Accounting and Accountability in the "New European Public Sector" EIASM, Edinburgh, UK.

Lim, S., & Hong, S. (2012). Analysing the determinants of local borrowings in Korea. *The Korean Journal of Local Finance*, *17*(1), 83–106.

Liu, C., Moldogaziev, T. T., & Mikesell, J. L. (2017). Corruption and state and local government debt expansion. *Public Administration Review*, *77*(5), 681–690. doi:10.1111/puar.12711

Local Government Act, New Zealand Statutes (2002).

Local Government Amendment Act. (1996). *No 3*. New Zealand Statutes.

Local Government Borrowing Act, New Zealand Statutes (2011).

Local Government Rates Inquiry Panel (LGRI). (2007). *Funding Local Government: Report of the Local Government Rates Inquiry*. Available at: http://ndhadeliver.natlib.govt.nz/ArcAggregator/arcView/

Local Government (Rating) Act, New Zealand Statutes (2002).

Mautz, R. K. (1988). Editorial: Monuments, mistakes and opportunities. *Accounting Horizons*, *2*(2), 123–128.

McCrae, M., & Aiken, M. (2000). Accounting for infrastructure service delivery by government: Generational issues. *Financial Accountability & Management*, *16*(3), 265–287. doi:10.1111/1468-0408.00108

Mulgan, R. (2000). 'Accountability': An Ever-Expanding Concept? *Public Administration*, *78*(3), 555–573. doi:10.1111/1467-9299.00218

Myerson, R. B. (2015). Moral hazard in high office and the dynamics of aristocracy. *Econometrica*, *83*(6), 2083–2126. doi:10.3982/ECTA9737

Navarro-Galera, A., Buendía-Carrillo, D., Lara-Rubio, J., & Rayo-Cantón, S. (2017). Do Political Factors Affect the Risk of Local Government Default? Recent Evidence from Spain. *Lex Localis*, *15*(1), 43–66. doi:10.4335/15.1.43-66(2017)

New Zealand Treasury. (2015). *Thirty Year New Zealand Infrastructure Plan 2015*. Available online: https://treasury.govt.nz/publications/infrastructure-plan/thirty-year-new-zealand-infrastructure-plan-2015

New Zealand Treasury. (2018). *New Zealand Infrastructure Plans*. Available online: https://treasury.govt.nz/information-and-services/nz-economy/infrastructure/new-zealand-infrastructure-plans

NZIER. (2012). *Is local government fiscally responsible? NZIER report to Local Government New Zealand, 11 September 2012*. NZIER.

Office of the Auditor-General. (2012). *Matters arising from the 2012-22 local authority long-term plans*. Available at: http://www.oag.govt.nz/2012/ltps-2012-22/docs/long-term-plans-2012-22.pdf

Office of the Auditor-General (OAG). (2013). *Managing Public Assets*. Available at: https://www.auditnz.govt.nz/publications-resources/asset-management/asset-management-for-public-entities/appendix.htm

Office of the Auditor-General (OAG). (2014). *Water and roads: Funding and management challenges*. Available at: https://www.oag.govt.nz/2014/assets

Office of the Auditor-General (OAG). (2015). *Matters arising from the 2015-25 local authority long-term plans*. Available at: https://www.oag.govt.nz/2015/ltps

Pallot, J. (1990). The nature of public sector assets: A response to Mautz. *Accounting Horizons*, *4*(2), 79–85.

Pallot, J. (1992). Elements of a theoretical framework for public sector accounting. *Accounting, Auditing & Accountability Journal*, *5*(1), 38–59. doi:10.1108/09513579210008244

Pallot, J. (1997). Infrastructure accounting for local authorities: Technical management and political context. *Financial Accountability & Management*, *13*(3), 225–242. doi:10.1111/1468-0408.00035

Pallot, J. (2001). Transparency in local government: Antipodean initiatives. *European Accounting Review*, *10*(3), 645–660. doi:10.1080/09638180126794

Park, J. H. (2013). Local government reform: Is it effective on debt burdens? *Public Finance and Management*, *13*(3), 195–214.

Pereira, C., & Bhavnani, R. (2008). *Private Gains for Public Benefits: Reelection, Accountability, and Corruption*. Michigan State University.

Pilcher, R. (2018). Depreciation in local government—still the problems continue. In Public Sector Accounting, Accountability and Governance (pp. 30-42). Routledge.

Pitesa, M., & Thau, S. (2013). Masters of the universe: How power and accountability influence self-serving decisions under moral hazard. *The Journal of Applied Psychology*, *98*(3), 550–558. doi:10.1037/a0031697 PMID:23379913

Poterba, J. M. (1996). Budget Institutions and Fiscal Policy in the US States. *The American Economic Review*, *86*(2), 395–400.

Poterba, J. M. (1997). Do Budget Rules Work? In A. Auerbach (Ed.), *Fiscal Policy: Lessons from Empirical Research* (pp. 53–86). MIT Press.

Premchand, A. (1993). *Public Expense Management*. Washington, DC: International Monetary Fund.

Rowles, T., Hutton, B., & Bellamy, S. (1998). Accounting for infrastructure assets: The case of land under roads. *The Annual Conference of Accounting Association of Australia and New Zealand*, Adelaide, Australia.

Sinclair, A. (1995). The chameleon of accountability: Forms and discourses. *Accounting, Organizations and Society*, *20*(2-3), 219–237. doi:10.1016/0361-3682(93)E0003-Y

Stewart, D. (1984). The Role of Information in Public Accountability. In A. Hopwood & C. Tomkins (Eds.), *Issues in Public Sector Accounting* (pp. 13–34). Oxford, UK: Philip Allen.

Tan-Kantor, A., Abbott, M., & Jubb, C. (2017). Accounting Choice and Theory in Crisis: The Case of the Victorian Desalination Plant. *Australian Accounting Review*, *27*(3), 273–284. doi:10.1111/auar.12149

Ter-Minassian, T., & Craig, J. (1997). Control of subnational government borrowing. In T. Ter-Minassian (Ed.), *Fiscal Federalism in Theory and Practice* (pp. 156–172). Washington, DC: International Monetary Fund.

Van Daniker & Kwiatkowski. (1986). *Infrastructure Assets: An Assessment of User Needs and Recommendations for Financial Reporting*. GASB.

Van Daniker, R. P., & Harris, J. (1999, Summer). Reporting about infrastructure: A preparer perspective. Public Budgeting and Finance, 111–17.

Vera, J. O. (2018). Explanatory factors and limitations of Spanish local debt. *Academia (Caracas)*, *31*(2), 360–377. doi:10.1108/ARLA-12-2015-0330

Walker, P. (2002). Understanding accountability: Theoretical models and their implications for social service organizations. *Social Policy and Administration*, *36*(1), 62–75. doi:10.1111/1467-9515.00270

Walker, R. G., Clarke, F. L., & Dean, G. W. (1999). Reporting on the state of infrastructure by local government. *Accounting, Auditing & Accountability Journal*, *12*(4), 85–102. doi:10.1108/09513579910283477

Walker, R. G., Clarke, F. L., & Dean, G. W. (2000a). Use of CCA in the public sector: Lessons from Australia's experience with public utilities. *Financial Accountability & Management*, *16*(1), 1–32. doi:10.1111/1468-0408.00095

Walker, R. G., Clarke, F. L., & Dean, G. W. (2000b). Options for infrastructure reporting. *Abacus*, *36*(2), 123–159. doi:10.1111/1467-6281.00057

Walker, R. G., Dean, G. W., & Edwards, P. J. (2004). Infrastructure reporting: Attitudes of preparers and potential users. *Financial Accountability & Management*, *20*(4), 351–375. doi:10.1111/j.1468-0408.2004.00199.x

Walls, J. (2018). *The scale of New Zealand's infrastructure deficit is 'massive' and can't be fixed without billions of dollars of private capital.* Available online: https://www.interest.co.nz/news/93445/scale-new-zealand%E2%80%99s-infrastructure-deficit-massive-and-cant-be-fixed-without-billions

Winters, M. S., & Weitz-Shapiro, R. (2013). Lacking information or condoning corruption: When do voters support corrupt politicians? *Comparative Politics*, *45*(4), 418–436. doi:10.5129/001041513X13815259182857

XRB. (2017). *PBE IPSAS 17 – Property, Plant and Equipment. External Reporting Board.* Wellington, New Zealand: XRB.

Yang, L. (2017). Financial management conservatism under constraints: Tax and expenditure limits and local deficit financing during the Great Recession. *Local Government Studies*, *43*(6), 946–965. doi:10.1080/03003930.2017.1365711

Zimmerman, J. L. (1977). The municipal accounting maze: An analysis of political incentives. *Journal of Accounting Research*, *15*, 107–144. doi:10.2307/2490636

ENDNOTES

1 We use local councils, local governments and local authorities interchangeably through the course of the chapter.

2 Five territorial authorities are also unitary authorities, which perform the functions of a regional council in addition to those of a territorial authority. In New Zealand, a unitary authority is a territorial authority (district or city) that also performs the functions of a regional council. The five unitary authorities are: Gisborne District Council, Nelson City Council, Tasman District Council, Marlborough District Council, and Auckland Council. Chatham Islands have a council with its own special legislation that makes it very like a unitary authority.

Related Readings

To continue IGI Global's long-standing tradition of advancing innovation through emerging research, please find below a compiled list of recommended IGI Global book chapters and journal articles in the areas of public administration, e-government, and citizen engagement. These related readings will provide additional information and guidance to further enrich your knowledge and assist you with your own research.

Agostino, D., Arnaboldi, M., & Azzone, G. (2018). Social Media Data Into Performance Measurement Systems: Methodologies, Opportunities, and Risks. In G. Azevedo, J. da Silva Oliveira, R. Marques, & A. Ferreira (Eds.), *Handbook of Research on Modernization and Accountability in Public Sector Management* (pp. 254–275). Hershey, PA: IGI Global. doi:10.4018/978-1-5225-3731-1.ch012

Aladalah, M., Cheung, Y., & Lee, V. C. (2018). Towards a Model for Engaging Citizens via Gov2.0 to Meet Evolving Public Value. *International Journal of Public Administration in the Digital Age*, *5*(1), 1–17. doi:10.4018/IJPADA.2018010101

Anand, D., & Khemchandani, V. (2017). An Analytical Method to Audit Indian e-Governance System. *International Journal of Electronic Government Research*, *13*(3), 18–37. doi:10.4018/IJEGR.2017070102

Anthony, S. M., & Zhang, W. (2017). Alternative Tweeting: A Comparison of Frames in Twitter's Political Discourse and Mainstream Newspaper Coverage of the Singapore General Election of 2011. In M. Adria & Y. Mao (Eds.), *Handbook of Research on Citizen Engagement and Public Participation in the Era of New Media* (pp. 324–343). Hershey, PA: IGI Global. doi:10.4018/978-1-5225-1081-9.ch018

Bandeira, A. M., Meira, D., & Tomé, B. (2018). Reflections on the Accounting Framework of Public Interest Cooperatives in Portugal. In G. Azevedo, J. da Silva Oliveira, R. Marques, & A. Ferreira (Eds.), *Handbook of Research on Modernization and Accountability in Public Sector Management* (pp. 433–445). Hershey, PA: IGI Global. doi:10.4018/978-1-5225-3731-1.ch020

Boachie, C. (2017). Public Financial Management and Systems of Accountability in Sub-National Governance in Developing Economies. In E. Schoburgh & R. Ryan (Eds.), *Handbook of Research on Sub-National Governance and Development* (pp. 193–217). Hershey, PA: IGI Global. doi:10.4018/978-1-5225-1645-3.ch009

Bolívar, M. P. (2018). Governance in Smart Cities: A Comparison of Practitioners' Perceptions and Prior Research. *International Journal of E-Planning Research*, *7*(2), 1–19. doi:10.4018/IJEPR.2018040101

Borrego, A. C., Lopes, C. M., & Ferreira, C. M. (2018). The Perception of Tax Complexity Within Local Authorities' VAT Framework: Evidence From Portugal. In G. Azevedo, J. da Silva Oliveira, R. Marques, & A. Ferreira (Eds.), *Handbook of Research on Modernization and Accountability in Public Sector Management* (pp. 384–405). Hershey, PA: IGI Global. doi:10.4018/978-1-5225-3731-1.ch018

Buyana, K., & Lwasa, S. (2017). Infrastructure Governance at Sub-National Level: The Case of Kampala City in Uganda. In E. Schoburgh & R. Ryan (Eds.), *Handbook of Research on Sub-National Governance and Development* (pp. 324–342). Hershey, PA: IGI Global. doi:10.4018/978-1-5225-1645-3.ch015

Carini, C., Teodori, C., & Giacomini, D. (2018). A New Useful Tool or a Further Misunderstood Obligation?: Perceptions on the LG Consolidated Report. In G. Azevedo, J. da Silva Oliveira, R. Marques, & A. Ferreira (Eds.), *Handbook of Research on Modernization and Accountability in Public Sector Management* (pp. 55–76). Hershey, PA: IGI Global. doi:10.4018/978-1-5225-3731-1.ch004

Chigwata, T. C. (2017). Fiscal Decentralization: Constraints to Revenue-Raising by Local Government in Zimbabwe. In E. Schoburgh & R. Ryan (Eds.), *Handbook of Research on Sub-National Governance and Development* (pp. 218–240). Hershey, PA: IGI Global. doi:10.4018/978-1-5225-1645-3.ch010

Costanza, F. (2018). Governing Patients' Mobility to Pursue Public Value: A System Dynamic Approach to Improve Healthcare Performance Management. In G. Azevedo, J. da Silva Oliveira, R. Marques, & A. Ferreira (Eds.), *Handbook of Research on Modernization and Accountability in Public Sector Management* (pp. 276–299). Hershey, PA: IGI Global. doi:10.4018/978-1-5225-3731-1.ch013

Cruz, A. C. (2018). Portal for Employees in the Public Sector: A Tool for Knowledge Management in Human Resources. In G. Azevedo, J. da Silva Oliveira, R. Marques, & A. Ferreira (Eds.), *Handbook of Research on Modernization and Accountability in Public Sector Management* (pp. 342–362). Hershey, PA: IGI Global. doi:10.4018/978-1-5225-3731-1.ch016

Cunha, A. M., Ferreira, A. D., & Fernandes, M. J. (2018). The Impact of Accounting Information and Socioeconomic Factors in the Re-Election of Portuguese Mayors. In G. Azevedo, J. da Silva Oliveira, R. Marques, & A. Ferreira (Eds.), *Handbook of Research on Modernization and Accountability in Public Sector Management* (pp. 406–432). Hershey, PA: IGI Global. doi:10.4018/978-1-5225-3731-1.ch019

del Mar Gálvez-Rodríhuez, M., Haro-de-Rosario, A., & Caba-Pérez, M. D. (2017). A Comparative View of Citizen Engagement in Social Media of Local Governments from North American Countries. In M. Adria & Y. Mao (Eds.), *Handbook of Research on Citizen Engagement and Public Participation in the Era of New Media* (pp. 139–156). Hershey, PA: IGI Global. doi:10.4018/978-1-5225-1081-9.ch009

Demirbas, T. (2018). The Role of Annual Reports in Ensuring Accountability: The Case of Development Agencies in Turkey. In G. Azevedo, J. da Silva Oliveira, R. Marques, & A. Ferreira (Eds.), *Handbook of Research on Modernization and Accountability in Public Sector Management* (pp. 446–469). Hershey, PA: IGI Global. doi:10.4018/978-1-5225-3731-1.ch021

Dhamija, A., & Dhamija, D. (2018). Motivational Factors and Barriers for Technology-Driven Governance: An Indian Perspective. In A. Manoharan & J. McQuiston (Eds.), *Innovative Perspectives on Public Administration in the Digital Age* (pp. 194–211). Hershey, PA: IGI Global. doi:10.4018/978-1-5225-5966-5.ch010

Drulă, G. (2017). Citizen Engagement and News Selection for Facebook Pages. In M. Adria & Y. Mao (Eds.), *Handbook of Research on Citizen Engagement and Public Participation in the Era of New Media* (pp. 122–138). Hershey, PA: IGI Global. doi:10.4018/978-1-5225-1081-9.ch008

During, R., Pleijte, M., van Dam, R. I., & Salverda, I. E. (2017). The Dutch Participation Society Needs Open Data, but What is Meant by Open? In M. Adria & Y. Mao (Eds.), *Handbook of Research on Citizen Engagement and Public Participation in the Era of New Media* (pp. 304–322). Hershey, PA: IGI Global. doi:10.4018/978-1-5225-1081-9.ch017

Fernandes, T. M., Gomes, J., & Romão, M. (2017). Investments in E-Government: A Benefit Management Case Study. *International Journal of Electronic Government Research, 13*(3), 1–17. doi:10.4018/IJEGR.2017070101

Ferreira, A. D., Santos, C., Azevedo, G. M., Gonçalves, J., & da Silva Oliveira, J. (2018). Performance Indicators and Accountability in Portuguese Public Universities: Socio-Economic Perspective. In G. Azevedo, J. da Silva Oliveira, R. Marques, & A. Ferreira (Eds.), *Handbook of Research on Modernization and Accountability in Public Sector Management* (pp. 210–233). Hershey, PA: IGI Global. doi:10.4018/978-1-5225-3731-1.ch010

Gatchair, S. D. (2017). Collaborative Governance and the Implementation of Fiscal Responsibility Frameworks. In E. Schoburgh & R. Ryan (Eds.), *Handbook of Research on Sub-National Governance and Development* (pp. 463–482). Hershey, PA: IGI Global. doi:10.4018/978-1-5225-1645-3.ch021

Gomes, J. P., & Laureano, R. M. (2018). Impacts of Electronic Public Procurement in the Portuguese Construction Sector: Several Years After Implementation. In G. Azevedo, J. da Silva Oliveira, R. Marques, & A. Ferreira (Eds.), *Handbook of Research on Modernization and Accountability in Public Sector Management* (pp. 363–383). Hershey, PA: IGI Global. doi:10.4018/978-1-5225-3731-1.ch017

Grant, B., Woods, R., & Tan, S. F. (2017). Subnational Finance in Australia and China: The Case for Municipal Bond Banks. In E. Schoburgh & R. Ryan (Eds.), *Handbook of Research on Sub-National Governance and Development* (pp. 150–166). Hershey, PA: IGI Global. doi:10.4018/978-1-5225-1645-3.ch007

Gray, N., & Pugalis, L. (2017). Place-Based Subnational Development: Unpacking Some of the Key Conceptual Strands and Normative Dispositions. In E. Schoburgh & R. Ryan (Eds.), *Handbook of Research on Sub-National Governance and Development* (pp. 34–53). Hershey, PA: IGI Global. doi:10.4018/978-1-5225-1645-3.ch002

Groshek, J. (2017). Organically Modified News Networks: Gatekeeping in Social Media Coverage of GMOs. In M. Adria & Y. Mao (Eds.), *Handbook of Research on Citizen Engagement and Public Participation in the Era of New Media* (pp. 107–121). Hershey, PA: IGI Global. doi:10.4018/978-1-5225-1081-9.ch007

Guarini, E., & Pattaro, A. F. (2017). Fiscal Responsibility and Multi-Level Governance: Bridging the Gap between Policy and Management. In E. Schoburgh & R. Ryan (Eds.), *Handbook of Research on Sub-National Governance and Development* (pp. 167–192). Hershey, PA: IGI Global. doi:10.4018/978-1-5225-1645-3.ch008

Hansson, K., & Ekenberg, L. (2018). Embodiment and Gameplay: Situating the User in Crowdsourced Information Production. In A. Manoharan & J. McQuiston (Eds.), *Innovative Perspectives on Public Administration in the Digital Age* (pp. 239–255). Hershey, PA: IGI Global. doi:10.4018/978-1-5225-5966-5.ch013

Heaton, L., & Días da Silva, P. (2017). Citizen Engagement in Local Environmental Issues: Intersecting Modes of Communication. In M. Adria & Y. Mao (Eds.), *Handbook of Research on Citizen Engagement and Public Participation in the Era of New Media* (pp. 1–19). Hershey, PA: IGI Global. doi:10.4018/978-1-5225-1081-9.ch001

Heisler, E. (2017). Measuring Enclosures and Efficacy in Online Feminism: The Case of Rewire. In M. Adria & Y. Mao (Eds.), *Handbook of Research on Citizen Engagement and Public Participation in the Era of New Media* (pp. 389–409). Hershey, PA: IGI Global. doi:10.4018/978-1-5225-1081-9.ch021

Hodgson, J., McKinlay, P., & Knight, B. (2017). Subnational Governance and Development: A New Perspective. In E. Schoburgh & R. Ryan (Eds.), *Handbook of Research on Sub-National Governance and Development* (pp. 407–431). Hershey, PA: IGI Global. doi:10.4018/978-1-5225-1645-3.ch019

Ismailova, R., Muhametjanova, G., & Kurambayev, B. (2018). A Central Asian View of E-Government Services Adoption: Citizens' Trust and Intention to Use E-Services. In A. Manoharan & J. McQuiston (Eds.), *Innovative Perspectives on Public Administration in the Digital Age* (pp. 212–226). Hershey, PA: IGI Global. doi:10.4018/978-1-5225-5966-5.ch011

Iwasaki, Y. (2017). Youth Engagement in the Era of New Media. In M. Adria & Y. Mao (Eds.), *Handbook of Research on Citizen Engagement and Public Participation in the Era of New Media* (pp. 90–105). Hershey, PA: IGI Global. doi:10.4018/978-1-5225-1081-9.ch006

Jackson, T., Nel, E., & Connelly, S. (2017). A Comparison of Resource Equalization Processes for Subnational Rural Governance and Development: Case Studies of England, Scotland, Canada, Australia, and New Zealand. In E. Schoburgh & R. Ryan (Eds.), *Handbook of Research on Sub-National Governance and Development* (pp. 117–149). Hershey, PA: IGI Global. doi:10.4018/978-1-5225-1645-3.ch006

Ji, Q. (2017). A Comparative View of Censored and Uncensored Political Discussion: The Case of Chinese Social Media Users. In M. Adria & Y. Mao (Eds.), *Handbook of Research on Citizen Engagement and Public Participation in the Era of New Media* (pp. 269–282). Hershey, PA: IGI Global. doi:10.4018/978-1-5225-1081-9.ch015

Jovita, H., Mutiarin, D., & Nurmandi, A. (2018). Covering the Cost of the Past: Disaster Management in the Most Typhoon-Affected Region in the Philippines. *International Journal of Disaster Response and Emergency Management, 1*(2), 49–63. doi:10.4018/IJDREM.2018040104

Kang, W., & Wang, Y. (2018). China Digital Governance Development Review Over the Past Two Decades. *International Journal of Public Administration in the Digital Age*, *5*(3), 92–106. doi:10.4018/IJPADA.2018070107

Kassen, M. (2017). E-Government Politics as a Networking Phenomenon: Applying a Multidimensional Approach. *International Journal of Electronic Government Research*, *13*(2), 18–46. doi:10.4018/IJEGR.2017040102

Lawrie, A. (2017). The Subnational Region: A Utopia? The Challenge of Governing Through Soft Power. In E. Schoburgh & R. Ryan (Eds.), *Handbook of Research on Sub-National Governance and Development* (pp. 96–115). Hershey, PA: IGI Global. doi:10.4018/978-1-5225-1645-3.ch005

Luk, C. Y. (2018). The Impact of Digital Health on Traditional Healthcare Systems and Doctor-Patient Relationships: The Case Study of Singapore. In A. Manoharan & J. McQuiston (Eds.), *Innovative Perspectives on Public Administration in the Digital Age* (pp. 143–167). Hershey, PA: IGI Global. doi:10.4018/978-1-5225-5966-5.ch008

Ma, L. (2018). Digital Divide and Citizen Use of E-Government in China's Municipalities. *International Journal of Public Administration in the Digital Age*, *5*(3), 16–31. doi:10.4018/IJPADA.2018070102

Madsen, C. Ø., & Kræmmergaard, P. (2018). How to Migrate Citizens Online and Reduce Traffic on Traditional Channels Through Multichannel Management: A Case Study of Cross-Organizational Collaboration Surrounding a Mandatory Self-Service Application. In A. Manoharan & J. McQuiston (Eds.), *Innovative Perspectives on Public Administration in the Digital Age* (pp. 121–142). Hershey, PA: IGI Global. doi:10.4018/978-1-5225-5966-5.ch007

Maulana, I. (2017). Social Media as Public Political Instrument. In M. Adria & Y. Mao (Eds.), *Handbook of Research on Citizen Engagement and Public Participation in the Era of New Media* (pp. 231–247). Hershey, PA: IGI Global. doi:10.4018/978-1-5225-1081-9.ch013

Maxwell, S., & Carboni, J. (2018). Foundations' Civic Engagement With Stakeholders: Leveraging Social Media Strategies. In A. Manoharan & J. McQuiston (Eds.), *Innovative Perspectives on Public Administration in the Digital Age* (pp. 25–41). Hershey, PA: IGI Global. doi:10.4018/978-1-5225-5966-5.ch002

McNeal, R. S., Schmeida, M., & Bryan, L. D. (2017). Smartphones and their Increased Importance in U.S. Presidential Elections. In M. Adria & Y. Mao (Eds.), *Handbook of Research on Citizen Engagement and Public Participation in the Era of New Media* (pp. 283–303). Hershey, PA: IGI Global. doi:10.4018/978-1-5225-1081-9.ch016

Melo, A. I., Santinha, G., & Lima, R. (2018). Measuring the Quality of Health Services Using SERVQUAL: Evidence From Portugal. In G. Azevedo, J. da Silva Oliveira, R. Marques, & A. Ferreira (Eds.), *Handbook of Research on Modernization and Accountability in Public Sector Management* (pp. 300–318). Hershey, PA: IGI Global. doi:10.4018/978-1-5225-3731-1.ch014

Mensah, I. K. (2017). Tackling the ICT Infrastructure Gap for the Successful Implementation of E-Government Projects. *International Journal of Strategic Information Technology and Applications*, *8*(2), 40–56. doi:10.4018/IJSITA.2017040104

Mensah, I. K. (2018). E-Government Services Adoption: The Important Elements of Trust and Transparency. *International Journal of Electronic Government Research*, *14*(3), 12–31. doi:10.4018/IJEGR.2018070102

Miller, K. L. (2017). Local Government Reform in Jamaica: A New Paradigm for Participatory Local Governance. In E. Schoburgh & R. Ryan (Eds.), *Handbook of Research on Sub-National Governance and Development* (pp. 520–542). Hershey, PA: IGI Global. doi:10.4018/978-1-5225-1645-3.ch024

Mohammed-Spigner, D., Porter, B. E., & Warner, L. M. (2018). States' Budget Investments in Technology and Improving Criminal Justice Outcomes. In A. Manoharan & J. McQuiston (Eds.), *Innovative Perspectives on Public Administration in the Digital Age* (pp. 90–105). Hershey, PA: IGI Global. doi:10.4018/978-1-5225-5966-5.ch005

Monteiro, R. P., & Pinho, C. (2018). Cost Accounting in Brazil's Public Sector: Importance, Use, and Level of Deployment. In G. Azevedo, J. da Silva Oliveira, R. Marques, & A. Ferreira (Eds.), *Handbook of Research on Modernization and Accountability in Public Sector Management* (pp. 319–341). Hershey, PA: IGI Global. doi:10.4018/978-1-5225-3731-1.ch015

Morim, A. C., Inácio, H., & Vieira, E. (2018). Internal Control in a Public Hospital: The Case of Financial Services Expenditure Department. In G. Azevedo, J. da Silva Oliveira, R. Marques, & A. Ferreira (Eds.), *Handbook of Research on Modernization and Accountability in Public Sector Management* (pp. 77–102). Hershey, PA: IGI Global. doi:10.4018/978-1-5225-3731-1.ch005

Moura e Sá, P., Lourenço, R. P., & Veloso, S. (2018). Are Public Administration Institutions Willing to Disclose Their Performance Through Data Portals?: The Case of the Portuguese Directorates-General. In G. Azevedo, J. da Silva Oliveira, R. Marques, & A. Ferreira (Eds.), *Handbook of Research on Modernization and Accountability in Public Sector Management* (pp. 234–253). Hershey, PA: IGI Global. doi:10.4018/978-1-5225-3731-1.ch011

Mupepi, M. G. (2017). Developing Democratic Paradigms to Effectively Manage Business, Government, and Civil Society: The African Spring. In E. Schoburgh & R. Ryan (Eds.), *Handbook of Research on Sub-National Governance and Development* (pp. 432–462). Hershey, PA: IGI Global. doi:10.4018/978-1-5225-1645-3.ch020

Nam, T. (2017). Achievable or Ambitious?: A Comparative and Critical View of Government 3.0 in Korea. *International Journal of Electronic Government Research, 13*(1), 1–13. doi:10.4018/IJEGR.2017010101

Nam, T. (2019). Does E-Government Raise Effectiveness and Efficiency?: Examining the Cross-National Effect. *Journal of Global Information Management, 27*(3), 120–138. doi:10.4018/JGIM.2019070107

Nathai-Balkissoon, M., & Pun, K. F. (2018). E-Government of Occupational Safety and Health: Improvement Prospects for a Developing Nation. In A. Manoharan & J. McQuiston (Eds.), *Innovative Perspectives on Public Administration in the Digital Age* (pp. 65–89). Hershey, PA: IGI Global. doi:10.4018/978-1-5225-5966-5.ch004

Nemec, J., Meričková, B. M., Svidroňová, M. M., & Klimovský, D. (2017). Co-Creation as a Social Innovation in Delivery of Public Services at Local Government Level: The Slovak Experience. In E. Schoburgh & R. Ryan (Eds.), *Handbook of Research on Sub-National Governance and Development* (pp. 281–303). Hershey, PA: IGI Global. doi:10.4018/978-1-5225-1645-3.ch013

Nistor, C. S., Oprisor, T., & Crisan, A. R. (2018). Implications of Accountability Through the Prospect of Integrated Reporting Adoption in the Public Sector. In G. Azevedo, J. da Silva Oliveira, R. Marques, & A. Ferreira (Eds.), *Handbook of Research on Modernization and Accountability in Public Sector Management* (pp. 189–209). Hershey, PA: IGI Global. doi:10.4018/978-1-5225-3731-1.ch009

Noor, R. (2017). Citizen Journalism: News Gathering by Amateurs. In M. Adria & Y. Mao (Eds.), *Handbook of Research on Citizen Engagement and Public Participation in the Era of New Media* (pp. 194–229). Hershey, PA: IGI Global. doi:10.4018/978-1-5225-1081-9.ch012

Ogonek, N., & Hofmann, S. (2018). Governments' Need for Digitization Skills: Understanding and Shaping Vocational Training in the Public Sector. *International Journal of Public Administration in the Digital Age, 5*(4), 61–75. doi:10.4018/IJPADA.2018100105

Okada, A., Ishida, Y., & Yamauchi, N. (2018). In Prosperity Prepare for Adversity: Use of Social Media for Nonprofit Fundraising in Times of Disaster. In A. Manoharan, & J. McQuiston (Eds.), Innovative Perspectives on Public Administration in the Digital Age (pp. 42-64). Hershey, PA: IGI Global. doi:10.4018/978-1-5225-5966-5.ch003

Ökten, S., Akman, E., & Akman, Ç. (2018). Modernization and Accountability in Public-Sector Administration: Turkey Example. In G. Azevedo, J. da Silva Oliveira, R. Marques, & A. Ferreira (Eds.), *Handbook of Research on Modernization and Accountability in Public Sector Management* (pp. 18–39). Hershey, PA: IGI Global. doi:10.4018/978-1-5225-3731-1.ch002

Othman, R., Nath, N., & Laswad, F. (2018). Environmental Reporting and Accounting: Sustainability Hybridisation. In G. Azevedo, J. da Silva Oliveira, R. Marques, & A. Ferreira (Eds.), *Handbook of Research on Modernization and Accountability in Public Sector Management* (pp. 130–158). Hershey, PA: IGI Global. doi:10.4018/978-1-5225-3731-1.ch007

Perelló-Sobrepere, M. (2017). Building a New State from Outrage: The Case of Catalonia. In M. Adria & Y. Mao (Eds.), *Handbook of Research on Citizen Engagement and Public Participation in the Era of New Media* (pp. 344–359). Hershey, PA: IGI Global. doi:10.4018/978-1-5225-1081-9.ch019

Pinterič, U. (2017). ICT as the Path Beyond Bureaucracy?: The Use of ICT by Ignorance of the Citizens. *International Journal of Public Administration in the Digital Age, 4*(2), 33–42. doi:10.4018/IJPADA.2017040103

Quinn, B. C. (2017). Integration, Innovation, and Intimidation?: Linking the Third Sector and Local Government in Ireland. In E. Schoburgh & R. Ryan (Eds.), *Handbook of Research on Sub-National Governance and Development* (pp. 75–95). Hershey, PA: IGI Global. doi:10.4018/978-1-5225-1645-3.ch004

Rahman, M. S. (2017). Politics-Administration Relations and the Effect on Local Governance and Development: The Case of Bangladesh. In E. Schoburgh & R. Ryan (Eds.), *Handbook of Research on Sub-National Governance and Development* (pp. 256–279). Hershey, PA: IGI Global. doi:10.4018/978-1-5225-1645-3.ch012

Rana, T. (2018). New Public Management Reforms and Modernization Changes in Australia. In G. Azevedo, J. da Silva Oliveira, R. Marques, & A. Ferreira (Eds.), *Handbook of Research on Modernization and Accountability in Public Sector Management* (pp. 1–17). Hershey, PA: IGI Global. doi:10.4018/978-1-5225-3731-1.ch001

Reddy, P. S. (2017). Political-Administrative Interface at the Local Sphere of Government with Particular Reference to South Africa. In E. Schoburgh & R. Ryan (Eds.), *Handbook of Research on Sub-National Governance and Development* (pp. 242–255). Hershey, PA: IGI Global. doi:10.4018/978-1-5225-1645-3.ch011

Ryan, R., & Woods, R. (2017). Decentralization and Subnational Governance: Theory and Praxis. In E. Schoburgh & R. Ryan (Eds.), *Handbook of Research on Sub-National Governance and Development* (pp. 1–33). Hershey, PA: IGI Global. doi:10.4018/978-1-5225-1645-3.ch001

Ryan, R., & Woods, R. (2017). Women's Political Empowerment: Lessons for Subnational Levels of Government – Nepal, Pakistan, Rwanda, and Indonesia. In E. Schoburgh & R. Ryan (Eds.), *Handbook of Research on Sub-National Governance and Development* (pp. 385–405). Hershey, PA: IGI Global. doi:10.4018/978-1-5225-1645-3.ch018

Santos, C., Ferreira, A. D., Marques, R. P., & Azevedo, G. M. (2018). EAGLE_Index: Enhancement of an Accountability Guide for Learning E-Government. In G. Azevedo, J. da Silva Oliveira, R. Marques, & A. Ferreira (Eds.), *Handbook of Research on Modernization and Accountability in Public Sector Management* (pp. 103–129). Hershey, PA: IGI Global. doi:10.4018/978-1-5225-3731-1.ch006

Schoburgh, E. D. (2017). Challenges in Institutionalizing Democratic Governance via Popularly Elected Mayor: The Case of Jamaica. In E. Schoburgh & R. Ryan (Eds.), *Handbook of Research on Sub-National Governance and Development* (pp. 344–367). Hershey, PA: IGI Global. doi:10.4018/978-1-5225-1645-3.ch016

Schoburgh, E. D. (2017). The Institutional Imperatives of Local Economic Governance: Lessons from a Small Island Developing State. In E. Schoburgh & R. Ryan (Eds.), *Handbook of Research on Sub-National Governance and Development* (pp. 54–74). Hershey, PA: IGI Global. doi:10.4018/978-1-5225-1645-3.ch003

Serna, C. A., Pineda, A. A., & Rojas, O. A. (2017). Subnational Governance Model from the Integration of Online Media and Social Networks: The Case of Medellin City, Colombia. In E. Schoburgh & R. Ryan (Eds.), *Handbook of Research on Sub-National Governance and Development* (pp. 483–498). Hershey, PA: IGI Global. doi:10.4018/978-1-5225-1645-3.ch022

Sforza, V., Mechelli, A., & Cimini, R. (2018). Towards the Modernisation of EU Public Sector Accounting Standards: Lessons From the Reconciliation Between National and Governmental Accounting. In G. Azevedo, J. da Silva Oliveira, R. Marques, & A. Ferreira (Eds.), *Handbook of Research on Modernization and Accountability in Public Sector Management* (pp. 40–54). Hershey, PA: IGI Global. doi:10.4018/978-1-5225-3731-1.ch003

Shan, Z., & Tang, L. (2017). Social Media and the Public Sphere in China: A Case Study of Political Discussion on Weibo after the Wenzhou High-Speed Rail Derailment Accident. In M. Adria & Y. Mao (Eds.), *Handbook of Research on Citizen Engagement and Public Participation in the Era of New Media* (pp. 410–425). Hershey, PA: IGI Global. doi:10.4018/978-1-5225-1081-9.ch022

Sharma, V., & Sengar, A. (2018). Mobile Governance for Affordability and Profitability/Feasibility. In A. Manoharan & J. McQuiston (Eds.), *Innovative Perspectives on Public Administration in the Digital Age* (pp. 227–238). Hershey, PA: IGI Global. doi:10.4018/978-1-5225-5966-5.ch012

Sihi, D. (2018). Friending and Funding Through Facebook: Social Media Use of Regional Nonprofit Organizations. In A. Manoharan & J. McQuiston (Eds.), *Innovative Perspectives on Public Administration in the Digital Age* (pp. 256–283). Hershey, PA: IGI Global. doi:10.4018/978-1-5225-5966-5.ch014

Song, M. Y., & Abelson, J. (2017). Public Engagement and Policy Entrepreneurship on Social Media in the Time of Anti-Vaccination Movements. In M. Adria & Y. Mao (Eds.), *Handbook of Research on Citizen Engagement and Public Participation in the Era of New Media* (pp. 38–56). Hershey, PA: IGI Global. doi:10.4018/978-1-5225-1081-9.ch003

Soverchia, M., & Fradeani, A. (2018). The eXtensible Business Reporting Language: A Digital Tool to Enhance Public Sector Accountability. In A. Manoharan & J. McQuiston (Eds.), *Innovative Perspectives on Public Administration in the Digital Age* (pp. 106–120). Hershey, PA: IGI Global. doi:10.4018/978-1-5225-5966-5.ch006

Spada, P., & Allegretti, G. (2017). Integrating Multiple Channels of Engagement in Democratic Innovations: Opportunities and Challenges. In M. Adria & Y. Mao (Eds.), *Handbook of Research on Citizen Engagement and Public Participation in the Era of New Media* (pp. 20–37). Hershey, PA: IGI Global. doi:10.4018/978-1-5225-1081-9.ch002

Staiou, E., & Gouscos, D. (2018). The Evolution of Self-Organized Social Solidarity (SoSS) Initiatives in Greece and Their Relationship to Online Media: A Longitudinal Research. In A. Manoharan & J. McQuiston (Eds.), *Innovative Perspectives on Public Administration in the Digital Age* (pp. 168–193). Hershey, PA: IGI Global. doi:10.4018/978-1-5225-5966-5.ch009

Strekalova, Y. A., Krieger, J. L., Damiani, R. E., Kalyanaraman, S., & Wang, D. Z. (2017). Old Media, New Media, and Public Engagement with Science and Technology. In M. Adria & Y. Mao (Eds.), *Handbook of Research on Citizen Engagement and Public Participation in the Era of New Media* (pp. 57–72). Hershey, PA: IGI Global. doi:10.4018/978-1-5225-1081-9.ch004

Syväjärvi, A., Leinonen, J., Kivivirta, V., & Kesti, M. (2017). The Latitude of Information Management in Local Government: Views of Local Government Managers. *International Journal of Electronic Government Research, 13*(1), 69–85. doi:10.4018/IJEGR.2017010105

Tan, S. F. (2017). Local Representation in Australia: Preliminary Findings of a National Survey. In E. Schoburgh & R. Ryan (Eds.), *Handbook of Research on Sub-National Governance and Development* (pp. 368–384). Hershey, PA: IGI Global. doi:10.4018/978-1-5225-1645-3.ch017

Tavares, M. D., & Rodrigues, L. L. (2018). Strategic Responses of Public Sector Entities to GRI Sustainability Reports. In G. Azevedo, J. da Silva Oliveira, R. Marques, & A. Ferreira (Eds.), *Handbook of Research on Modernization and Accountability in Public Sector Management* (pp. 159–188). Hershey, PA: IGI Global. doi:10.4018/978-1-5225-3731-1.ch008

Thomas, M. A., & Elnagar, S. (2018). A Semantic Approach to Evaluate Web Content of Government Websites. In A. Manoharan & J. McQuiston (Eds.), *Innovative Perspectives on Public Administration in the Digital Age* (pp. 1–24). Hershey, PA: IGI Global. doi:10.4018/978-1-5225-5966-5.ch001

Toscano, J. P. (2017). Social Media and Public Participation: Opportunities, Barriers, and a New Framework. In M. Adria & Y. Mao (Eds.), *Handbook of Research on Citizen Engagement and Public Participation in the Era of New Media* (pp. 73–89). Hershey, PA: IGI Global. doi:10.4018/978-1-5225-1081-9.ch005

Towner, T. L. (2017). Information Hubs or Drains?: The Role of Online Sources in Campaign Learning. In M. Adria & Y. Mao (Eds.), *Handbook of Research on Citizen Engagement and Public Participation in the Era of New Media* (pp. 157–178). Hershey, PA: IGI Global. doi:10.4018/978-1-5225-1081-9.ch010

Tshishonga, N. (2017). Operation Sukuma-Sakhe: A New Social Contract for Decentralized Service Delivery and Responsive Governance in KwaZulu-Natal. In E. Schoburgh & R. Ryan (Eds.), *Handbook of Research on Sub-National Governance and Development* (pp. 304–323). Hershey, PA: IGI Global. doi:10.4018/978-1-5225-1645-3.ch014

Vie, S., Carter, D., & Meyr, J. (2017). Occupy Rhetoric: Responding to Charges of "Slacktivism" with Digital Activism Successes. In M. Adria & Y. Mao (Eds.), *Handbook of Research on Citizen Engagement and Public Participation in the Era of New Media* (pp. 179–193). Hershey, PA: IGI Global. doi:10.4018/978-1-5225-1081-9.ch011

Vrettos, K., & Gouscos, D. (2019). Evaluating the Presence of Greek Tourism-Related Public Sector Entities in Online Social Networks. *International Journal of Public Administration in the Digital Age, 6*(1), 15–40. doi:10.4018/IJPADA.2019010102

Waller, P. (2017). Co-Production and Co-Creation in Public Services: Resolving Confusion and Contradictions. *International Journal of Electronic Government Research, 13*(2), 1–17. doi:10.4018/IJEGR.2017040101

Weng, S. (2018). Internet Political Participation and Public Agenda-Setting: Social Network Analysis of PX Event in Zhangzhou. *International Journal of Public Administration in the Digital Age, 5*(3), 60–75. doi:10.4018/IJPADA.2018070105

Woods, R. (2017). Not Forgetting the Public Servants: Capacity-Building to Support Subnational Governance and Development Implementation. In E. Schoburgh & R. Ryan (Eds.), *Handbook of Research on Sub-National Governance and Development* (pp. 499–519). Hershey, PA: IGI Global. doi:10.4018/978-1-5225-1645-3.ch023

Yang, K. C., & Kang, Y. (2017). Social Media, Political Mobilization, and Citizen Engagement: A Case Study of the March 18, 2014, Sunflower Student Movement in Taiwan. In M. Adria & Y. Mao (Eds.), *Handbook of Research on Citizen Engagement and Public Participation in the Era of New Media* (pp. 360–388). Hershey, PA: IGI Global. doi:10.4018/978-1-5225-1081-9.ch020

Yavuz, N., Karkın, N., Parlak, İ., & Subay, Ö. Ö. (2018). Political Discourse Strategies Used in Twitter during Gezi Park Protests: A Comparison of Two Rival Political Parties in Turkey. *International Journal of Public Administration in the Digital Age, 5*(1), 82–96. doi:10.4018/IJPADA.2018010105

Yuan, Y. (2017). A Gradual Political Change?: The Agenda Setting Effect of Online Activism in China 1994-2011. In M. Adria & Y. Mao (Eds.), *Handbook of Research on Citizen Engagement and Public Participation in the Era of New Media* (pp. 248–268). Hershey, PA: IGI Global. doi:10.4018/978-1-5225-1081-9.ch014

About the Contributors

Ana Maria Cunha has a PhD in Accounting Master in accounting and public administration Full researcher at the Research Center on Accounting and Taxation Invited Teacher at the Polytechnic Institute of Cávado and Ave.

Augusta Ferreira completed his first degree at the Higher Institute of Accounting and Administration of Aveiro; she got his Masters Degree in Business Management Specialization in Corporate Finance at Minho University and she holds a PhD in Accounting at Aveiro University and Minho University. Currently she teaches Accounting within the accounting scientific area at Higher Institute Accounting and Administration of Aveiro (Aveiro University) and she is interested in researching public accounting, accounting information systems, disclosure of financial information and accountability. She has presented and published many articles in national and international journals and conferences.

Maria Fernandes has a PhD in management sciences Professor at the Accounting and Taxation Department Research interests: public accounting; public finance

Patricia Gomes has a PhD in Accounting Master on accounting and auditing Full researcher at the Research Center on Accounting and Taxation Professor at the Polytechnic Institute of Cávado and Ave.

* * *

Paolo Biancone is a Professor of Business Administration at the University of Turin. Biancone is an expert in Islamic Finance. Coordinator of the PhD in Business Management at the University of Turin. Observatory responsible on Islamic Finance at the University of Turin. Member of the Social Entrepreneurship Committee (formerly the Civil economy Observatory - Committee for social entrepreneurship) of the Chamber of Commerce of Turin. Promoter and member of the organizing committee of the Turin Islamic Economic Forum TIEF 2014-2015-2017. He is scientific director of the methodology on Popular Financial Reporting in local government- experimental project City of Turin.

Marco Bisogno is an associate professor in Accounting at the University of Salerno. He received his PhD from the University of Naples "Federico II." His current research interests are on public sector accounting, transparency and accountability, financial sustainability and financial distress, intellectual capital. He is a member of the editorial board of several international journals.

Nives Botica Redmayne is a scholar at Massey University, New Zealand. Her main area of research and expertise is in financial reporting, governance and assurance, in particular, financial reporting in for-profit and public sector as well as in assurance services market regulation and audit in public and not-for-profit sectors. Her recent research focus has been on the introduction of International Financial Reporting Standards (IFRS) and International Public Sector Accounting Standards (IPSAS) in public sector reporting and the effects of these standards on the quality and cost of reporting, governance and auditing in public sector. Nives contributes to the development of professional standards, guidance and policies for practising auditors in New Zealand.

Valerio Brescia has a PhD in Business and Management at the University of Turin, he is fellow in research in Italy with the research topic in the Consolidated Financial Statements of the municipality, accounting standards and Popular Report. He holds a master's degree in Economic Sciences Company - firms Administration and Control at the School of Management and Economics in Turin with full marks and has a Master in Management of local health facilities and hospitals from the University of Turin. He is part of the methodology Application Committee on Popular Financial Reporting in local government - experimental project City of Turin.

Francesca Citro is an Assistant Professor in Accounting at the University of Salerno, Italy. Her research interests include public accounting and disclosure quality measurement. She currently teaches business administration.

Beatriz Cuadrado-Ballesteros is Associate Professor of Accounting at the University of Salamanca (Department of Management and Business Economics & Multidisciplinary Institute for Enterprise), where she earned her PhD in Business. Her research interests are public administration and public sector reforms. In particular, she focuses on efficiency, accountability, governance, financial distress and accounting systems. Her work has been published in top international journals. She has attended several international conferences in accounting and public sector, as well as she was visiting researcher at the Edinburgh University Business School, the Coimbra Business School, and the University of Salerno.

Dimu Ehalaiye is a Senior Lecturer in the School of Accountancy, Massey University, New Zealand. His current research interests focus on financial accounting and reporting, accounting standards setting, public sector accounting, accounting in financial institutions and accounting in emerging markets. His research has been published in prominent journals like Pacific-Basin Finance Journal, Public Money and Management, Applied Economics, Emerging Markets Finance and Trade, Australian Accounting Review and Pacific Accounting Review.

Margarita Labrador is an Associate Professor in the Department of Accounting and Finance, University of Zaragoza, Spain.

Fawzi Laswad is a Professor and Head of School of Accountancy at Massey University, New Zealand. His research interests include financial reporting for the private and public sectors. He also has research interests in accounting education.

Carla Martinho is a Professor in higher education since 1993. Currently at ISCAL she teaches the curricular unit of calculation and financial operations and is regent of Mathematics I and II in the degree of Management. Graduated in Mathematics Applied to Actuarial Sciences by FCT / UNL, Master in Mathematics Applied to Economics and Management by ISEG / UTL and PhD in Education and Development by FCT / UNL. It develops applied research and quantitative methodologies, evaluation metrics and performance evaluation. He is a member of SPM, SPE, FORGES and AEDEM.

Serena Santis is an Assistant Professor in Accounting at the University of Campania "Luigi Vanvitelli", Italy.

Paula Santos has a PhD in Management. Coordinator Professor of Accounting in ISCAL.

Silvana Secinaro is a Researcher of the Department of Management at the University of Turin, chartered accountant, a freelance journalist, author of numerous publications on public and private accounting, as well as crowdfunding. Component of National Commission of Italian Ministry of finances on IPSAS. Member of the editorial staff of Press, the national magazine of the Chartered Experts Accounting, October 2014. She is part of scientific committee of the methodology on Popular Financial Reporting in local government- experimental project City of Turin.

José Zafra-Gómez is an associate professor in accounting at the University of Granada. His research interests focus on local government. He has had papers published recently in journals including Regional Studies, Urban Studies, European Journal of Operational Research. Journal of Public Administration Research Theory and OMEGA, among others.

Index

N

P

R

S

IGI Global
DISSEMINATOR OF KNOWLEDGE
www.igi-global.com

Publisher of Peer-Reviewed, Timely, and Innovative Academic Research Since 1988

IGI Global's Transformative Open Access (OA) Model: **How to Turn Your University Library's Database Acquisitions Into a Source of OA Funding**

In response to the OA movement and well in advance of Plan S, IGI Global, early last year, unveiled their OA Fee Waiver (Offset Model) Initiative.

Under this initiative, librarians who invest in IGI Global's InfoSci-Books (5,300+ reference books) and/or InfoSci-Journals (185+ scholarly journals) databases will be able to subsidize their patron's OA article processing charges (APC) when their work is submitted and accepted (after the peer review process) into an IGI Global journal.*

How Does it Work?

1. When a library subscribes or perpetually purchases IGI Global's InfoSci-Databases including InfoSci-Books (5,300+ e-books), InfoSci-Journals (185+ e-journals), and/or their discipline/subject-focused subsets, IGI Global will match the library's investment with a fund of equal value to go toward subsidizing the OA article processing charges (APCs) for their patrons.

   Researchers: Be sure to recommend the InfoSci-Books and InfoSci-Journals to take advantage of this initiative.
2. When a student, faculty, or staff member submits a paper and it is accepted (following the peer review) into one of IGI Global's 185+ scholarly journals, the author will have the option to have their paper published under a traditional publishing model or as OA.
3. When the author chooses to have their paper published under OA, IGI Global will notify them of the OA Fee Waiver (Offset Model) Initiative. If the author decides they would like to take advantage of this initiative, IGI Global will deduct the US$ 1,500 APC from the created fund.
4. This fund will be offered on an annual basis and will renew as the subscription is renewed for each year thereafter. IGI Global will manage the fund and award the APC waivers unless the librarian has a preference as to how the funds should be managed.

Hear From the Experts on This Initiative:

"I'm very happy to have been able to make one of my recent research contributions, 'Visualizing the Social Media Conversations of a National Information Technology Professional Association' featured in the *International Journal of Human Capital and Information Technology Professionals*, freely available along with having access to the valuable resources found within IGI Global's InfoSci-Journals database."

– **Prof. Stuart Palmer**, Deakin University, Australia

For More Information, Visit: www.igi-global.com/publish/contributor-resources/open-access or contact IGI Global's Database Team at eresources@igi-global.com

www.ingramcontent.com/pod-product-compliance
Lightning Source LLC
LaVergne TN
LVHW081322300926
849161LV00008B/1854